CONSCIOUS LIFE
Creating Your Reality

An Alexander Book
by
Ramón Stevens

ISBN-10: 0-9639413-2-1
ISBN-13: 978-0-9639413-2-9

Revised Edition
Originally published 1991
ISBN: 0-9639413-5-6

Cover design: Andy Hughes

Pepperwood Press
www.alexandermaterial.com

Printed in the United States of America

Contents

Preface 5

Introduction.. 7

Part One: Physical Universe Construction

1. "Camouflage" and "Direct" Physical Systems 11
2. The Primal Cells 14
3. The Primal Pulse 16
4. The Laws of Vibration 20
5. The Axis and the Sphere 26
6. The Nature of Vibration 29
7. Bedrock, Water, and Air 34
8. Earth, Moon, and Sun 41
9. Water Planet Life 48

Part Two: The Human Seed

10. Families of Consciousness 55
11. The Stage of Duality 59
12. The Human Blueprint 63
13. Earth Clay and Star Dust 70
14. Air, Food, and Water 74
15. The Four Vibrational Bodies 82
16. The Senses 88
17. The Coordinate 104

Part Three: The Nature of Events

18. Master Events and Probabilities 111
19. Thought, Experience, and Object 118
20. Space-Time.. 122
21. The Event-Body Link 124
22. Event Gravity 131
23. Evolution of the Species... 137
24. The Space-Time Seesaw 144

Part Four: The Power of Mind

25. The Electric Belief Screen 155
26. The Event Magnet 162
27. The Belief Screen Quiz 168
28. Belief Hierarchies 172
29. Emotion 177
30. Human Vibrations 185
31. Bedrock Vibrations 193
32. Memory 206
33. Fear 211

Part Five: Conscious Life

34. A New Creation Myth 219
35. Affirmation 224
36. Visualization 233
37. Health 239
38. Abundance 257
39. Love and Relationships 263
40. Ritual 276
41. Being Peace 289
42. The Revolution 293

Preface

When spirit teacher Alexander dictated *Conscious Life* twenty years ago, the notion that we create our reality was just that: a notion, an intriguing idea, perhaps a philosophy. It lay far outside the five-sensory realm of science, whose concrete cosmos reduces us to ciphers battered about by forces beyond our control, with a dollop of raw chance tossed in to keep us on edge.

Over the years it has been my pleasure to hear from scientists in a variety of disciplines. These scientists—often "closet metaphysicians"—find themselves butting up against their fields' materialist boundaries. Convinced there is "more" to life and the universe than the mechanical play of Newtonian forces—consciousness, perhaps?—they seek a more inclusive, comprehensive cosmology, and some find their way to the Alexander Material.

Fortunately, with such visionaries leading the way, science is beginning to explore the previously heretical realm of consciousness. The field of energy psychology looks especially promising. But I have always been skeptical of, or indifferent to, efforts to "prove" the existence of energy fields or the power of intention because such research uses the methodology and technology of mainstream science, which denies their existence. It is like asking the pope to validate evidence that the Bible is a fraud. As Alexander writes:

> Your culture's rejection of any "nonrational" thought reduces you to the mentality of robots, stumbling around helter-skelter, prey to any breeze that blows your way. From our perspective, nothing could be more *irrational* than denying yourself the steady flow of wisdom from the auric body as it guides your path through life...You might cast a glance about your society and consider whether your exclusive emphasis on "rational" thought has brought you contentment, a healthy environment, food and shelter for all, and a world at peace.

In the years since *Conscious Life* was published, the idea that we create our reality has taken root and blossomed, most recently popularized as the "Law of Attraction." It is a liberating notion, yet it also carries great responsibility: there are no more excuses, no more blame hurled at the cold cruel world or malevolent others: *we* have made our lives what they are. And if we are not happy with what we have created, we can change it. Yet Alexander cautions that there are limits:

> The novice metaphysician may latch onto the New Age rallying cry of "You create your own reality," and, in the first heady rush of liberation, declare, "Nothing can affect me! I am invincible! I create my own reality!"

> If our young pupil were to stand naked in a snowstorm and defiantly cry, "You can't hurt me! I create my own reality!", what would the likely outcome be? Enlightenment or frostbite?

Alexander's contribution is a meticulously detailed, "nuts and bolts" exploration of physical universe construction, consciousness, and how they intersect to form our experienced reality. For those compelled by the notion of living in a self-created reality, yet wanting an explanatory "how," *Conscious Life* is your guide.

You create your own reality whether you believe you do or not—you might as well have a conscious hand in the process!

Ramón Stevens

Introduction

You create your own reality.

While this phrase is the foundation of the human race's evolving consciousness, it strikes many as ridiculous, confusing, bewildering, even threatening. How do I create my own reality? many ask. Am I not born into a world of sturdy structure and pattern, merely taking my place among the established rhythms of society and family, affected by others, by twists of nature, by God's plan for my life?

Because "you create your own reality" is the cornerstone of the Era of Conscious Life, and at the same time is so difficult for many to comprehend and actively implement in their lives, we devote this book to exploring precisely how your thoughts and beliefs create your life and world, both individually and collectively.

Above all, the approaching Era of Conscious Life is one in which personal power will be reclaimed, restored to the individual, rather than projected outward. Institutions of religion, science, and government, which now dominate and manipulate society to their advantage, will shrink in importance as individuals reclaim the personal power formerly projected onto others. Morality, ethics, lifestyle, relationships, health, sexuality, the meaning of life itself: all these will arise from within, echoing in the chambers of each private heart, rather than being dictated from without.

The time preceding your age can be described as the Era of Unconscious Life, when power was projected outward, onto gods and demons, healers and priests, the twists of fate, the caprice of God. You now stand at the cusp of the Era of Conscious Life, when the chimeric surface of life evaporates to reveal the fundamental truths formerly hidden from awareness. To understand these truths, to actively implement them in directing the flow of life events, is to reclaim personal power and embrace a higher order of life, a Conscious Life.

We will first explain physical universe construction, the principles and processes upon which the universe is built. Next, we will explore human consciousness and how it is seeded into the physical system as a unique medium of growth and learning. We follow by examining the nature of events, their source, their meaning, and your power to attract and repel potential events. We then explore the power of mind, touring through the realm of thought and belief and their effects on the physical world. In the final section we narrow our focus to you, an individual, offering practical tools and techniques empowering you to create your life's events; and encouraging you to offer a healing presence during this time of transition, the grinding of spiritual gears as the race struggles toward a higher order of life.

To those willing to take the journey toward the freedom and responsibility of Conscious Life, this book is dedicated.

Alexander

Part One

PHYSICAL UNIVERSE CONSTRUCTION

One

❧

"Camouflage" and "Direct" Physical Systems

Beyond your world, your solar system, your galaxy, your universe, beyond the farthest reaches of space and time, beyond dimensions of which you hold no awareness, lies the Source of all creation. In Its unquenchable thirst for growth and new experience, It creates a limitless realm of pulsating, expanding, perpetual growth, casting off uncountable fields of exploration. From this infinite range of activity the Source spins off a unique, highly specialized crucible of creation: physical universe construction.

However vast and unknowable your universe appears, it stands as but one of many versions of physical universe construction, each set upon its unique and private path, each contributing its store of growth to the ever-expanding drama of creation.

Flowing from the Source's unquenchable hunger for an infinite variety of experience, physical universe construction spills into two primary fields of activity: "camouflage" and "direct."

Your universe—its unknowable vast distances, its drama of life and death, its fiery supernovas, its imploding black holes, its infinite variety of life, its swirling, pulsing, rhythmic, cosmic dance—all this stands as one precious, unique, and irreplaceable corner of creation within the "camouflage" physical system.

Let us look closely at the two primary varieties of physical universe construction, and their purpose.

At base, all is vibration.

Your eyes drink in a magical world rich with color and shape and form. Your ears carry the laugh of a child, the distant call of the wolf, the music of the ages. Your tongue and nose sample the world before you and inside you. Your skin carries songs of warmth and pain and ecstasy.

However rich the world your senses weave may seem, at their base all such images and sounds and sensations are vibration, interpreted by your senses in their unique and highly specialized fashion. The world you know is not a bedrock reality, but an impressionist painting brought to life with the sure strokes of your intimate artists, your senses.

Yours, then, is a "camouflage" physical universe: You do not perceive vibration directly, but camouflaged by the interpretation of your senses.

What of the "direct" physical universes?

Just as your planet and universe play host to families of consciousness finding their greatest fulfillment and challenge within a camouflage physical system, so are there also those whose growth is best fulfilled through expression in a direct physical system.

A direct physical system is one in which vibration is perceived directly, without the interpretations and distortions of physical senses.

It is most difficult for you to imagine such a system, and for us to describe it. A planet is perceived as a swirling ball of vibration, densest at the core, gradually tapering off to a "surface" vibration of density sufficient to allow motion to the conscious species upon it, while also holding them to the surface (in your camouflage system this is gravity). Pockets of unstable energy, swirling masses and excrescences from deep inside the core, are perceived directly, where you might find earthquake faults and mountains. Travel is virtually instantaneous, as beings can select a locale based upon its known coordinates and instantly be pulled to the desired location. Thought transmission from one individual to another occurs instantaneously, without distortion, without the need for symbolic expression through speech.

You may wonder, is the camouflage physical system a poor, orphaned cousin of the direct physical system? How much easier to navigate through life perceiving vibration in its pure form, rather than through the symbolism of sense!

If you were asked what is most precious to you, what all the world's peoples yearn for daily, what so breaks your spirit when taken from you, what would you answer? Freedom.

Freedom, free will, is the purpose of a camouflage physical system. In a direct physical system, all thoughts are known instantaneously. There is no right to silence, nor to privacy, nor to solitude. There is no need for such either, for the families of consciousness inhabiting direct physical systems enjoy challenges fundamentally different from yours, in which all beings on a planet are embarked on highly cooperative ventures, where fulfillment is found through communal effort, not individual initiative.

Those families of consciousness choosing to inhabit camouflage systems, such as your universe, channel their growth through the primacy of the individual. While the great underlying commonality of your species and world often escapes you, it is upon this rich communal bed that you each spring to life as unique sparks of desire and intent. You find your challenges through individual effort, through uniqueness in form, upbringing, education, geography, and life experience. Your two sexes, your numerous races, your clatter of tongues, your realms of religion: You divide and divide and divide, ensuring that each individual will be utterly unique, never duplicated, that each life cries out to the depths of the universe with its unique song of private experience.

Freedom, free will, can be ensured only in a system where your thoughts are yours alone, to be shared only when you wish to offer crumbs of private experience to the world at large. Your thoughts, your dreams, your hopes, your unique worldview: all these are your intimate private possessions.

Thoughts are vibration. In a direct physical system, where all bands of the vibrational spectrum are perceived by all others, to hold one's counsel and silence is impossible. Only in a camouflage physical system can one find solitude and the privilege of a private inner life.

Those families of consciousness feeding into a camouflage system, of which you are a member, seek growth and expansion through the medium of individual identity, unique life experience, and private inner life. Your thoughts hum on frequencies no human sense can detect, to be shared only when you choose to express them through the recognizable vibration of sound. Thus are your privacy, your uniqueness, and your freedom ensured.

This is the fundamental purpose behind your choice to enjoy life on planet earth.

Two

❧

The Primal Cells

The fundamentals of physical universe construction hold for both camouflage and direct physical systems. Since all is vibration, the mechanics of how vibration is created, transferred, and stored are identical in both systems.

Consider your universe. You perceive an incomprehensibly vast sea of empty space, punctuated at random intervals by stars and planets, comets and ice fields. You perceive a realm of stuff and nothing, of matter miraculously suspended in the vacuum of space.

This is how the universe appears to your camouflaged eyes. The reality is quite different.

There is no "empty space." There is no cubic inch of the universe that is not pulsating with life.

Weaving a three-dimensional web throughout the vast reaches of space are the fundamental building blocks of physical universe construction: infinitesimally minute pockets or cells, transmitters of vibration, floating contiguously and uniformly from one end of the universe to the other. These fundamental units of space we shall term the "primal cells." Primal cells are of uniform shape and size, locked into position by surrounding brethren cells. Each primal cell is oblong in shape, rounded at the ends, its length four times its diameter. Each is braced by one other cell at each end, with four others lying contiguous along the north, south, east, and west angles. Each primal cell is thus held into place by six others lying immediately contiguous to it.

The primal cells do not create matter. They contain it. They are receptacles and transmitters of information, of vibration. Where you perceive greater density, as in planets and stars, this does not mean that the primal cells are crowding together to create such mass. Again, the primal cells always retain uniform shape and size, and always the identical number will inhabit a given unit of space.

An analogy would be a chunk of honeycomb. Here you find individual pockets or cells holding their position in the larger matrix, allowing passage to bee and honey while each cell maintains its individual integrity and stance.

Each primal cell holds its position in the larger framework, allowing passage to vibration from one to the other, particularly along the axis leading from the two rounded ends.

Primal cells are far tinier than anything your scientists have been able to perceive, or ever will. Indeed, they are invisible to your eye in any case for they have no mass or weight; they contain matter while not sharing matter's properties. Billions of primal cells are required to maintain the stance of a single electron. The primal cells required to maintain the contours and bulk of your body are simply beyond counting.

The primal cells are the foundation of the physical universe. How else does your planet, your solar system, stay in place? How do all the stars maintain their stance? What holds them in sure and steady position? Stepping back from your view of the universe as pockets of matter floating in empty space, you can see that the primal cells create a three-dimensional structure containing both spheres of matter and the reaches of space. Both matter and space are contained within the primal cells' matrix, which holds the features of the universe in place.

Your universe, then, is not a vast, dull void enlivened by a few random chunks of spinning ice and mud, but is instead a living fabric pulsing with life and energy, sizzling with vibration at every point, creating the rich humming sea in which your planet floats.

Three

The Primal Pulse

You hang suspended in an illusory web of time and space, clinging to its comfortable, familiar strands of a physical world and the passage of time, convinced of these bedrock parameters of your existence. Space and time—they form the fundamental foundation upon which your lives rest. Your mind cannot grasp the possibility of existence without them; they are the glue with which you bind place to moment, event to season, life to death.

Could you mark off time in a universe devoid of matter, with no mechanism for counting the moments, for observing the constant flow of change? Could matter exist without time, marking off neither beginning nor end nor decay of its existence?

Space and time are inseparable, inextricably bound to one another, the two-armed embrace upholding your world's stance in space and course through time.

Space and time, the twin siblings of your existence, spring from a common womb: the primal pulse.

The Source does not cast off fields of activity only to watch them wind down, collapse, and expire. All realms are perpetually replenished with a fresh flow of energy and intent. In the physical universe system, this energy and intent are fed through the fundamental building block of space and time, the primal pulse.

Energy does not flow smoothly and constantly from the Source into the physical system. Instead, it pulsates constantly between the physical system and the Source, back and forth, in a perpetual, rhythmic dance. Each pulsation from your system to the Source carries every detail of the condition and progress of your universe; every new burst from the Source brings fresh energy and sustenance, carrying also encouragement and support for those avenues of exploration leading to the fulfillment and growth of all those embarked on the experiment of physical universe construction.

The universe is created fresh and new in every moment. Every beat of the primal pulse creates a unique version of the universe, never to be duplicated, each such instant powered by a thundering, fresh bolt of energy from the Source.

Your world, your universe, blinks on and off in a constant pulsing dance impossible for you to discern. Your mind leaps the gaps of non-being, convincing you of a smooth, constant flow of moments, when instead the passage of time is like frozen frames of film pulled continuously through a projector, convincing you of a steady march of moments.

You live in a three-dimensional world and universe of space and time. Beyond your universe lies the fourth dimension, the primal dimension, the creator of time and space, the ultimate building block of your reality: the primal pulse.

We have seen how the physical universe is a matrix of primal cells, minute carriers and transmitters of vibration, floating uniformly throughout the reaches of space, sustaining the planets and stars and all your eyes can fathom when you gaze skyward.

This matrix of primal cells receives its information, its instructions as to the condition and progress of the universe, each time the primal pulse blinks "on" into your system.

Each primal cell within your system has a counterpart in the nonphysical dimensions lying beneath and beyond your world, those vaster realms of activity of which physical universe construction is but one slice. Each primal cell in your system carries a nonphysical twin, then, in these deeper dimensions standing behind the universe you know.

During the constant rhythmic dance of pulsation from physical universe to the Source and back, each nonphysical cell receives information from its physical twin, calculates all information relevant to the physical cell, then feeds that information back into the physical system with the next pulse from the Source. Each primal cell in your system thus receives a constant flow of information apprising it of its position in the overall matrix, and of the vibration it must emit in order to maintain the even flow of time and the sturdy stance of space undergirding the universe.

For it is vibration, remember, that the primal cells carry. It is vibration transmitted back to the nonphysical twin cells, and vibration which pulsates in return to each primal cell.

With every beat of the primal pulse, each primal cell in your system receives stimulation provoking emission of a highly specific vibration, a wave pattern or burst of electrical energy. In deepest terms all such configurations can be reduced to mathematical equations, though such calculations are performed on the nonphysical side of the pulse, with their physical expression manifesting in the fundamental patterns of physics and electromagnetism.

The pulse each cell receives from its nonphysical twin has two primary attributes: charge and pattern. The charge is a measure of how intensely a cell is stimulated, how much information is transmitted to it, how "full" it becomes with the beat of the pulse. A primal cell holding its position in a reach of empty space may receive no more charge than is necessary to sustain the contour of its walls, ensuring its continued stance in the overall matrix. A primal cell contributing to the sustenance of a physical object, in contrast, will be flooded with a charge of information, of vibration, the primal genesis of physical matter. So the charge is a measure of the physical structure to which a primal cell is contributing: empty space or the earth's solid crust.

The pattern of the charge is the second parameter of each primal pulse. The pattern is a highly specialized configuration granted to the charge which further shapes and molds it. The pattern is a three-dimensional wave form, a vibrational sculpture carved into the charge, shaping its unique contribution to the overall matrix. The degree of charge determines how much a primal cell contributes to the physical universe at its specific point in space. The pattern determines the shape and flavor of that information.

In addition, each primal cell is in constant communication with all others. Most intensely, each primal cell communicates its charge and pattern to those two cells abutting it at either end. All primal cells lying in a row, end to end, are connected by a strand or filament flowing through the center of each cell and binding each to its immediate neighbors. To a lesser degree, each primal cell offers information to the four cells lying along its flanks; the degree of information imparted is determined by the intensity of the charge.

The primal pulse is the womb from which space and time spring.

By sparking each primal cell with charge and pattern, the primal pulse creates the most elemental building blocks of the physical universe; from these primal building blocks are built particles, atoms, elements, molecules, matter, life, planets, stars, solar systems, galaxies. All are constructed from the charge and pattern of the primal cells, each cell making its unique contribution to the universe's construction.

The primal pulse blinks back and forth from your system to the nonphysical realms beyond your awareness, a steady rhythmic beat. Here is the fundamental unit of time, the most basic "moment" of your system.

All measures of duration are built upon this primal moment, this sure and steady rhythm from the Source.

The primal pulse is the fundamental, elemental, primary unit of physical universe construction. It is a four-dimensional burst carrying the seeds of both space and time within its pulsation.

Every pulse from the Source creates the universe anew; each beat begets a fresh and eternal moment of limitless potential, a precious crucible of creation seeded with space and time and your hopes and dreams, carrying you forward on your march to growth and enlightenment.

Four

❧

The Laws of Vibration

Now that we have established a matrix of primal cells creating and sustaining the structure of the physical universe, and have seen how the primal pulse fed from the Source into your system and then back again begets both space and time with its archetypal heart beat, we can begin to explore the nature of vibration—what it is, how it works, and the fundamentals of how vibration creates the universe you know.

Remember that the primal cells carry the fundamental unit of vibration, each beat of the primal pulse sparking a burst measured by charge and pattern. The charge describes the burst's intensity; the pattern informs its shape.

Remember also that primal cells lying in a line, end to end, are connected by a filament, making passage of information easiest along this steady axis.

This constant communication among primal cells, this exchange of information, leads to the first fundamental law of vibration: A given primal cell will always influence neighboring cells to assume its charge. The information exchange is not simply a neighborly way of saying hello, but is designed to ensure a consistency of vibration in a given area, for the purpose of creating and sustaining physical matter. We will delve into this much more deeply later, but for now understand that the constant exchange among cells is one in which each transmits its charge for the purpose of creating a sympathetic vibration in the others.

Imagine three primal cells lying in a row. If the two cells on either end carry a charge of 10, and the cell in the middle carries a charge of 5, there will be irresistible pressure on the middle cell to meet the outer cells' charge of 10. While the numbers are arbitrary and essentially meaningless, the point is that the stronger charge will always raise the vibrational charge of neighboring cells carrying a lower charge.

Three cells in a row, with the outer cells carrying charges of 5 and the center cell a charge of 10, will find on the next pulse that the outer cells raise their charge to 6 or 7, while the center cell retains a charge of 10. The process is not one of averaging, not one of regression toward the mean, but instead is one in which the highly charged cells induce their neighbors to raise their charge and form a continuous line of identical high charge.

You might ask, if the nonphysical twin cells are controlling the energy fed to each of the cells, how can the primal cells, those in the physical universe, influence each other? Are they not manipulated and fed their information solely from the nonphysical side of the pulse?

Remember that the pulse is a two-way street, with information both being fed to the physical universe, and the physical universe sending back a constant stream of information as to its stance and situation. The primal pulse sends a constant fresh flow of energy into the physical system. It is the physical system that determines the charge and pattern of each such burst; such determinations remain on the physical side of the process. While the nonphysical side receives information about the alterations and status of the primal cells' charge, they do not seek to manipulate it, to force a new configuration upon the physical system.

The purpose of a physical camouflage system such as yours is freedom, free will. This is not limited to the human species. It begins at the very base, the fundamental building block, the primal cell: here begin free will and self-determination.

A second law of vibration, closely related to the first, is that sympathetic vibrations attract. This is the next step up in our physical system, away from the contiguous cell-to-cell communication described in the first law. Stepping back to a larger picture, we find that agglomerations of primal cells holding sympathetic vibrations will attract.

Now, remember, the cells themselves do not move. They do not travel through the universe. The cells are merely the transmitters and containers of vibration. So when we say similar cells attract, understand that the physical structure of cells remains secure while the vibrational charges they carry do move from cell to cell, along highly specific laws.

Imagine in this case a three-dimension matrix of a thousand cells, ten on a side, forming a square. If two opposite corners of the square contain cells carrying charges of 10, while the inner cells vary from 3 to 7, the natural tendency is for the two agglomerations carrying charge 10 to meet in the middle. Remember that it is the charges traveling, not the cells themselves.

Because all cells are in constant communication with all others, and most intensely with their immediate neighbors, two agglomerations of charge 10 will know of each other's existence across the intervening field of lower charge. They will attempt to move toward each other and meet.

Imagine that one such string of primal cells carrying charge 10 is five cells long. On either side of this string are cells holding charge 5. Now, if the intent to meet with the other string of charge 10 is sufficiently strong, the five-cell string moves with each beat of the primal pulse. In other words, every time the primal pulse bursts into the physical system, that five-cell string of charge 10 will have moved over by one cell. If you imagine it moving to the right, then on the next pulse we will have two cells on the left carrying charge 5 and the five-cell string to the right. On the next pulse, three cells carrying charge 5, and the five-cell string over one more cell to the right.

Again, the cells themselves are not moving. It is the charge they contain that moves with each beat of the primal pulse, each pulse allowing a charge to move one cell's distance.

Ultimately, two agglomerations of charge 10 will work their way through the field of lower charge and meet, creating a matrix of twenty cells carrying charge 10.

You may ask how this relates to the first law. Will those strings of charge 10 not attempt to influence all surrounding cells to also raise their charge to 10? Yes, they will, but they do not always succeed. In addition, we are building a basic model here and must explain it piece by piece before we plug it all in for a three-dimensional demonstration!

A third law of vibration builds from the second: A field of identical charge is stronger than a field carrying various charges. A field of uniform charge 5 is stronger than a random assortment of charges 1 through 10. In part this relates to law one, whereby neighboring cells attempt to influence the charge of the others. To do so requires, in itself, expenditure of energy or vibration. Now, we are using terms more native to the human species, like "intend" and "attempt," and while there is little consciousness involved in the process, still the "intent" to influence one's neighbors does involve an expenditure of energy, or a diversion of energy from simply sustaining the stance of the cell.

Therefore, in a field of uniform, identical charge, each cell finding itself surrounded by sympathetic vibration will expend no energy to influence its neighbors. Locked into a tight embrace of familiar vibration, each cell can commit its full energy to sustaining its charge and pattern, and contribute to the structure of which it is a part.

You have a saying for this: strength in numbers. Your understanding flows from this fundamental law, that fields carrying identical charge are stronger than fields of random charge.

Flowing from the preceding is our next law, that of resistance. Again, while imposing human attributes on the primal cells because it eases your understanding, a cell being influenced by its neighbor carrying a higher charge will "resist" raising its charge to the higher. Otherwise, you see, within a few beats of the primal pulse the entire physical universe, every primal cell, would carry a charge of 10. And your precious physical world, its enormous variety of shape and size and form, would instantly become a solid slab of rock!

A cell "resists" the urgings of its neighbor to raise its charge. It seeks always to maintain its stance in its present condition, for there is strength in time as well as in numbers. Therefore, the greater the number of primal pulses during which a cell retains an identical charge, the "stronger" that cell's contribution to the structure of which it plays a part. Again, to alter one's level of charge requires a certain loss of energy, a diversion of intent from the primary purpose of sustaining a charge. If a primal cell can be said to have consciousness at all, it is this: to retain its stance, to carry an identical charge, for as many beats of the primal pulse as possible. This is how matter endures through time, through the intent of each cell to maintain its stance, hold its charge, as long as possible.

And whence swells that primal cell's lusty shout of individuality? We must cross the barrier into the nonphysical realm, back to the very Source, Whose purpose in creating fields of physical universe construction can manifest and be sustained only if each cell declares and defends its independence. We are scraping the bottom of the explanation barrel; we can go no further, cannot scrape the barrel itself as a way of understanding its contents. We tell you that each cell strives to maintain its stance, its charge and pattern; the "why" is answered: Because if it didn't, physical universe construction would be impossible.

How is the process of resistance maintained? Ultimately, over time, wouldn't the highest-charged cells' tenacious exhortations toward their neighbors to join them result in a universe of uniform charge 10 cells? And, once again, your blue-green crucible of life becomes a meteor.

The fifth law of vibration is that the total vibration, or energy, seeded into the physical system with each primal pulse is constant. The overall level and intensity of vibration fed into the universe is identical with each beat of the pulse.

This means that any gain in charge in one cell must be balanced with an equal loss in another cell elsewhere. The overall charge of the universe must be, will always be, maintained.

This ensures that the universe does not rise to a uniform charge 10 existence (or nonexistence, in your case). No magnanimous cosmic banker doles out a limitless store of vibration on demand. Instead, a constant, uniform charge is imparted to the entire physical system, and any loss in one area must be balanced with a gain in another.

Again, you have a version of this law on your planet; you know that no energy is ever lost, but simply transformed. You know that no matter is ever lost, but simply transformed. The overall relative arrangement of elements and molecules remains identical; the structures and forms they support vary.

You may ask, if each primal cell maintains free will, are they not forced, coerced, into gaining and losing charge as necessary for the overall balance of the physical system? Where lies the free will in such a system?

Remember the constant tug-of-war between cells to retain charge or to influence one's neighbors. In every such transaction, a minute amount of energy is lost. Lost? Never. It is returned to the system with the next beat of the primal pulse, and fed to those cells in the process of raising their charge to a higher value. Those reducing their charge also contribute to this pool of free-floating energy, which will be directed precisely to those cells requiring it.

In addition to the energy required to maintain the overall uniform charge of the physical system, there is a floating "pool" or "reserve" of energy. Depending upon the alterations in charge on a given beat of the pulse, this reserve will either be replenished or diminished. So there is no rigid command that energy must be fully distributed to every cell with each beat of the pulse, for there is built into the system a certain leeway, a certain bank of free will, in this free-floating store of energy.

Again, this store is not a bottomless cookie jar into which the primal cells may dig. The overall energy imparted to the physical system with each pulse still remains identical, and the reserve of energy is included in the overall equation. So the energy imparted remains constant, but the reserve allows the interactions among cells to continue unhindered and undirected by any omniscient overseer: Once again, free will is restored to the cosmos and all the primal cells rest easy!

A sixth law of vibration arises from the distinction between each cell's charge and its pattern, or wave form. These are the two fundamental parameters of the burst every cell receives with each beat of the primal pulse. They concern our prior laws in this manner: Charge creates resistance, while pattern allows attraction.

It is a cell's charge that determines its attempt to "influence" its neighbors, or to resist their influence. The charge is the intensity of a cell's pulsation, and it is this which determines one's "relationship" with one's neighbors. One can rest securely in a sea of cells carrying identical charge; one can induce a neighbor cell to raise its charge; one can resist the urge of a neighbor to increase one's charge. So the degree to which a cell is embroiled in "resistance" at a given pulse beat is a function of its charge. The second principle of vibration, that similar charges attract, remains valid in light of the sixth law, if the charges' patterns are similar. Indeed, the strongest vibrational field is one of consistent charge bound by sympathetic pattern.

It is a cell's pattern that determines its sympathy with others, its recognition of likeness, its urge to combine into a cohesive body of uniform vibration, seeking strength in numbers. Pattern is the unique flavor of a charge, and here again you recognize this: like attracts like. It is pattern that influences this constant dance of attraction, of motion toward those cells carrying sympathetic vibration.

Each primal cell thus carries the basis for both attraction and resistance, and each cell is involved in both processes constantly. They are the fundamental processes, the archetypal dynamic of physical universe construction. As an example, if a given group of cells shares a common pattern and has joined together on the basis of attraction, within that grouping there will also be elements of resistance as those of higher charge seek to boost the intensity of their neighbors. So two cells can attract and resist simultaneously; indeed, this is the very root of what prevents your system's collapse into a homogeneous and deadly uniformity. Attraction and resistance—these are the fundamental processes, the fundamental relationships.

We have very briefly and superficially sketched the six fundamental laws of vibration and how it manifests in its most primal form in your physical system. There is no purpose in digging deeper into further detail, for doing so would serve no purpose in a book such as this. Our intention is to ultimately lead you to understand how to create your own reality; to do so, you must understand the fundamental building blocks of physical universe construction, how vibration works, and the fundamental principles governing its ever-swirling dance. While seemingly esoteric at this point, ultimately you will find these principles to be of immeasurable value in understanding how human consciousness creates your world and its events.

Five

♋

The Axis and the Sphere

With a rudimentary understanding of the principles of vibration under our belts, we can now take a step back and examine how the primal units of vibration, of energy, combine and interact in order to create and sustain the physical universe and its reaches of space and matter. We will focus on the fundamental patterns and shapes native to physical universe construction, the building blocks of all matter.

There are two primal shapes or patterns native to every physical system. First and most fundamental is the shape of the primal cell. Remember that it resembles a tube, rounded at both ends, its length four times its diameter. This is the fundamental pattern of all matter. We will call it the *axis*.

Not every manifestation of an axis pattern will hold to the precise dimensions of the primal cell. So we define an axis as being any pattern with an oblong, tubular shape, its length at least four times its diameter. This is the primal pattern: the axis.

The second fundamental pattern is built upon the axis: the *sphere*. A sphere is a globe built upon an axis. Any object which is perfectly round or slightly pear-shaped we will consider a sphere.

Let us now examine why these two patterns, the axis and the sphere, are the fundamental shapes in the physical universe, and what principles of the physical system flow from these primal building blocks.

Vibration travels most efficiently in a straight line. Any diversion, any detour from the straight line, necessarily results in a loss of energy. Since, as we have seen, each primal cell works to retain its charge at its highest level, any sapping of that charge will be resisted. So the transmission of vibration along a straight line is the most efficient and the most natural direction for vibration to flow.

It stands to reason, then, that the principal building block of the physical system, the primal cell, is shaped in such a way as to allow the maximal flow of energy along a straight line, given the total area of the cell. A sphere, for instance, would not allow as great a length of linear travel as the same area shaped as an oblong.

You might ask, why not then squeeze the primal cell still further, so its length equals eight times its diameter, while still retaining the same total area? The reason relates to the need for a certain amount of "room" around the filament to allow a cell's expression of its charge and pattern, the pattern particularly. There must be space for a virtually infinite variety of expression of pattern, and the primal cell's diameter is constructed to allow precisely that freedom of expression. So the primal cell is as "skinny" as it can be and still allow each burst to fully express itself in charge and pattern.

A primal cell, then, is the fundamental shape of physical matter, allowing maximum transmission of vibration with minimal energy loss. Every primal cell is an axis, the archetypal axis of your system.

If you were to hold a primal cell between your hands and squeeze your hands together, what would result? A sphere. The ends are rounded, and under the pressure of your hands the center portion would bulge out, resulting in a sphere. The sphere, then, is the second fundamental shape of the physical system.

Because the archetypal shape of matter is the primal cell, an axis, it follows that any sphere will be a more complex construction than an axis. For every sphere is built around an axis, and the cells contributing to construction of a sphere must work harmoniously to create and sustain that shape. The sphere is one step away from the axis, a step toward greater complexity of design. A sphere must always be an agglomeration of charge, even the tiniest one, while the primal cell, beyond which no further division is possible, is an axis simply for existing.

In other words, since it is the fundamental shape, it can be said that an axis just happens—as it is most natural for charge to travel along a straight line—while there must be some intent behind the creation of a sphere, some purpose to the enterprise. It is a more complex construction, and the individual cells or charges involved must step outside their most natural desire to link into a linear energy flow, contributing instead to the less efficient sphere.

A sphere is still a highly efficient design. Think of an onion and its layers. Every cell contained in a given layer can communicate in a lineal fashion with the others in its layer, thus retaining the preference for energy to transmit linearly. No cell is stranded in a remote corner, as is possible in a square, where the outermost cell would have no tangent neighbors to communicate with end to end. Think again of the onion; imagine peeling off each layer and laying them flat. You have a series of fields in which the cells can communicate linearly, those fields decreasing in size as you approach the core, the axis.

This is the construction of a sphere, then: fields of linear cells curving or wrapping about an axis. Each cell communicates most intensely with those in its own field, while also communicating with those cells in adjacent layers. This way information from the core, the site of greatest energy, is dispersed throughout the sphere with the greatest efficiency.

The axis and the sphere are the fundamental, primal shapes and patterns of physical universe construction. The axis is the ultimate archetype; the more complex sphere is the most natural and efficient shape built upon an axis.

While the axis is the fundamental shape of the physical system, and the sphere is the most efficient form built upon it, there is an intermediate construction which we alluded to in dissecting our onion: the horizontal field.

In its most basic form, a field consists of primal cell strings lying snug against neighboring strings, creating a horizontal plane of contiguous strings. The smallest possible field would have as its height the diameter of a single primal cell, while in breadth its size can vary from two strings to a virtually infinite series of strings; and each such string can vary in length depending upon the number of primal cells joining to form the string.

The field is the basic "layer" of physical matter. Vibration travels most efficiently along the filament connecting primal cells lying in a row, while communication is also possible laterally, to neighboring strings.

You can see how a field held in a horizontal plane is less efficient than one curving about an axis. Communication between cells in the far corners is much more difficult—meaning more energy is lost in the transmission—than if that field wraps itself into a spherical shape. So while the field is technically the next step up from the axis, it is most natural for fields to shape themselves in spherical fashion; thus the sphere remains the most natural step up from the axis.

The axis, the field, the sphere: this is the progression in basic building blocks of physical universe construction. The axis is the most basic shape, the most efficient; the sphere consists of fields curving about an axis, creating a more complex grid of vibration organized in as efficient a shape as possible.

From these basic patterns flow the blueprints for every particle of the universe.

Six

The Nature of Vibration

Stepping back from our examination of the basic shapes and patterns of physical universe construction, now is the time to take a look at the fundamental qualities of the swirling dance that springs to life with every beat of the pulse.

The first quality of vibration is *cooperation*. No matter how grand the design, your system could not persist for two beats of the primal pulse without a respect for the communal venture upon which all primal cells and their charges are embarked. While each cell declares its free will, this assertion of independence rides upon a recognition of the deep, cooperative embrace upholding your system. It is only by pooling their charge, communicating constantly, operating on the agreed-upon laws of vibration, that the primal cells can create and sustain the fundamental building blocks of space and time.

This may appear to conflict with the law of resistance—in which a cell of lower charge "resists" the urge of its neighbor to raise its charge. This is not a David-and-Goliath scenario, a predator-prey stalking game, a drama of victor and vanquished. While again attributing human consciousness to a process so as to make it more familiar to you, the cell carrying a higher charge urges its neighbor—*urges* its neighbor—to match its charge. It does not force, it does not threaten, it does not destroy. The urge is a gentle, familiar, neighborly exhortation, not an ultimatum carrying veiled threats of violence.

The cell carrying lower charge demurs, declines the offer, declares its determination to retain its charge, however minuscule. Its integrity is never threatened, nor need it be defended. Knowing that its charge is strengthened by uniformity over time, each cell wishes to retain its charge for as long as possible, as many beats of the primal pulse as possible. It therefore respectfully declines the coaxing of its neighbor.

The key word is *respect*. Beginning at the primal level of cells and their charges, and the swirling dance of vibration, at no point does force or its dark cousins of threat and violence ever come into play. Respect for the unique integrity and stance of all other cells—this is the fundamental nature of vibration as it manifests in the physical system, to the extent that such cells and vibration carry "consciousness."

Cooperation is the fundamental quality of physical universe construction.

A second feature of the physical system's construction is *there are no boundaries*. There is no point where a pool of sympathetic vibration jealously stakes its claim to a matrix of primal cells, refusing to allow entrance or passage to others. While it is natural for vibrations of sympathetic pattern to congregate, it does not follow that they set up fences and walls, barring entry to other vibration.

The process of attraction and resistance results in agglomerations of vibration clumping together in a respectful flowing dance, a cosmic game of musical chairs—and no one is left out when the music stops! So while the natural tendency is for sympathetic vibrations to attract, never does this manifest as fence, padlock, or boundary.

Flowing from this is a third quality of the primal vibrational dance: While it is true that sympathetic vibrations attract, and find strength in numbers, the physical system is strongest when bolstered by *variety*. Earlier we said that the strongest structures are those carrying a uniform charge; to expand on that model, in truth the very strongest structure is one in which a field of uniform charge is enhanced at points by cells carrying diverse charge.

Remember that a cell's pattern governs attraction, while charge triggers resistance. In a field of sympathetic vibration, cells may be attracted on the basis of common pattern while carrying dissimilar charges; those carrying higher charge will seek to raise the charge of their neighbors. This primal dynamic, while it does result in a minute loss of energy, also creates a bond between the cells involved, as they communicate back and forth with each beat of the pulse. Such cells are linked, locked together for the duration of their exchange. And this bond strengthens the overall matrix of which the cells are a part.

There is a certain ratio, or percentage of uniform charge to diverse charge, that determines whether the dynamic over resistance strengthens or weakens a matrix. In a field of random charge, with all the cells either cajoling their neighbors or declining the invitation, so much energy is dissipated that the structure itself will be weakened. In a field of relatively uniform charge, with a few strays declaring their right to carry low charge, the resultant bonds will strengthen the overall structure. In a three-dimensional matrix, the ideal mix is about one pariah cell to twenty uniform cells. Such a matrix is stronger than a field of entirely uniform cells, and certainly stronger than a field of floating random charge.

So while sympathetic vibrations attract, and create strong fields of uniform charge, that strength is further bolstered by the presence of a few varying charges, the dynamic bonds between them gluing the matrix together.

In summary, the swirling dance of physical universe construction is governed by the three fundamental qualities of cooperation among all elements and cells, the free-flowing passage of energy and information without hindrance or barrier, and the spice and power of variety. At the primal dawn of creation, the universe is an exuberant, cooperative dance knowing neither wall nor boundary, enhanced by the limitless variety of form the primal pulse assumes on bursting into physical life.

If the universe is governed by the qualities of cooperation, free passage, and variety, on what lofty level was the determination made to establish these as the ground rules? Did such characteristics randomly arise from the primordial soup of the universe's first dawn, crystallizing into tradition over eons? How is it that such qualities are infused into the universe with every beat of the primal pulse?

For the first time we must cross the threshold of the primal pulse, venturing to the "other side," to the realms beyond time and space and definition. We must return to the Source.

The Source Itself is unknowable. No consciousness of any level or realm is broad and deep enough to fully apprehend and fathom the very Source of all Creation. Knowing this, knowing that at best we can perceive only fragments and hints of the greater Source from which the universe springs, we find Its tracings etched upon the fabric and design of your world.

Since the Source creates all of which you are aware, it follows that all qualities of life upon earth are reflective of their greater Source. Nothing can exist which does not spring from the Source. We find symbols and clues of the Source's nature by examining the world It has created.

You will grant that the human species holds consciousness as its primary attribute. You also grant other species a degree of consciousness, however rudimentary.

Knowing that any quality found in your world must flow from its Source, you can deduce that the Source is the originator and creator of consciousness. And since the Source feeds Its grand design into your universe with every beat of the primal pulse, it naturally follows that consciousness bursts into life at the fundamental element of matter, the primal cell.

You divide your world into "animate" and "inanimate," granting consciousness to yourselves and other species, while denying it to the earth that sustains you. This division reflects not a bedrock reality, but your skewed perception.

The Source creates consciousness. The Source creates your universe. With every primal pulse It feeds Its consciousness into the smallest building block of time and space, the primal cell. Each burst of the pulse, each spark of breath and life, is suffused with consciousness.

You live not on a lonely planet spinning through cold, dark space, but float in a sea of life sizzling with consciousness and exuberance at every point. You walk not upon a crust of cold, dead rock, but on a pulsing, organic fabric whose consciousness eludes you.

Because the Source is the font of all consciousness, because It thrusts Its energy and intent into your world with every primal pulse, every corner of creation glows and bubbles with consciousness, beginning at the fundamental level of the primal cell and its dancing, spinning charge. Primal cells communicate. They resist. They attract. They ache to join with others. At the first breath of physical life, the dim horizon of time and space, your universe pulsates with consciousness.

Even granting consciousness to the primal cells, we still have not explored why their natural expression is cooperation, free-flowing energy, and variety. Why should these qualities, and not others, govern the primal dance of physical universe construction?

Again we must leap the primal pulse, back into the realms unknown to time and space, back to the Source. And here we find the single most fundamental and essential ingredient of your system, from which all else flows: *intent*.

The universe exists because the Source *intends* it to be. Your world spins because the Source *intends* it to spin. You live because the Source *intends* you to live. Nothing is random, nothing is accidental; nowhere do coincidence or fate or chance enter the process. Everything happens for a reason, everything has a purpose; the reason and purpose flow from the *intent* of the Source to create and sustain your universe.

Of the infinite realms of exploration created by the Source from Its unquenchable thirst for new experience and growth, your system is cast as a unique and irreplaceable medium of exploration. Your universe is not cast off in the vast, dark reaches of creation, left to sputter itself out to deathbed whimpers of spinning ice, but is perpetually suffused with the Source's intent for you and your world: to be and to grow.

Do you suppose that human consciousness is the accidental creation of the primal cells as they sustain your body and brain, that their primal consciousness multiplies exponentially to become the miracle of the human soul?

You exist because the Source intends that you exist; It finds growth and fulfillment through your private life and your experience with others as you tread the path of time and space. Every other element of your system, from the birds soaring overhead to the rock you crumble underfoot, exists as a unique and precious focus, a singular slant on the intent to be and to grow.

The three fundamental qualities governing creation and sustenance of your system—cooperation, free-flowing energy, variety—flow from the Source's *intent* that such shall be the nature of the physical system. This intent rides atop the consciousness infused into the system with every beat of the pulse. It informs and governs the primal interactions and processes of the physical system, the swirl of vibration breathing space and time to life.

Consciousness and intent carry neither weight nor mass; they do not create and sustain the primal interactions of matter, but ride above them, organizing the flow into patterns of coherence, consistency, and endurance. To be and to grow—this is the purpose of your physical system, and that purpose finds truest expression through cooperation, free-flowing energy, and variety.

Each beat of the primal pulse carries this intent to your world with fresh vigor and power, feeding the Source's design into the patterns of matter and the trickle of moments, buoying the unique and precious expression of intent that finds fulfillment through your world and life.

Seven

༉

Bedrock, Water, and Air

Now that we understand the fundamental principles of vibration, and see how its organization flows from the Source's intent to create your world as a unique crucible of growth, and has granted you and your world the breath of life—to be and to grow—we now turn to an examination of the underlying structure of your planet, with an eye toward appreciating precisely how it serves as the stage on which you play out the drama of your lives.

Remember that the sphere is the most efficient organizational structure vibration can take, other than the axis. Let us take a brief look at how vibration manifests in these two basic patterns.

Axis energy is generally of uniform charge and pattern. Information travels most easily along the filament connecting primal cells end to end, and therefore the processes of attraction and resistance pulse with greater urgency along the axis. The process of resistance—of cells inducing neighbors to raise their charge—is easiest along the axis, and cells carrying lower charge are more likely to accede to their neighbors' urging, for there is less energy loss in altering one's charge linearly rather than laterally. So the urge to carry uniform charge is most easily expressed along the axis. The same also holds true for the cells' pattern, where sympathetic vibrations are most easily transmitted along the filament.

As a result, axis energy is almost always of a fairly uniform consistency, both in charge and pattern. The axis is a stronger, tighter bond of cohesion, as a rule, than a sphere.

As we have seen, a sphere is constructed as layers of charge, fields of charge, wrap around an axis. The advantage to the field—to the extent it retains individual purpose—is that communication among its cells is easiest this way, resulting in the least loss of energy. At the same time, communication between layers is possible through the lateral relationships, allowing free passage of information and charge throughout the matrix of the sphere.

We have already seen that a sphere is a more complex design than an axis, for each layered field of charge maintains a certain integrity and stance, while still contributing to the overall structure. As a result, a sphere gives rise to a greater variety of charge and pattern and structure, supporting various fields and pockets of vibration, all contained within the matrix. You see how this differs from axis energy—uniform, consistent, tenacious.

For this reason you live on a sphere, not an axis. For this reason almost all objects in space are spheres, not axes. A sphere allows greater variety, and as variety is the spice and spark of the physical system, it naturally follows that the structure that is both most efficient and most conducive to variety will be the "standard" model of matter.

If you consider your planet for a moment, you realize that it is not a construction of gradually decreasing density, with the greatest density at the core, tapering off layer by layer to the random puff of stratosphere. Instead, you find relatively sharp demarcations of density: The earth you walk upon is solid under your feet, yet one inch above the surface your foot moves unhindered through the lightness of air. The soil does not gradually taper off, then, but resolves itself firmly, breaking cleanly to form the crust.

The surface of the globe is covered more by water than by soil or rock. Again, the ocean breaks away neatly at the shore; it does not blend with beach or cliff to an indistinguishable mixture; each states the limits of its purpose and stakes no further claim.

The three primary densities of matter on the surface of your planet are thus soil and rock, water or other liquid, and atmosphere. These three levels of density, of vibration, ride in distinct and discrete patterns, rarely blending with others, creating not a homogenous soup of commingled vibration but your varied world of mountain and river and sky.

The three densities of matter on your planet reflect the three basic vibrational patterns employed in physical universe construction. Let us now examine these three patterns.

The densest material is bedrock, the firm foundation undergirding your soil. Given your understanding of vibration and how it combines to weave patterns of varying strength and endurance, you should be able to deduce the vibrational composition of bedrock.

First, such a field is of relatively uniform charge. Remember that such a field is strong because its members carry identical charge and therefore need dissipate no energy in the game of resistance. All energy is focused on sustaining the charge of the cell, and the structure of which it is a part.

The very strongest density is a field enlivened by a few stray cells of diverse charge, sparking a soft flavoring of resistance whose bonds further strengthen the structure. This, then, is the vibrational pattern of bedrock: uniform charge carrying a few strays.

This uniformity holds not only in a given layer of cells, but also to neighboring layers. You see a reflection of this when you hold a rock and observe its striated layers lying sharp and even, never undulating, gluing the rock to its impervious, dense form.

The charge of the primal cells sustaining bedrock will be on the high end of the scale. Using our simplified model of 0 to 10, bedrock carries a uniform 9 or 10 charge. There is greater bulk to the burst each primal cells carries; more "space" is taken up by the charge, and thus a given matrix carries that much more "stuff" with each beat of the pulse. We are dealing now with the most basic level, the level of vibration, not even approaching the complexity of electron and proton which govern the specific elements creating bedrock. At the level of vibration, each primal cell carries a large burst, filling the cell to the walls with intent, creating the original units of bulk, mass, and weight.

While primal cells sustaining bedrock carry the greatest charge of all physical densities, they also carry the softest or most attenuated pattern to that charge. Remember that pattern is the flavor or song of each charge, the unique stamp and shape the charge assumes. The more dramatically and uniquely contoured a pattern is, the more unstable the matrix of which it is a part—for the urge of pattern is attraction, to find sympathetic vibrational companions. Therefore, the more distinct and variable a cell's pattern, the more compelling the urge to move, to seek out sympathetic vibration. And, therefore, the more "unstable" is the structure of which it plays a part.

For this reason, bedrock charges carry relatively uniform, consistent pattern, undulating softly from cell to cell; not erupting with volcanic bursts of uniqueness, but remaining in quiet sympathy with neighboring cells. This uniformity of pattern means the cells can rest at ease, secure in the familiar comfort of sympathetic vibration, and therefore sustain a structure enduring through space and time.

Here is a key quality of your world: A given density reflects its stability both in solidity in space and endurance through time. If you hold a rock, you can state that at this moment it is of hard, dense structure, impervious to your efforts to squeeze or break it with your hands. At the same time, you acknowledge that this rock will endure through time long beyond your last breath. So a given density manifests equally in space and time, for both such measures spring from the primal pulse, the spark of physical life begetting moment and matter.

Can you hold a cloud of steam in your hands and find it impervious to your grasp? And how long does it last in time? Again, space and time are inextricably linked when shaping the patterns of matter.

Bedrock, the foundation upon which you live, is constructed of layered fields of uniform high charge, carrying a few randomly charged cells, woven into a harmonious and gentle pattern of vibration.

The next density of matter you recognize is liquid. Water stands as the mediator between bedrock and atmosphere: You can feel it against you, as with rock, while also moving freely through it, as with air.

Water is constructed in a fundamentally different pattern, though. It is not merely diluted bedrock, nor condensed air. It has a unique pattern of vibration.

Rather than building from the primacy of the layer, as with bedrock, water's pattern requires a larger three-dimensional matrix in which agglomerations of sympathetic vibration can attract and resist. While bedrock is sheets or layers built one atop the other, water's primal building block is chunks or masses of charge floating through the three-dimensional matrix of primal cells, giving far greater play to the game of attraction and resistance.

As example, imagine a cube of a thousand primal cells, ten on a side. You might have a few clumps of vibration at the high and low end, toward 0 and 10, while the bulk of the cells support clusters of charge around the mean, around charge 5. Floating clumps of charge ranging from 3 to 7 will predominate, swirling about each other in the perpetual dance of attraction and resistance. This pulsating swirl of vibration is enlivened by the few clusters of charge at either end of the scale, for the higher charges seek to raise the level of the whole lot, while the lower charges resist the entreaties of the majority.

Because the fundamental pattern of water is one of floating clusters of varying charge, the structure cannot solidify in space and time as bedrock does. Too much energy is dissipated in the game of attraction and resistance. Further, the majority of cells carry charges around the mean, the average. Thus, each burst of the primal pulse fills each cell halfway, contributing equal parts of "stuff" and "nothing" to the brew which becomes water. As such, there will be less solidity in space, and less endurance in time.

Water swirls, dances, leaps, flows, rains, cascades, trickles, gushes, erupts, showers, bathes. The oceans wash constantly upon the shore; the river eats forever at its banks; the tides ebb and flood the whole globe over. If water has one fundamental characteristic, it must be this: motion. Water always flows downhill, flowing to the ocean or seeping into the ground. Water is never still, never complacent for a moment, always doing, creating, destroying, pulsating.

All such qualities flow from the fundamental vibrational pattern creating water, that of a constant dance of attraction and resistance, of clumps of charge bouncing about in exuberant play.

Just as the charges creating water are of varying intensity, hovering about the mean, so are the patterns describing the shape of those charges of greater uniqueness and independence than those sustaining bedrock. For it is pattern that governs attraction, and therefore pattern that calls the players to dance. The greater diversity of pattern in a given matrix, the greater the pull of attraction. As each cell's pattern searches for sympathetic partners to embrace, the cell's urge to move brings it in contact with similarly mobile cells of varying charge—varying charge, the source of resistance. So a field of highly individual patterns, unless it also carries uniform charge, will be one given to an exuberant dance of attraction and resistance.

Thus, water carries less solidity in space and less endurance through time. The vibrational pull of attraction and resistance is too costly in energy loss to sustain the firmness of bedrock or its permanence through time. Water's fundamental quality is motion; alone of the three densities it can leap through all three density levels—ice, water, vapor—in a matter of moments.

Motion, change, variety, a pulsating urge to travel and transform— these are the fundamental qualities of water, born of its primal play of attraction and resistance.

Air is the lightest of the three basic earth densities. In its natural state it has neither color nor smell; you rush through it without hindrance, never giving it a moment's thought. While you know it carries elements and molecules, these travel in patterns beyond the reach of your senses; to you a glass holding no liquid is "empty."

Let us see just how empty that glass is.

The charge and pattern of air are the inverse of those sustaining bedrock. That is, air's charge is negligible, while its pattern is wildly and fantastically varied. Remember that charge is a measure of the intensity of the primal pulse feeding into the primal cells. The greater the charge, the more "stuff" the cell contains. The cells creating and sustaining air remain virtually empty with each beat of the pulse, receiving just enough charge to reinvigorate the walls of the cell, to maintain its stance, while sparking little else. There is little charge imparted to the cells creating air.

At the same time, however, the pattern or shape of what little charge is imparted carries the greatest variety of all three densities. Each air cell carries a starkly unique and independent pattern.

Bedrock carries layer upon layer of uniform pattern; water flows from clumps of charge scurrying about; air buoys the supreme individualists, the nonconformists, the misfits, the pariahs of the physical system. Each is radically different; each travels alone most of the time. For when pattern differs so radically from cell to cell, the inevitable swirl of attraction will rarely result in two or more cells meeting and bonding in compatible harmony. When two air cells approach, they may well recognize a common theme in the pattern of the other, but upon closer examination will find a unique variation the other cannot match. And so they part and begin the search anew.

Because air cells carry so little charge, resistance plays virtually no part in air's swirling dance. There is no charge to compare with one's neighbors, to urge or decline. The process is pure attraction, and because the patterns are so radically different, and so rarely result in sympathetic bonding, the motion is constant and unhindered.

This is why you are unhindered when you walk through air. Resistance plays no part in the vibrational structure underlying it. And because there is so little charge to the cells, there is no "stuff" for you to knock your head against.

You can see that air is not simply the "opposite" of bedrock, for in both cases resistance plays little part. Bedrock carries uniform charge, so resistance never arises; air carries no charge, so resistance is unknown.

As with every corner of the universe, "empty space" pulsates with consciousness, life, and intent at every point. Because the process holds no mass or resistance, it escapes the scope of your senses. Hold your breath for five minutes if you still consider air devoid of life!

In summary, the three basic densities of your planet are bedrock, water, and air. Bedrock carries high charge and little resistance. Water carries an equal play of attraction and resistance among clusters of moderately varying charge. Air is a fantastical dance of attraction among cells of low charge, a perpetual and ultimately futile search for sympathetic companions.

Again, these processes lie far below the most elemental atoms and molecules that create the earth and its features. These are the patterns from which the elements are cut and sewn into your planet's fabric.

When it snows, hold out your hand and catch a souvenir of earth's three densities, compressed into the gently falling shape of a snowflake. Like air, each is unique, distinct, never to find its twin. Like water, it is born of attraction and resistance, condensing in the clouds. And it holds, for however brief a moment, the stability and endurance of bedrock, glistening like a diamond in your hand before surrendering to your heat, spilling its form into a droplet upon the earth, returning in the verdant disguise of spring's first scent.

Eight

∽

Earth, Moon, and Sun

Now that we understand the three basic densities of matter underlying the earth's construction, let us turn our attention to an examination of how these elements are arranged and weaved to form your home. Doing so will offer clues as to the purpose of life on earth, and of the human species.

Your planet is a sphere spinning on an axis. Axis energy is generally of highly uniform, consistent, and enduring vibration, while a sphere is a more complex arrangement allowing greater variety. Because variety is a fundamental quality of vibration as it manifests in the physical system, and because the Source seeks fulfillment through diversity, it stands to reason that a body of matter playing host to life will assume the shape most conducive to a variety of life forms, the sphere.

Given your understanding that every primal cell, every corner of the universe, pulsates with consciousness, to question whether other planets "support" life is vain. Every planet *is* alive, pulsing with life, and the support of independent life forms upon the surface, where it occurs, is literally the icing on the cake. No planet floats "dead" through space; consciousness suffuses them all, finding purpose and fulfillment in the variety of structures and densities and journeys of each around its sun.

Life on planet earth is no accident, then, no serendipitous roll of the dice in a cosmic crap shoot, but instead flows from the Source's intent to explore physical reality in as wide a range of activity as possible. To create a planet and then grant millions of species upon its surface, each with a unique consciousness and purpose, provides an infinitely rich crucible of creation.

To allow for the drama of surface life, a planet must have a highly specialized core of energy in its axis. For axis energy always works its way out through the layers of bedrock into the atmosphere; during this passage it invigorates and balances the life forms upon the surface. Thus, a planet sustaining surface life necessarily carries axis energy of a specific configuration.

The first quality of such a planet's axis energy is its pulse. The frequency of a planet's axis pulse determines whether or not it can sustain surface life. Now, an axis pulse is not of the same duration or intensity as the primal pulse which bursts into your physical system, creating the entire universe. Each planet, each body of matter, creates a unique, secondary pulse which rides atop the primal pulse.

The purpose, always, is to "slow down" the primal pulse to a frequency supportive of life forms whose perceptual mechanisms (your senses) can perceive frequencies only along certain narrow bands of vibration. Because these bands of vibration are relatively slow, at least compared with the beat of the primal pulse, the axis energy of your planet slows down the primal pulse, fashioning it into a beat compatible with the vibrational spectrums of your senses.

Technically, a planet's axis does not slow the primal pulse. This fundamental rhythm never varies. Understanding that an axis also pulsates at a consistent rate, the process is one in which a planet's axis absorbs a certain number of primal pulsations while emitting a steady "on" vibration, then an equal number of pulsations while in the "off" condition.

In other words, as a crude example, if a planet's axis slows the primal pulse at a ratio of a hundred to one, this means that every hundred "on" and "off" primal pulsations translate into a single uniform "on" axis pulse, followed by the next hundred primal pulsations being rendered as a single "off" axis pulse. The technicalities of how this is achieved are not necessary for your understanding that a planet's axis "slows" the primal pulse to a rate necessary for sustaining the planet's purpose—in your case, among others, sustaining surface life.

So your planet pulsates from its axis with a unique vibration designed to allow you and all other species to thrive and grow. This "earth pulse," as we shall hereafter call it, is a slowing of the primal pulse down to a frequency conducive to sustaining surface life.

A sphere is constructed of layers or fields of charge curving about an axis. A planet such as yours will carry fields of highly specific configuration.

First, they must allow relatively unfettered passage to the earth pulse emanating from the axis. There are planets where the activity of the intermediate fields is so intense, drinks up so much vibration, that little or no energy can rise to the surface, to be released into atmosphere. Since all surface species depend on a constant flow of energy from the axis, such a planet can support no surface life; to you it appears dead and cold. In truth, such a planet concentrates its life and vibration in the intermediate layers between axis and surface, finding its challenge and growth at these layers.

Your planet, then, is one in which the intermediate layers of vibration allow sufficient passage of energy that surface life can be sustained. As such, the bedrock layers act as transmitters of vibration rather than serving as the primary focus of the planet's purpose.

The intermediate layers act as filters. While allowing relatively free passage to the earth pulse, the layers do not simply pass that energy on, but color and flavor it into highly specific fields. The purpose, again, is to enhance variety, the immense variety of species upon your planet's surface. The intermediate layers thus find their growth and challenge in absorbing the uniform earth pulse, and while still allowing free flow to its frequency, they shape and sculpt that energy into an infinite variety of pattern before passing it along to the surface.

Returning to our qualities of charge and pattern, the process is one in which the layers allow regular and consistent transmission of charge to rise toward the surface, while configuring that charge into pockets and areas of specific and unique pattern. This allows for the enormous variety of topography, plant and animal life, and variations on the theme of human consciousness which enrich your globe.

Your planet rides on an axis slowing the primal pulse down into the earth pulse, the heart beat of all life, while the bedrock layers shape that pulse into specialized pockets of energy, giving rise to the richness and variety of life upon the surface.

How is the varied terrain, the variety of topography, created and sustained upon the earth's surface?

Remember that energy travels most easily along an axis, along the filament connecting primal cells lying in a row. The transmission of charge laterally, along the cells' flanks, results in some loss of energy and fidelity of the charge and pattern.

You can see, then, that as a sphere is constructed of layers of charge wrapped about an axis, energy rising from the axis toward the surface is transmitted laterally, layer to layer. The energy thus cannot help but be dissipated, altered, for its travel through the layers of bedrock. In addition, the charge and pattern are altered by the deliberate work of the bedrock layers to shape a variety of energy fields upon the surface.

The result, on your planet and most others, is that the surface is not a uniform, smooth, glassy layer, polished to a sheen, numbing in its monotonous homogeneity. Instead, by the time the earth pulse reaches the surface, it has been so altered and fractured by its travels that the surface becomes an uneven, broken, ragged jumble of mountain, plain, and ocean floor. Imagine for a moment that the earth's oceans have evaporated; consider now the enormous peaks and valleys, the pitted gullies and trenches, which form the surface of the planet.

You credit the condition of the planet's surface to erosion, uplift, volcanic activity, earthquakes, the movement of the tectonic plates, the battering of rain and wind. While these forces all legitimately shape and mold earth's surface, they all spring from one fundamental cause: the earth's pulse losing its firm, consistent axis energy as it emanates through the bedrock layers, crumbling to increasing instability as it nears the surface, further flavored by the deliberate scrambling into unique fields. The result is your fantastically varied planet's surface.

Now, understand the distinction between the earth pulse's *frequency* and its *configuration*. The frequency is the fundamental vibrational pattern of the planet, squeezing the primal pulse down into a rhythm conducive to life. This never alters, never varies, anywhere on the planet's surface. It remains consistent and constant. The frequency is a measure of how many pulsations per unit of time pump from the earth's core.

It is the configuration—the charge and pattern—this vibration assumes that is altered and degraded for its passage through the bedrock. This is the flavor, the color of the earth's vibration shaped by the filters of bedrock.

So while the rhythm of the earth pulse never varies, the charge and pattern riding atop it assume virtually infinite configurations upon reaching the surface.

That explains bedrock and its peaks and valleys. But they alone cannot sustain life upon the surface. Whence arises the elixir of life, the primordial fountain of existence, the play of rain and tide?

We must now leave the earth's surface and embrace its two celestial neighbors who join in partnership with the earth to spark the breath of life: the sun and the moon.

Let us first review what has been explored earlier. Axis energy is always of a highly specific, consistent pattern. Its endurance in space and through time depends upon its regular, constant pulsation of uniform energy.

Bedrock energy is also of a highly uniform configuration, a high charge flavored by consistent pattern, with resistance playing virtually no part.

The composition of a planet's material always reflects the energy of its axis. A planet such as yours—constructed of bedrock—can spring only from an axis energy sympathetic to bedrock: high charge, consistent pattern, little resistance.

There are "planets" consisting entirely of liquid, and those made of gas, each reflecting the nature of its axis energy.

Would life be possible on a planet composed entirely of bedrock, breaking cleanly into atmosphere, devoid of liquid? Life, as you know it, would be impossible on such a sphere. And yet that is precisely the foundation of your planet, as determined by its axis energy.

Bedrock and atmosphere know little of resistance. A planet of these two densities alone cannot support life.

To be and to grow: this is your purpose. To grow, most fundamentally, is a process of resistance, of effort expended against the extant elements. To move at all is to shove aside the atmosphere that surrounds you. To grow roots breaks up the soil, overriding its bedrock desire to maintain solidity and permanence. To eat and drink is to alter the composition and stance of the natural world, transforming the elements of nutrition into bone and blood.

Because the fundamental urge of every primal cell, and of every structure it creates, is to maintain its stance for as long a time as possible, and because the processes of life ineluctably lead to alterations in the natural world, it follows that the fundamental quality of life, of growth, is resistance.

A planet of bedrock and atmosphere knows no resistance. It can know no life. Only liquid, only water, carries the lively dance of attraction and resistance. Only water can sustain and buoy life.

Since a planet's composition reflects its axis energy, and since your planet is almost entirely bedrock, you know that your planet's core energy is one knowing little resistance. For there to be life at all upon the surface, therefore, the play of attraction and resistance must be imposed from without.

Here enter the sun and moon.

The moon shares the earth's composition, does it not? It is a hard, dusty crust of bedrock, supporting no animate life, seemingly cold and dead. You thus know that its core axis energy is of uniform high charge, with little variation in its pattern. And resistance plays even less of a role than in your planet's core, virtually none. The result is a surface of uniform bedrock, sculpted into peaks and valleys like the earth, but devoid of animate life.

Now picture the sun. It is an explosive, fulminating ball of gas, a volcano imploding on itself, spewing tendrils of gaseous lava from its surface, a swirling, angry cacophony of action and battle.

And resistance. Remember that resistance always results in a loss of energy, dissipated to the atmosphere, weakening the structure. A swirling ball of gas like the sun, knowing nothing of bedrock or stability or permanence, reflects its fundamental nature: a sphere pulsating with resistance.

Where charge is concerned, the most unstable field is one of random charge, an equal distribution along the spectrum, allowing no one vibration to congregate and dominate. Such a field gives rise to a perpetual dance of resistance, of primal cell against primal cell, cajoling and resisting in an endless and futile urge to build structures of uniform charge.

Pattern governs attraction, the joining of sympathetic vibration. The most unstable field in terms of pattern will be cells of highly individualistic configuration, a sea of iconoclasts searching in vain for sympathetic companions.

Thus you may deduce the composition of the sun: a swirling sphere of random charge unable to create and sustain structure, each charge carrying a unique and distinct pattern forcing a perpetual instability. The struggle of resistance releases energy; the urgent search for similar pattern releases energy. Thus the sun expends all of its energy on the process of attraction and resistance, leaving none to build and sustain structure.

The result is a ball of explosive activity spewing energy far into the reaches of space—and to the surface of your planet.

The moon is a ball of bedrock, of stability, of permanence. The sun is a crash of resistance. Between them lies your earth.

Remember that vibration always attempts to induce its neighbors to assume its charge. Remember that like attracts like. As the earth's axis energy emanates from the surface, unstable, crumbling, drifting in random chunks, it is susceptible to influence both by the moon's steady high charge and by the sun's play of resistance.

The result is water.

Water is clumps of charge floating in a sea of attraction and resistance. Clusters of charge—a compromise between the strict uniformity of moon energy and the random dissipation of sun energy. Meeting the two pulls halfway, earth's unstable surface energy coagulates into clusters of charge, pockets of attraction and resistance.

The moon's uniform bedrock pulls toward the sturdy bedrock of earth. The furious random shower of sun energy bathes you with resistance. The forces meet on your planet, urging its unstable surface energy to assume their shape and form. The dynamic tension between moon and sun energy creates a unique blend, clusters of attraction and resistance, trickling, flowing, rushing, cascading, thundering, swelling, and roaring into the primal sea, the cornucopia of life, spilling its infinitude of leaf and flesh upon the plains and peaks and ocean depths.

None of this is accidental. The urge to be and to grow, which fuels every corner of the physical system, finds fulfillment through the infinite variety of matter and its configurations. A sphere of uniform, quiescent bedrock, like the moon, plays host to a specific energy finding its fulfillment in such stable permanence. A chaotic, random jumble of explosive impermanence, like the sun, offers fulfillment to another flavor of matter's expression. And strung between them, the earth, while bedrock stable at the core, provides a surface of unstable fields and pockets, inviting suasion from moon and sun; the result is a field of attraction and resistance which allows and sustains the abundance of life blessing your planet.

The earth thus plays an intrinsic and invaluable part in the intent of the Source to create and explore the physical universe, and to seed it with consciousness. For it is consciousness which animates life, and therefore life which realizes the Source's intent that consciousness find free play and fulfillment in the physical system.

There are no accidents, least of all the blue and green spinning ball of your birth. Suspended between a sphere of stable bedrock and a sphere of random explosion, your planet melds their dynamic tension into the liquid bed of life, setting the stage for the blessing of conscious life.

Nine

உ

Water Planet Life

A water planet such as yours exists for the purpose of allowing the expression of consciousness through animate and inanimate life. While every primal cell in every corner of the universe—your planet's surface or the "empty" vastness of space—contains consciousness just for existing, a water planet's life forms play host to a rich variety of focuses or slants available nowhere else. Each form of life on your planet shares a certain common consciousness with other members of its species; and all species of the earth live cooperatively, linked in the common experience of water planet consciousness.

Let us examine the process by which life is created and sustained on a water planet. Ultimately, all depends on the process of photosynthesis, where plants convert the sun's energy into the basic building blocks required to sustain their lives and the animate species that consume them. We will begin our examination at this level, then.

All plants must have water or die. Aquatic plants live enfolded in an aqueous cocoon; terrestrial plants must drink up their life's essence through the roots. In both cases, water is essential to the growth and survival of plants.

Remember that water is the progeny of sun and moon as they exert their disparate pulls upon the earth's unstable surface energy. Water is the only element of the earth knowing resistance to any great extent; and as life itself is a process of resistance, water is essential to growth and survival.

You know that sunlight is necessary for photosynthesis to occur. Let us narrow our view to a single plant cell and examine precisely what occurs during this process.

A plant cell, composed almost entirely of water, plays host on a miniature scale to the tug-of-war between moon and sun that creates water. Clumps or clusters of charge swirl about the plant cell in a dance of attraction and resistance, with no one charge gaining sufficient strength to allow its dominance over all others.

When the sun rains its random shower of energy upon the earth and upon the plant, the "randomness" of the cell's charges is enhanced. Where before clumps of charge floated about, now those clusters are burst asunder by the sun's insistent pull. The result is a relative increase in the force of attraction—solitary units of charge of highly individualistic pattern scattering about in vain search for sympathetic companions. A plant cell absorbing direct sunlight finds its clusters of charge disintegrating into discrete units of charge, giving way to the force of resistance.

Resistance releases energy. Thus, when a plant's cell is under the sun's sway of resistance, and its clusters of charge disintegrate into solitary units, it releases energy. No energy is ever lost, as you know, and this released energy can go one of two places: into the atmosphere, or be reabsorbed by the plant. The bulk of released energy is just so captured by the plant. The excess energy, which is not required to sustain the plant in its present size, can then be channeled into physical growth—literally, the plant filling more primal cells with its bulk.

One fundamental characteristic of water planet life is its ability to recapture excess energy, rather than releasing it to the atmosphere, and to pour the excess into physical growth of the organism. Each form of consciousness, however rudimentary, revels in its earthly existence, and the more primal cells are filled with its bulk, the greater the exuberance of existence. The tendency is therefore to funnel excess energy into physical growth.

There are limits, of course, beyond which extra growth would serve to hinder an organism's fulfillment, and beyond which it will not grow. There is a reason why you are not all twelve feet tall, as we shall explore later, relating to maintaining your brain's distance from the earth's surface at an optimum height.

At its most basic level, growth of any organism flows from the sun's stimulating a battle of resistance, resulting in release of energy which is then funneled into physical growth—literally the annexation of primal cells previously holding "empty" space.

Intrinsically bound to a discussion of energy is its expression in terms of temperature—heat and cold. For while you cannot examine the process of photosynthesis, cannot hear or see the pull of resistance sparking a plant cell to release energy, you certainly feel the warmth of the sun and the chill of the wind.

In a camouflage physical system such as yours, you do not experience vibration directly, but symbolically through the interpretation of your senses. Heat and cold, sensations carried from your skin to your brain, reflect the constant play of disparate energy fields upon the earth's surface.

Every primal cell of whatever density—air, water, bedrock—under the sun's glare will be cajoled toward expressing resistance, and thus toward release of energy. This is a self-perpetuating system, as each cell's random excess energy will induce its neighbor to follow suit—and yet its neighbor is also being directly stimulated by the sun. So an area under the sun's glare grows increasingly similar to the composition of the sun itself—a field of random charge, of highly individualistic pattern, building in an increasingly frantic dance of resistance.

The result is excess energy released but finding no immediate home, no niche in which to ease itself, no structure to which it can contribute. For every other primal cell is equally spewing out excess energy, taking none in.

This you experience as heat—literally, the swirling clouds of random excess energy released by the sun's pull of resistance. As the day wears on—as the sun rises in the sky until it hangs directly overhead—the earth, water, and air under its gaze grow increasingly warm. The cycle feeds on itself, excess energy begetting more resistance, begetting still more excess energy. This reaches its apex with the sun directly overhead at noon, its beams shooting straight and true to earth, inducing the structures there to a frenzy of resistance.

By late afternoon, with the sun's rays at an oblique angle, its ability to provoke earth's elements toward resistance is diminished. And with night-fall comes release from the sun's grasp, a restoration to the "natural" state of the earth's elements, a quiescent, soothing return to the earth's bedrock energy as fed to you by the earth's steady pulse. With the splash of resistance retreating for another day, feeling instead the steady maternal heartbeat of earth about you, you lie down and take your rest, secure in the calm, soothing rhythm of earth.

Despite the sun's urgent pull toward resistance, earth's elements never give in completely, dissolving in the chaotic jumble of the sun. Their fundamental structures are too strong, and the sun too distant, for there to be danger of complete surrender. Bedrock and atmosphere carry little resistance, and are therefore little affected by the sun's entreaties. A rock will become warm to the touch; air will heat under the sun's glare. But water alone carries any appreciable measure of resistance; so water undergoes the greatest transformation: from ice to water to vapor, all under the sun's shower of resistance. Water most easily surrenders its energy and form to the sun's persuasion.

The earth rides on an axis of bedrock. As such, the areas of the surface closest to the axis—the poles—will be most influenced by bedrock's steady, constant pattern. As a result, the poles are covered with ice—water in its most quiescent state, the form closest to the stability of bedrock.

Farthest from the pull of the earth's axis lies the equator. Here the sun holds greatest influence; here the air sizzles with heat; here the rain forests sprout a thick tangle of verdure and support the greatest concentration of species on earth; here the cold, icy grip of winter stakes no claim.

Yet even in the sun's dominion, the moon asserts eminent domain in the sweep of the tides. As the earth revolves, that section directly facing the moon is literally pulled toward it. The moon's bedrock calls to the earth's bedrock axis; the axis bends toward the moon, squeezing itself toward its mate. The oceans, pools of attraction and resistance, sway to the moon's song of attraction, leaping and frothing toward the distant magnet, tossing their essence higher and higher upon beach and cliff.

The dance never ends. The sun's pull of resistance reigns at the equator; earth's bedrock rules the poles. The moon pulls ocean and crust toward it in a grip of attraction, while the sun showers the tides with random resistance. Every living organism feeds on the constant swirl of attraction and resistance; energy, the fundamental of life, springs free to weave an infinitude of living form, host to innumerable slants of consciousness.

It is within this crucible of creation that our main focus of interest, human consciousness, finds its home and expression. With the fundamentals of physical universe construction behind us, let us turn now to an examination of your species' place upon the water planet Earth, how your presence provides a unique and invaluable focus to the Source, and how you may exercise your free will to weave from earth's elements the conscious life of your design.

Part Two

THE HUMAN SEED

Ten

Families of Consciousness

You now understand the principles of vibration, how they order and build the universe. You understand how your water planet balances between moon and sun, allowing life to bloom. Thus is prepared the garden of your existence, awaiting the seed of consciousness, the germ of intent, from which you thrust your heads toward the stars and shoot brilliant blossoms of unique life experience.

All consciousness flows from the Source. We must now leap the primal pulse and nestle in the lap of all creation, the better to understand the origin and purpose of consciousness.

While each primal cell is suffused with consciousness and intent for its very existing, such consciousness is a rudimentary fragment of what even the lowest life forms experience. Flowing from the Source's intent that Its consciousness shall feed into an infinite variety of focuses, the Source spins off a host of families of consciousness, each with a unique flavor and perspective, with which to explore Its creations. Each such family of consciousness we shall term a "host consciousness." A host consciousness is the communal source of life perspective granted the various forms of life. Each such host consciousness carries within it further divisions of consciousness, all carrying the stamp of the host while splintering that communal intent into a multitude of unique facets. The host consciousness acts as an umbrella, drawing together unique slants of consciousness under one communal perspective.

Just as you divide and classify the earth's species by phylum, genus, and so forth, so are there similar divisions of consciousness. Indeed, the divisions of consciousness arise first, later spilling into physical form.

An example would be the feline host consciousness. All felines upon the earth share a certain standard perspective, senses perceiving vibration within a certain range, certain "instinctual" behaviors and rituals necessary for survival and fulfillment, a specific common purpose in assuming earthly form. Within the feline host consciousness we find divisions into jungle cats, mountain cats, plains cats, and also your domesticated cats. While they all share a common form and consciousness, each has taken a unique slant, depending on its locale and life conditions.

By now your race has enjoyed the company of domesticated cats for so long that it seems their "instinctual" behaviors should have died out. Why the fascination with chasing mice or flies, when the food bowl sits brimming in the kitchen? Why the constant preening, if there is no prey to detect the cat's scent? Such "instincts" will never die out because they are not genetically programmed into your cats, or any other animal. They have no physical source or base. They arise instead from the feline host consciousness, which flows into every cat and keeps it a "cat," whatever its circumstances.

This same principle holds true for all species of the earth. Think of the major divisions—first, plants and animals. Then mammals, fish, birds. Humans, apes, cats, dogs, marsupials. Each such division represents a finer focus or slant of a larger umbrella consciousness. Each stands utterly unique.

As consciousness originates beyond the realm of space and time, there can be no thought of "evolution," of human consciousness miraculously—or accidentally—springing from mutating apes. Human consciousness has always been—will always be—human consciousness and nothing else. The same holds true for every other species. Nothing *descended* from anything else; the blueprints for the earth's species have *always* existed—in your time terms—since before the planet's creation. These families of consciousness, created before the earth could sustain a single-celled organism, are fed into your world and its passage of moments. None commingles with any other; none descends from any other. All were created as equally unique and precious focuses of consciousness with which to explore the earth.

What is human consciousness? What is the purpose and meaning behind this particular focus?

While all animals of the "higher" orders can be considered capable of reason, capable of learning from experience and altering behavior accordingly, human consciousness is a distilled, finely focused expression of the quality of reason. Rational thought is the unique perspective of humanity, its purpose for being. Most fundamentally, human consciousness exists to learn to manipulate symbol—for as all physical objects are symbols (as we shall later explore), and as speech and art and music are all symbol, the human race's unique contribution is to actively manipulate the symbols of the physical world rather than merely using them as the medium of life, as other species do. Other families of consciousness use the physical world as the basis for explorations without seeking or needing to actively manipulate the environment, beyond nest building and so forth. Human consciousness stands alone as the master manipulator of symbol. This is your purpose.

More is involved, however, than simply the ability to shove the earth's elements around in novel configurations. Remember the purpose of a physical camouflage system such as yours: freedom, free will. While at base all is vibration—every hope and dream and love and plan—all such are hidden from your fellows unless you choose to share them, through the symbol of speech or pen and paper. So the "rational" host consciousness feeds itself into both direct and camouflage physical systems; in your case, with the added slant of allowing each individual a highly private experience.

In basic terms it is true that all species of the earth create their own reality. For one thing, every living creature has "chosen" to become that creature, chosen the host consciousness of which it will be a part, chosen the circumstances of birth and so on. Most species carry no awareness of this once ensconced in physical form. To do so would be to violate the very purpose of a camouflage system: freedom and uniqueness.

Human consciousness allows you to strip away the facade of a physical world and explore the very origins of your existence. This is the basis of religion, the urge to wrestle into symbol and myth the source of life, recognizing that you flow from a greater Consciousness than your own and that your life has purpose and meaning. The human race has always had a far greater ability to "create its own reality" as each individual makes his life choices.

What has been largely hidden from your awareness, until recently, is the immense power and potential of human consciousness to consciously create both an individual life and the larger world, to literally pull into being the events of one's life. This you do in every moment, though the process is shrouded behind the veil separating you from your deeper source. The time upon you now, the overture to the Era of Conscious Life, will at last allow you to strip the veil away, to understand and utilize the power of your mind to consciously create your life.

In a sense, the facade of a camouflage physical world is being stripped away, leaving you with the choice—always, the *choice*—to directly glimpse the machinery and mechanics behind your world and to understand and manipulate its events according to your desire. The era upon you, commonly called the New Age, is at base a reclaiming of personal power, an upsurgent affirmation of the primacy of the individual. In a sense you are reclaiming your birthright, the purpose for incarnation upon a camouflage earth—to experience a unique and private life—while also stripping away the camouflage wrappings. The best of both worlds, you see! Such is the age upon you.

The simple fact that you can consciously comprehend that yours is a camouflage physical system means that the camouflage has partially been stripped away. Yet the fundamental purpose of a camouflage reality can never be overridden—the intent that you should each live highly private lives, sharing your experience with others only to the extent of your choice. Until the day when all of your species can communicate telepathically at all times with perfect fidelity, the purpose behind your camouflage system remains intact and valid—and we do not anticipate its demise any time soon!

Human consciousness, the manipulator of symbol, flows from the host human consciousness into a shower of sparks, each unique and never duplicated in all of time, each living its private experience while sharing its journey with others through the expression of symbol. Such is your purpose on earth, your unique contribution to the fulfillment of your Source.

Eleven

ھ

The Stage of Duality

Human consciousness stands under the larger umbrella or rubric of "rational" consciousness. Such rational consciousness feeds into a multitude of forms throughout your universe, and into those dimensions of which you have no awareness. On your own planet, the human race is the rational species living upon the bedrock crust, while the cetaceans are the rational species exploring the depths of the sea.

As rational consciousness feeds itself into a virtually infinite variety of settings or bases from which to symbolically explore reality, each site will sustain a unique slant of rational consciousness, specifically tailored to manipulate effectively in the extant environment. In other words, first the physical universe is constructed, with its myriad foundations—planets of water, ice, gas, bedrock, other liquid chemicals—and then consciousness feeds itself into these structures, assuming a unique slant in each different environment.

Human consciousness was not randomly tossed onto planet earth, then, but was deliberately fed into form here precisely because earth's elements and structure provide a unique milieu for a rational species, available nowhere else in the universe.

To understand the configuration of human consciousness upon your planet, let us review earth's construction. Yours is a water planet. Water is the result of the dual pull between the bedrock attraction of the moon and the random resistance of the sun, exerting their force on the unstable surface energy, forcing an aqueous compromise. As physical growth is a process of resistance, earth's one level of density carrying resistance—water—is essential for life.

You see what a unique stage this sets on which to play the drama of human life. Most planets don't know the sway of moon and sun energy in balanced strength. They know nothing of the opposing pulls of attraction and resistance. While this results in the substance necessary for the survival of physical organisms—water—more importantly, it provides a field of vibration allowing growth and fulfillment to your consciousness.

Yours is a life of duality. Building on the fundamental duality underlying your system—the primal pulse with its steady on and off—your earth is influenced by the duality of moon and sun, the pulls of attraction and resistance. Your day is marked by night and day, light and dark; your consciousness follows this rhythm into wakefulness and sleep; your physical form finds its fundamental division in male and female.

Suspended between the moon and sun, your bodies composed of the aqueous, life-giving issue of their disparate pulls, human consciousness seeds a world whose fundamental quality, shaping and marking every form of life upon it, is duality. It is not that human consciousness exists for the purpose of experiencing a life of duality, but that the earth's fundamental duality plays host to a variety of consciousness, and flowing into that structure, "rational" consciousness assumes human form. This is your unique perspective, informing every moment of your lives, as your very bodies depend upon and are composed of the liquid result of the moon-sun nexus.

When considering questions and issues such as the purpose and meaning of human life upon your planet, it is important to keep in mind which "side" of the primal pulse we are on. For the play of duality exists solely on the physical side, born of your solar and lunar companions. Yet the intent to incarnate on your planet, and the great families of consciousness which squeeze into the denizens of the human race, lie on the nonphysical side of the primal pulse where "duality" does not exist, except as a concept.

Very briefly, let us discuss human consciousness at its source, from beyond the primal pulse, and how its qualities manifest in the physical world.

First, there is the host consciousness, the umbrella under which all human experience stands. The intent and purpose of this host consciousness is to seed your water planet with a rational species and to explore and manipulate the environment symbolically. That is the overall or fundamental purpose of human life.

This host consciousness is then broken down into smaller families of consciousness. This is the first division into unique perspectives on human life, unique roles which can be assumed and played out on earth. There is a family of consciousness to which most political leaders belong, for instance. Another claims the artists as its progeny. One family specializes in nurturance of earth, child, and animal. Another revels in physical construction and manipulation.

We might term each such family of consciousness a "master consciousness," meaning these are the fundamental divisions of human consciousness, the original bodies of intent, each of which plays a necessary role in sustaining human civilization and the earth you share.

Each master consciousness will again divide, specializing further and further, squeezing into a multitude of unique perspectives, each sharing the intent of the master consciousness. These bodies of consciousness, stepping closer toward the primal pulse and more finely focusing on the possibilities of human life, we will term "greater entities."

Greater entities stand at the portal of the primal pulse, peering down into the historical passage of earth, sifting and sorting among the virtually infinite historical periods and geographical locales available for experiencing human life.

As the primal pulse is the originator of space and time, any body of consciousness lying on the "other" side will necessarily be beyond such parameters. Beyond the primal pulse, time and space do not exist. These are the root parameters of your system into which the larger bodies of consciousness feed. The greater entity level of consciousness, standing as it does at the portal between physical and nonphysical realms, exists outside of space and time, while fully aware of and utilizing these parameters to find fulfillment of its purpose.

All "time" is simultaneous from the perspective of the greater entities' consciousness. All historical periods of earth, and all possible variations on the temporal passage of earth, are available for review, just as you might stand before a display of apples and select the half dozen you find most appealing. Given the perspective of the master consciousness fed into its myriad greater entities, and given the unique purpose and desired growth of each greater entity, a variety of historical periods will be selected as most likely to provide venues for fulfillment and learning.

Here is where the barrier is crossed, consciousness feeding itself into the physical system, leapfrogging the primal pulse into space and time. When a greater entity makes its choices, it feeds them into physical being, creating a series of human incarnations over the entire time line of earth. You are one such incarnation. You exist because it serves the intent of your greater entity to have you here now, in your time and place, with your qualities and characteristics and talents contributing to the overall growth and fulfillment of your greater entity's purpose.

You can see how the traditionally understood concept of reincarnation falls a bit short of reality. It is true that "you" have lived before and will live again, in the sense that your greater entity has also created human lives in other historical periods—both past and future. At the same time, you stand utterly unique, created afresh for the specific purpose of being who and where you are. Your soul is not recycled, then, tossed into another body fifty years after your death. In time terms, all such incarnations are created "at once," beyond the beat of the primal pulse, beyond the flow of time. So while you share a certain common link with your other incarnations, flowing as you do from a common source, you stand utterly unique and unduplicated, not another step on the path to fulfillment but the very source of fulfillment.

You now understand the basic divisions of consciousness. First is the host "rational" consciousness, feeding itself into the limitless avenues of exploration available in the physical and nonphysical realms. From this flows the overall "human" consciousness, specifically tailored to populate and explore planet earth through the manipulation of symbol. Next come divisions into master consciousnesses, basic families of intent and purpose. Each such master consciousness creates a huge series of greater entities, each carrying the stamp of the master consciousness but with a unique perspective. These greater entities stand at the portal of the primal pulse, gazing onto earth's historical passage and selecting those periods most conducive to growth. Riding the primal pulse into space and time, each individual spark becomes a life, a human form and consciousness, playing out the unique drama of its private experience upon the stage of duality.

Twelve

୨ବ

The Human Blueprint

Let us now examine the physical manifestations of consciousness on your earth. For the shape, size, and other parameters of each life form offer much toward understanding the greater consciousness from which they flow.

Given the universe's setup, its three-dimensional matrix of primal cells transmitting vibration with greatest fidelity in a straight line, and with less efficiency laterally, we find the fundamental shapes of matter to be the axis and the sphere. The axis is the fundamental form matter takes, a highly efficient organization and design. The next step up in complexity is the sphere, fields of charge curving about an axis.

We have seen that most celestial bodies of matter—stars, planets, moons—are spheres built upon an axis. The same holds true for the expression of animate and inanimate life upon your planet: a sphere built upon an axis.

You may well protest that, while the mirror fails to reflect the very ideal of human form, it hardly reveals you to be a sphere! Let us assuage your outraged ego with a further explanation.

Because life on earth is a constant process of resistance, because simple physical existence requires "struggle" in the sense of ingesting nutrients and water, it was important that the design of most life forms assume the most efficient physical shape, the axis. This is readily apparent in the plant kingdom: flowers, grasses, and trees all standing straight and tall toward the sun.

Among the animal kingdom there is more variation. Yet the very definition of a vertebrate is that it carries a spine, a backbone. Thus is the axis ossified into place within every vertebrate animal. The spine's purpose, as you know, is to protect the spinal cord and its constant communications from the brain to all cells of the body, and back again. Energy, vibration, travels most efficiently along an axis; so this fundamental flow of information, of electrical impulse, flows along the axis of the spine.

The shapes built upon the spine's axis vary tremendously. The fish, the bird, and the mammal carry starkly different life purpose, are required to manipulate in vastly different ways, and their shapes reflect this. Upon the common axis of backbone is built a wealth of form in flesh. Each such form is specifically designed to harbor the unique slant of consciousness from which it flows.

As the various shapes and forms of life are "designed" on the levels of higher consciousness, beyond the portal of the primal pulse, they are beyond the reach of time. "Evolution," a fallacy even in your historical flow, plays no part in the shape and form of the earth's species. You are not a naked ape. You are a human being. Every other life form exists because it has been specifically designed to carry a unique consciousness, its physical shape reflecting the greater intent and purpose from which it springs.

The human body is an axis. Few are the terrestrial animals who can match the streamlined efficiency of the human body, the tight, compact bundle of flesh upon its sturdy axis. For you are the manipulator of symbol, the nomad, the inventor, the artist: you have a world to explore. To do so means the body must be efficient, require as little food as possible, and that the food be utilized economically. Some of your fellow creatures must ingest several times their body weight every day in food. If you had to do the same, what time would you have left to explore and shape the world? The closer a body's shape approximates an axis the more efficient it will be, and the less food it will need for a given weight. Thus the human body is a lean, tight engine upon its axis, using its fuel so efficiently that most of the day can be spent engaged in matters of the heart and mind, rather than the stomach.

Yet this construction, the human shape, is only part of your total physical reality. While your body ends neatly and firmly at the flesh—like bedrock meeting air—you carry about you a larger energy field, enveloping your denser body. In the area of your torso, where this energy field is most active and intense, it assumes the shape of a sphere. Just as your axis is solidified into backbone, so are the flow and direction of your energy field ossified into rib. The energy field originates at the backbone, flows out slightly behind the back of the body, then meets several feet before the chest. These separate flows retain their distinct patterns as they flow back into the body, returning to the backbone. Your energy field is two separate flows, one on either side of the body, their path etched into the granite of your rib cage.

We will explore the purpose and function of this energy field in more detail later. We raise its presence now only to demonstrate that you are, in fact, built as a sphere upon an axis. This is the fundamental form of matter, animate and inanimate, and while variations do occur, all life forms share this common pattern.

If you had to name the fundamental difference between plant and animal life, what would you say? That plants are tied to the earth, literally, and must build a sturdy network of roots, meaning the site of that first triumphant sprout and the last withering leaf shall be one and the same. Animal life is marked by mobility, the ability to move, to fly, to walk, to crawl, to swim, to jump. Animate life puts down no roots, springing from the cradle to a peripatetic romp about the globe.

The earth's axis pumps a steady, rhythmic beat of energy and intent, the earth pulse. This energy rises through the layers of bedrock, emanating at the surface in specialized pockets or fields, but always at the same steady, rhythmic pulse.

Plants, bound to the earth, anchored in soil, are constantly bathed by the energy of the earth pulse. Every planet's axis carries a unique vibration specifically tailored to the planet's purpose. As earth's purpose is to sustain life upon the crust, this steady flow of energy from the axis provides the bedrock stability necessary for life. The earth pulse reverberates through every particle of soil; plants, rooted to the crust, are fed a steady stream of vibration, of energy, suffusing them with the Source's intent that they shall be and grow.

Many plants cannot survive indoors. Transplanted into pots and placed on your windowsill, they wither and die. Among the plant family there are divisions of consciousness; some can thrive in a pot of soil, suspended several feet or more above the earth, while others must have the direct, steady earth pulse fed into their veins. Some can begin as sprouts started indoors, urged to life by warmth and water, but must later feel the solid earth about them or die.

But what of the animate species? Why are they free to move about the earth, seemingly divorced from the steady earth pulse sustaining the plant kingdom?

Every animate creature carries inside its body a unique and private source of pulsation: the heart. From the rudimentary wash of the insect to the thundering squeeze of the whale, all creatures divorced from the bedrock crust must carry their private pacemaker, its design and rhythm tailored to the body's form.

Flowing from the primal pulse, flowing from the earth pulse, you carry inside you the human pulse—squeeze and rest, squeeze and rest—a hammering sphere of muscle setting the rhythm for your body's processes.

Without it, you die. With it you stand united, beat by beat, with the rhythms of the earth and of the very source of the universe.

Freedom, free will is the purpose of human life in your camouflage physical system. Carrying your pulse inside you frees you from the bedrock gripping the plants, bathing them with the steady earth pulse. Your heart, your human pulse, allows you to run, jump, skip, leap, and swim without a moment's thought to sustaining your tie to the earth. For the heart pulse rides atop the earth pulse, squeezing its rhythm into a unique surge and pattern designed to sustain your form—your highly efficient form—and grant you the freedom to pursue your purpose: to manipulate your world without restriction.

One of the major flaws in the theory of evolution, positing as it does a steady line from ape to human, is that it betrays itself when considering why the human body has so little hair upon it. Since apes are covered with hair, and this is obviously a distinct advantage in keeping the body warm and free from everyday cuts and bruises, why has the human species "lost" this beneficial attribute? Does natural selection not propose that only the most salutary strands survive?

Again, you are not a naked ape, and there is no evolutionary line between human and ape. You are a distinct species, the human race, created at the very first along with every other species upon the earth. Why, then, are you hairless?

The human species' role in the world drama is to play the part of reason, of symbolic manipulation. This stands you apart from the other species in that it allows you to adapt the environment to you—rather than simply adapting to the environment. In cold climes you can construct dwellings safe from icy blasts, huddle around a fire, and wrap your bodies in fur. Yet those at the equator revel in their nakedness, for the balmy breezes and sizzling sun play gently upon the skin, making raiment unnecessary.

Thus, the human species bears little hair precisely as a way of ensuring its ability to spread about the globe, infusing each nook and cranny with the gift of reason and the power of symbolic manipulation, fashioning garments suitable for every climate. Yours is the most flexible and adaptable body on earth in terms of the extremes you can endure, for your power of reason enables you to don an armor of fur or a modest loincloth, as the climate requires. This ensures your adaptability, your power to populate every corner of the globe, blessing every climate and zone with the boon of reason.

You alone walk upright. Your two legs carry you through life without a single assist from your arms, once diapers have been abandoned. If the human species was created from the start to amble the earth on two legs, what is the purpose behind this distinct divergence from the animals' construction?

The bedrock energy emanating from the earth begins to dissipate rapidly once it meets atmosphere. This is the energy pumped from the earth's axis by the earth pulse, rising through the layers of bedrock to provide an anchor to the surface species. Once it meets air, it disintegrates rapidly. Inch by inch above the soil, this energy diffuses and crumbles, wisping into fragments of its former cohesiveness.

As a general rule, the "higher" the brain is off the ground, the "higher" the level of consciousness possessed by a species. Slugs and worms and ants contain little in the way of your brand of consciousness, though they do know social structure and organization. As mammals become larger, their bodies' bulk raising the brain higher from the earth's surface, the cohesive embrace between earth pulse and surface life begins to weaken—that is, the species are less "anchored" to the earth. Their bodies and brains receive less earth energy washing over them. As a result, "reason," which flows not from the earth but from the swarms of host consciousnesses feeding their intent into the earth plane, can hold greater sway.

As the brain is held higher and higher from the ground, "reason" and "consciousness" rise proportionately. The limits on the level of consciousness attained flow from the host consciousness, its purpose and intent in assuming mammalian form. While the giraffe and elephant hold their heads high above yours, they possess far less "reason" than you—for such is not the purpose of their species. You alone possess the finely focused filter of reason with which to explore the earth.

Most crucial to the upright stature of the human species is this: Animals walking on four legs carry their spine, their axis, parallel to the earth's surface. Think of a cat, a dog, a deer—all carry the axis parallel to the earth's curve. Most significantly, this means that the site of reproduction and the site of reason are held at the same distance from the earth's crust. In other words, both brain and reproductive organs receive the same level of earth energy, dissipating as it rises from the surface. This ensures that *reason*—the brain—and the *connection to the natural order*—via reproduction—are held in equal importance. All such animals remain forever deeply rooted to the natural order, for their act of propagation—the primal cycle of life—and their use of reason—sited in the brain—receive earth energy in equal strength.

Because the human species stands alone holding reason supreme above its connection to the natural order, the human species literally stands alone, on two legs. Doing so hoists the brain several feet above the reproductive organs. Thus, the brain receives much less earth energy through-out the day; the sway and pull of the earth upon the site of reason is diminished. This allows you to step apart from the natural order, make a symbolic leap out of the cocoon in which all other species dwell, and hold reason as your supreme attribute. No longer is there an equal wash of energy along the spine, along the axis, equally bathing the nexus with the natural order and the site of reason. Reason, centered in the brain, stands above, apart from, the earth pulse.

Consider the times when you do hold your spine parallel to the earth's surface. When you sleep, surrendering your reason and consciousness, relinquishing the grip of rational thought and restoring yourself to the natural order in the dream state. During sex—your connection with the natural order, restoring you to the natural cycle of life. So employing your reason, you can decide when to relinquish your reason! At such times you assume the spinal position of the animals, returning with them to the nat-ural order in which they are forever couched.

Holding your brain high above the earth, holding reason supreme, does not mean you are forever cut off from the natural order. You are not meant to stand apart from it, look down your elevated noses upon it, to scorn the creatures of the earth and their pitiable parallel spines!

The human species is meant to explore and manipulate the natural world while remaining fully a part of it. While reason is held supreme in your experience of life, it is to work in tandem with your understanding of, and appreciation for, the natural order which gives you life.

Your legs, particularly your feet, accomplish this. For they rest securely on the earth, at the same level as every eight-legged creature, and thus are your anchor to the natural world. The earth pulse beats steady rhythmic waves of energy to the surface, where your feet can receive the full force and benefit of its energy. Your feet keep you forever anchored in the natu-ral world, the natural order of which you are a part.

Consider which you find more enjoyable: walking barefoot through a meadow of grass, or clomping down a sidewalk encased in army boots? Subconsciously you feel the energy rising from the earth to meet your bare soles; you feel the warmth and vigor as your body revels in the unfiltered rush of warm earth energy. Subconsciously you feel yourself cut off from the steady invigorating waves as you march about in your boots, sealing yourself off from sustenance and warmth, your feet crying out in protest as their nourishment is lost, your body's vitality sapped, your reason twisted for the loss of its grounding to the natural world.

Earth energy travels up through the feet and legs, through the torso and head, finally being released through the crown. This is your grounding to the natural world, the steady rhythmic pulse of the earth rising through your body, bathing your brain—the shrine of reason—with a constant reminder of its natural source, the world you and all other species share.

Thirteen

Earth Clay and Star Dust

Riding the intrinsic duality of the earth as it floats suspended between sun and moon, the human species spills its form into two fundamental pillars: male and female. One rises from the bedrock stability of the earth. The other showers down from the stars.

Woman is sculpted from the clay of the earth. She rises from the soil and seasons to carry within her body the human young, tying her to the immutable cycle of earthly life. Woman energy is earth energy, bedrock energy, stable, steady, her heart beating in time to the pulse of the earth. Earth and moon embrace in a grip of attraction as bedrock pulls toward bedrock; woman joins earth and moon in creating a bedrock layer of human stability, reason inextricably linked to the natural order, a stable base of love and family from which the species can journey forth to explore the world.

Man is molded from star dust. Like the explosive release of the sun, man showers down upon the earth in a cacophony of random energy. Man carries from the stars the mystery and wonder of the universe, an exuberant search for truth and growth, an unquenchable thirst for exploration and creation. Man energy is star energy; like the stars and their life cycles, man is forever building, creating, destroying, creating anew. Like the random dissipation of the sun, man showers his diversity upon the bedrock stability of the earth, employing this crucible of creation as the medium into which he dives headlong, exploring manipulation and mastery of the physical universe.

Woman is tied to the tide. Her body flows with the natural rhythms of earth and moon. She carries from birth the seeds of her children, releasing them one by one in the hope and chance that they will embrace star dust and sprout to blossom inside her.

The lunar cycle approximates twenty-eight days. The menstrual cycle approximates twenty-eight days. Biologically, woman's cycle of reproduction is bound to the pull between earth and moon. As the oceans wash and swell under the moon's pull toward high tide, so is woman pulled toward conception: For a day or two out of each lunar-menstrual cycle, she swells with potential, her egg hovering in readiness, awaiting an infusion of star energy.

Man showers from the stars. Like the endless, perpetual fires and storms of the sun, man carries liquid star dust within him, forever fertile, forever ready. He joins with woman, planting his star dust inside her; if her rhythms allow the blessing of conception, a child sprouts to life.

Woman offers an egg. A sphere. A complex construction, built upon an axis, carrying genetic material and a liquid cocoon of nourishment sustaining the embryo in its first moments of life. Woman provides the bed—the bedrock stability, the nest, the sphere.

Man offers a sperm cell. An axis. A tight, bundled package of genetic material, swimming furiously toward the welcoming sphere like the energy of the sun showering toward earth.

When they meet—bedrock stability and a random shower of star energy—life sprouts in the aqueous medium of their bond. Bedrock attraction and solar resistance—such is how water is created. So float the young of your species from the very first, carried inside the mother in a malleable liquid cocoon, surrounded from the first moments by the primal sea from which all life springs.

Woman is the spiritual keeper of the earth. The human gift of reason is colored by her innate bond to the natural world, its immutable cycles played out within her womb. She stands shorter than man, her brain carried closer to the earth, bathing it in the earth's warm, maternal flow. Suspended between the natural world and human reason, she is the divine source of human life, the carrier and keeper of family, the nurturer of spirit and child.

Man is the material keeper of the earth. To him falls the task of building and sustaining the physical structures of civilization, joining human reason with the celestial drama of eternal creation and destruction, scaling the grand cosmic themes down to earth size. Man employs hammer and anvil to mirror the birth of galaxies, the eternal swirl of matter dancing across the universe, combining and breaking down in a perpetual swirl of creation. Man stands tall above the earth, his head closer to the stars from which he springs, his brain held further from the steady beat of earth, reaching toward the random shower of star energy that colors his consciousness. With feet rooted to earth, mind and spirit suffused with star

energy, man focuses his gift of reason toward creation of the physical arti-
facts of civilization.

Woman is the bearer of inner truth. Her gaze is turned inward, toward
nurturance of the soul.

Man is the bearer of outer truth. His eyes look outward, focused on
sustenance of the physical world.

Woman carries her seeds inside her. She carries her child inside her.
Her body's rhythms and organs are hidden from sight, as invisible to the
eye as is the spirit.

Man carries his seeds outside his body. He carries an arrow from the
stars, an organ protruding from his body with which he commits to
woman. Like the physical world, the organs he carries are visible to the
eye, capable of manipulation and of manipulating.

Man joins with woman; the arrow from the stars plunges into the hidden fire of earth. Each turns one's axis, the spine, toward one's source:
woman toward the earth, man toward the stars. Like the sun showering
earth with its perpetual blast of random energy, man showers the womb
with liquid star dust, millions of motile seeds shooting toward egg as comets streak through the sky. Star dust is released in the final thundering cat-
aclysm, as galaxies are born from the showering of energy and matter
through the reaches of space.

From this re-creation of the universe's birth—spirit and matter
melded in a loving embrace—egg and sperm, earth and star, sphere and
axis, meet in miniature genesis to fuse reason and divinity into the embryonic spark.

All human fetuses begin as female. All spring from the union of sperm
and egg to assume the form most closely tied to the natural world. Every
human being begins shaped as a bearer of inner truth, a keeper of the
spirit. If the star dust carries the intent to grow toward manhood, the fetus
later assumes the shape and form of man, stepping forward as a bearer of
outer truth, a keeper of the material world. Star energy is a diversion from
the steady maternal rhythms of earth, a deliberate growth toward the
heavens and their drama of creation.

If the range of human qualities and attributes is laid out on a spectrum, with the center point representing normalcy and the far poles the
extremes, woman generally clusters around the mean while man scatters
evenly throughout the spectrum. Woman springs from the bedrock consistency of earth and moon, whose central quality is stability, consistent
pattern and vibration. Man showers from the stars; like the sun, his energy

is randomly scattered across the spectrum, too diverse and independent to cluster in one area.

Man carries the extremes of human potential: the great thinkers and inventors, the heinous criminals and inquisitors, the sublime artists and authors, the depraved and insane. As star energy scatters randomly and evenly across the spectrum of human potential, it ignites into the wondrous variety of talent and behavior intrinsic to man.

Woman, flowing with the steady tide and spin of the earth, carries the bedrock stability necessary for sustaining human culture. Her energy is consistent, uniform, suffused with spiritual truth. Woman provides the steady base from which every human child sallies forth to explore the earth through reason and symbolic manipulation.

Even when the last vestige of sexism is eliminated from your culture, woman will rarely stray into the extremes of human potential, instead maintaining the steady familial hearth of human life. Man, urged forward by the random star energy suffusing his every cell, will spill into genius and idiot, sinner and saint, artist and fascist, healer and soldier, king and peasant, architect and arsonist.

As human consciousness—the intent to explore the physical universe through reason and symbolic manipulation—is fed into your planet and its intrinsic duality, the human species divides into male and female, star energy and earth energy.

Woman is tied to the tide. Man carries an arrow from the stars. Together you cover the globe, keepers of spirit and matter joined in love and companionship, each drawing from one's partner the strength of the other's unique focus, founding the human species upon the twin pillars of spirit and matter, reason and divinity.

Such is the purpose of male and female.

Fourteen

Air, Food, and Water

When we say that life is "struggle," we do not mean to affirm the puritanical notion that life is meant to be harsh and unpleasant, a relentless burden of trial and woe relieved only by the certainty of one's place in Heaven. Instead, our definition of "struggle" is simply that to remain alive, every organism must make an effort to sustain the life of its cells. You cannot sit in a corner, refusing to eat, drink, or breathe for months on end, and sustain your life. Life is "struggle" in the sense that you must make an effort to sustain your physical organism through breathing, drinking, and eating.

Every day you breathe, you drink, you eat. While breathing is regulated subconsciously, unless you deliberately override it, you must consciously seek out food and drink. You feel a thirst, feel a hunger pang, and must answer your body's signals with the nourishment and fluid it seeks.

The three densities of physical matter on the earth plane are atmosphere, liquid, and bedrock. Every day you ingest these three levels of density to sustain your body: as air, water, and solid food. In addition, every day you exhale or eliminate these same three densities: as exhaled breath, liquid and solid waste.

What is the purpose behind your constant ingestion and elimination of the three basic earth densities? Why should life be "struggle," in the sense of requiring a constant inflow and outflow of earth's basic densities?

Let us review the composition of these three levels of density, on the level of the primal cells lying behind the atoms and molecules composing them.

Air holds very little charge, yet those charges are of highly individualistic configuration, forcing a perpetual swarm of attraction as each charge searches futilely for identical companions. Resistance plays almost no part in the construction of air, as resistance flows from a field of high and low charge, and air cells carry virtually no charge.

Water flows from clusters of charge, most of them gathered about the mean, swirling and floating in an endless dance of attraction and resistance. The charges are not so starkly unique as with air, are configured more in consistent pattern, resulting in attracted clusters coagulating into cohesive groups. Yet within each such attracted group, cells of differing charge will meet, sparking the play of resistance as the cells carrying lower charge resist the pull of the higher charged cells. Water is the only density knowing resistance to any considerable degree.

Bedrock is atmosphere's opposite in terms of charge. Bedrock's primal cells swell with charge with every beat of the earth pulse, leaving very little empty space within the boundary of each cell, the charge bursting to the edges. These charges are highly consistent, of uniform pattern, meaning that attraction plays little part; there is no need to seek out sympathetic companions when all neighboring cells carry the same pattern. And resistance also plays little part, as all cells carry the same high charge.

These are the three basic patterns of the earth, from which atoms, molecules, and greater structures are built. Let us return now to the human body and why it must daily ingest substances born of all three levels.

If life is "struggle," in the sense of your needing to make a deliberate effort to sustain your body by ingesting the elements of the earth, it stands to reason that water should be your body's primary component. Water alone carries resistance, and resistance is the fundamental process of life, as resistance causes energy release, that energy being recaptured by the organism to annex neighboring primal cells. This is how the process of growth occurs, at the most fundamental level.

So your body is a private sea, your cells playing host to the dance of attraction and resistance known only to water. As the pull of resistance sparks energy release, the potential energy stored in water dissipates. The body no longer has the fuel to convert the bedrock elements into the material of the body's cells, and the energy driving its chemical reactions. Since the body requires a steady flow of fresh energy, the need for fresh water is constant, restoring one's supply of "attraction and resistance" from which all life springs.

On a hot day, under a broiling sun, you perspire and feel thirst. While it is true that perspiration helps cool the body as it evaporates from the skin, this is a secondary effect of perspiration, not the main purpose. Remember the sun's composition: a random cacophony of resistance, showering its energy upon the earth. When you stand directly within its rays, your body is stimulated to accelerate its play of resistance, held in the liquid of your cells. Resistance means release of energy, which is either reabsorbed or released as heat. Unable to recapture and utilize all the released energy, your body heats from within, literally in danger of raising its temperature.

The body's first priority is to sustain the brain, the heart, and other muscles. These can be damaged if your temperature rises even a few degrees above normal. So when under the sun's pull of resistance, the first order of business is to reduce the pool of excess water, lessening the sun's ability to spark resistance and its resultant heat. At the same time you feel a powerful thirst, for the water lost must be replaced quickly, as the energy released by resistance is required for all of the body's processes. On a hot day, when you stand under the sun for a prolonged period, your body is little more than a sieve, squeezing out all the excess water it can while constantly calling for more.

While you have been taught that energy is created when fuel, such as sugar, combines with oxygen, the fact is that water alone *creates* energy within the body, as water alone carries resistance. The other elements— oxygen and sugars, air and bedrock—ride atop water's play of resistance, absorbing the released energy into their reactions.

From which would you suffer first: water deprivation or food deprivation? Which would weaken you the fastest? You crave water more than food because water carries the play of resistance, latent energy driving all your body's functions and reactions. Without it, however rich your diet, however pure your air, you soon perish, for air and fuel alone cannot create energy; they must combine in the aqueous nexus of resistance water alone provides.

Turning to air, we find that you must inhale it on a far more frequent, regular basis than either water or solid. Deprived of air for more than four minutes, you can suffer permanent damage to the brain and other tissues. What is air's function in sustaining the body, and why do you require such a constant intake?

Air is a field of very low charge, of highly diverse pattern, forcing an endless swirl of attraction. Air's contribution to the body is attraction, the compelling urge to join with sympathetic companions. On a gross physical level, this helps the body's discrete organs and elements retain their cohesive shape and consistency. While there is a nonphysical blueprint for the body on the "other" side of the primal pulse, in which every element and organ is configured, on the physical side, the earth side, it is air's play of attraction that helps maintain the integrity of each discrete component.

In other words, as you think of your body and its different components, what is it that keeps them separate, in discrete organs and tissues? Why does the liver not disintegrate into random liver cells floating through the bloodstream? Why does it retain its cohesive identity? What holds it together?

As oxygen is carried to every cell of the body, so is the frantic swirl of attraction lying behind its atomic structure. Each cell is thus stimulated toward "attraction," cohesion with similarly contoured brethren. Every liver cell finds this urge to attraction fulfilled by clinging to the body's other liver cells—thus the liver retains its cohesiveness. Air's function in the body, the purpose of ingesting its field of attraction, is that air serves as the "glue" holding the body's organs and elements together. Each cell is stimulated to cling to those of similar construction.

The nonphysical blueprint for the body will carry the number of cells to manifest as "liver cells," given the body's age and condition. Thus, there is a "grid of intent" standing behind the liver, determining its size. This is all on the nonphysical side of the primal pulse. On the physical side, there must be a matching physical component working to ensure that the "grid of intent" manifesting as "liver" retains its cohesion. This is air's function: its play of attraction forces every cell to seek out and cling to similarly contoured cells.

This process of "like attracts like" is one of the fundamental qualities of vibration, as you will recall from our earlier discussion. In the case of the body, it ensures that an organ's cells cling cohesively together. Air, with its urgent swirl of attraction, bolsters every cell's natural urge to seek sympathetic companions.

If air carries so little charge, meaning it can release very little energy to the body, how is oxygen involved in the body's creation of energy? Remember that resistance occurs when cells attracted by similar pattern clump together, only to find themselves of differing charge, and thus attracting and resisting simultaneously. Air's contribution to the process is attraction: urging cells of like pattern to coagulate in cohesive embrace. When air's urge to attraction meets the body's high water content, it stimulates the play of attraction—thus sparking resistance, which results in release of heat and energy. So, in the body, air does not directly contribute to the creation of energy—it urges the body's water pool to do so.

While you ingest air and water in their pure, natural state, you do not as a rule fall to your knees to scoop up handfuls of bedrock soil and gleefully wolf it down. It is not bedrock itself you ingest, but those forms of life springing from the earth, carrying bedrock's characteristic of solidity. These are as essential to your body's health as air and water.

Anything that carries bedrock's solidity will necessarily share its fundamental construction: high charge, uniform pattern, little resistance. Each primal cell receives a blast of energy virtually filling the cell to its skin, leaving little empty space. This creates the "density," the solidity of bedrock and its expression in living form.

Your body also shares bedrock's solidity, to various degrees depending on the structures involved. Bone comes close to the tough, hard structure of rock. Organs and muscles stand between bedrock and liquid, malleable and flexible, yet of much firmer consistency than water. It is blood that most closely resembles water, flowing through your body as water flows to the sea.

Because your body is strung between liquid and bedrock in its construction, it stands to reason that you must regularly ingest "bedrock" substances as raw material to sculpt the body's parts. The tougher a substance is, the higher the charge imparted to the primal cells sustaining it. Bone, tough and inflexible, requires the ingestion of bedrock foods to replenish and sustain its structure.

Bedrock foods contribute the physical "stuff" of the body. Bedrock's highly charged primal cells sustain the body's structures to the degree they require solidity and endurance.

Remember that the primal cells are the most basic level of physical universe construction. Vitamins, minerals, and so on are far vaster and more complex constructions, requiring the space of billions or trillions of primal cells to assume their most fundamental shape. Our discussion is on the level of primal cells and how the different patterns they hold sustain the body. Issues of nutrition and so forth are an entirely separate matter, occurring on a far grander scale than the primal cells and their patterns of charge.

If we consider the foodstuffs of the earth, those springing directly from bedrock soil, we find an old theme played with a new variation. With rare exception, the earth's foods spring into two forms: the axis and the sphere.

Axis foods: corn, cucumber, carrot, celery, sprouts, broccoli, beans, wheat, lentils, rice, grains.

Sphere foods: apple, orange, plum, peach, grape, pumpkin, tomato, cantaloupe, melons.

Of course there are always a few who try to have it both ways: some pears and squashes.

You see how the two groups fall neatly into the recognized division of fruits and vegetables. Axis foods are almost always vegetables; sphere foods are almost always fruits.

Knowing that an axis is a bundle of highly compacted, uniform charge, and that a sphere is a more complex construction of layers built upon an axis, what can we deduce about the differences between axis and sphere foods?

First, axis foods have less water content than sphere foods. Axis foods are bundles of highly uniform high charge, allowing little "space" in their construction. Thus a carrot puts up far greater resistance to your attempt to chomp off a bite than does an apple. Because a sphere is a more complex construction than an axis, it follows that it requires more effort to "grow" into such a shape. It takes more energy to sustain a sphere than an axis, as energy is always dissipated laterally between the fields of charge. As water is the only density holding any appreciable resistance, resistance being necessary for growth, we find that sphere foods contain a higher water content than axis foods.

Second, as a sphere is a more complex construction than an axis, sphere foods are likely to entertain a greater variety of nutrients, reflecting the greater diversity of their construction. As energy travels most efficiently along a plane, each "field" curving about the axis—literally, the core—is able to maintain a separate stance from its neighbors. This allows for greater variety, sustains the presence of a wider range of elements, than can the tightly compacted construction of axis foods.

You know that you must ingest a wide variety of vitamins and minerals to sustain healthy balance in your body. Dropping down to the much more basic level of vibration, this reflects the truth that each of your body's structures—from blood to bone to muscle—emits a certain "vibration," and that it requires a constant influx of new material holding that vibration. When you eat a wide variety of substances from the earth, the different vibrational patterns manifesting as the different foodstuffs will each find their way to that area of the body most in sympathy with their patterns. The ingested foodstuff can then assume its place in the corporal structure, be it liver or heart or brain, easing into a body of similar vibration and sustaining its physical stance.

Let us examine this in more detail.

At its most basic level, your body is vibration. As the primal pulse slows to the earth pulse, so is the earth pulse further slowed and configured into the discrete elements and structures of your body. It is important to understand the difference between vibration and the energy imparted to the primal cells, with its qualities of charge and pattern.

Vibration refers to the frequency of a cell's stimulation, its constant dance from physical life to nonphysical retreat. How often it jumps between physical and nonphysical worlds, per a given unit of time, determines the frequency. In other words, the degree to which the primal pulse is "slowed" to sustain a given structure determines its frequency. Nothing can beat faster than the primal pulse, and everything physically discernible to your senses vibrates far, far slower than it; how much slower determines the structure's or cell's frequency.

Riding atop the frequency of pulsation are the qualities of charge and pattern. Charge determines how much "stuff" is imparted to a primal cell, while pattern determines the configuration of that charge. These two qualities flavor or color the charge imparted during the constant pulsation from nonphysical to physical worlds.

Each structure of your body vibrates at a different rate. Each has its unique frequency. Your body quite literally sings, though your ears cannot detect its song; each organ and muscle contributes its voice to the sublime harmony of the healthy human body.

Thus, the nonphysical blueprint for the body creates its organs by shooting forth into physical life a distinct and unique vibration for each organ and structure. A liver sings a different song than a kidney; the brain's sublime serenade cannot be mistaken for the warble of a toenail. Each separate structure is created and sustained by a blast of unique vibration from its nonphysical blueprint.

This vibration, by which we mean frequency per given unit of time, is then further colored by the qualities of charge and pattern. A vibrational pattern contributing to bone will carry high charge and uniform pattern, with little space in the primal cells, reflecting the need for a bedrock toughness. A stomach cell, in contrast, carries medium charge and greater variety to its pattern, resulting in a more pliable, malleable construction.

To reach physical expression, each vibration emitted by the nonphysical blueprint must find earth elements closely matching its vibration, charge, and pattern. This is how you are "fleshed out": Each point of intention vibrating with a unique frequency, charge, and pattern will attract to it those earth elements most closely matching its qualities. This creates and sustains the physical cells of your body, materials falling into place as instructed by the nonphysical blueprint.

You see in the bodies of those suffering from poor nutrition, particularly children, the effects when the body's nonphysical blueprint cannot find earth materials to grant expression to a given vibration. If the bones do not absorb sufficient bedrock foods—high charge, uniform pattern—they will be unable to assume the ossified toughness they should; the result will be weak and pliable bones. While the body will struggle to flesh out its structures, will fashion brain and heart and organs, these structures will be weakened for lack of sympathetic vibration absorbed in the food. The earlier in life this occurs the more dangerous the effect, for if a given vibration does not find itself matched by earth material of similar vibration, over time it will "give up," cease blinking into physical life in the expectation of meeting similar earth vibration. This results in the permanent growth stunting, mental retardation, and numerous other ailments common among those suffering malnutrition as infants.

Bedrock foods contribute the "stuff," the highly charged primal cells carrying little empty space. This contributes the "density" to the body, and the denser the structure, the more such bedrock will be required.

Air contributes the quality of attraction, the cohesive glue which urges cells of similar pattern to bond together. This is important because in many cases, different bodily structures will carry virtually identical frequency, or rate of vibration. What differentiates them is the pattern imparted by the nonphysical blueprint. Because air coaxes cells of similar pattern to adhere, you can support a multitude of different structures, all carrying a similar vibration, yet retaining their individual stance due to the different patterns carried on the charge. The body supports many different kinds of muscle, all of which hum at fairly identical frequency—it is the pattern behind the creation of those muscles that shapes each into its highly unique construction, and ensures its cohesion.

Water is the elixir of life, the source of all energy and growth. Water carries the sun's play of resistance to every cell, sparking release of energy, to be used as heat or fuel for growth. Without water, without the pool of latent energy carried in the play of resistance, life is impossible.

Bedrock, air, and water: the three levels of earth density, all of which must be consumed on a daily basis in order to sustain the life of your body. Each contributes a unique element. Bedrock contributes charge. Air urges attraction. Water sparks resistance. Charge, attraction, and resistance: these are the fundamental qualities of the primal pulse beating the universe to life. They suffuse every cell, every atom, every primal cell of your body, bonding you to the earth.

In good and vibrant health, your body's divine harmony echoes to the far reaches of the universe, exultant in the miracle of earthly life, contributing its unique note to the thundering symphony of creation, leaping the primal pulse back to the Source, Who cannot help but smile and tap Its foot in time to the divine rhythm of your existence.

Fifteen

§

The Four Vibrational Bodies

So far we have seen how the fundamental units of vibration in the universe, the primal cells, create and sustain every structure of which you are aware, your body included. We have also briefly touched on the Source's creation of myriad families of consciousness with which to explore life upon your planet. Now we must begin to examine the intersection of these physical and nonphysical sources of life, specifically relating to your species.

Hovering at the portal between physical and nonphysical realms, squeezing your greater entity's intent and desire into its first physical expression, stands the human psyche.

Our definition of the human psyche is that individualized spark of consciousness standing behind creation and sustenance of a single human being. Tumbling from the vast swirls of consciousness, squeezing down through the infinitely splintering varieties of human personality, the final, indivisible unit of consciousness is that dedicated to experiencing life through one body on its journey from birth to death. The psyche stands as the mediator between physical and nonphysical realities, overseeing the maintenance of the physical body, while also serving as the gateway to the vast, unseen seas of intent and consciousness informing the evolution and explorations of the race. While the psyche supervises your health and physical experience, it also is the portal to your dreams, your loves, your reincarnational bonds, your thread to the ultimate Source of all life.

Because the psyche is the intersection between physical and nonphysical worlds, focusing vast swarms of intent into one unique human spark, it is the first step in the hierarchy of consciousness to be governed by the physical properties of vibration. The vast families of consciousness, whether host, master, or greater entity, know no physical existence; they lie beyond the beat of the primal pulse. Stepping down to the level of a single human soul, the psyche squeezes across the primal pulse, hovering at the brink between physical and nonphysical worlds, assuming the properties of vibration while remaining hidden from your senses.

Let us examine the physical parameters of the human psyche. As the first expression of consciousness in the physical framework, it vibrates at a far faster frequency than any physical object. Just easing into the physical world, hovering at the intersection with the nonphysical source, it enters at a frequency far closer to the beat of the primal pulse than is manifest in perceivable objects.

Because the human psyche is the first expression of consciousness in the physical world, the principles and qualities of vibration hold little sway over its construction. While the qualities of charge, pattern, and frequency impress themselves upon the psyche, they do so only obliquely. There is no bedrock charge in the human psyche. In ways difficult to explain, the psyche vibrates at such a high frequency that there is not enough "time" within each vibration for a high charge to manifest and fill the primal cells with bulk. Because no "stuff" is imparted to the primal cells of the psyche, there can be little or no play of attraction and resistance, sparked by charge and pattern. The psyche's amorphous shape and high frequency allow for little suasion from the earth's vibrational principles.

Thought and consciousness hum on varying levels of frequency. Each step "down" closer to the physical earth requires a slowing of frequency. For instance, in the dream state, when you cross the psyche's portal into nonphysical realms and explore fields of intent and consciousness far beyond the physical earth, such experiences occur on levels of thought vibration far faster than your normal waking consciousness maintains. Dreams often seem nonsensical and fragmented because your waking consciousness struggles, upon awaking, to "slow down" the dream material to a frequency compatible with your conscious thought processes. To do so necessarily means a loss of fidelity, of coherence, of intent, such that you are left largely with symbol, rather than direct knowing, of what transpired in the dream state.

A more prosaic example would be when you squeeze your thoughts down into speech. Your thoughts hum on frequencies no one's ear can detect; to communicate, you must "slow down" your thoughts to a level of vibration—sound waves formed by your lips and tongue—that can be interpreted by the ears of others. You know how difficult it is sometimes to adequately and fully express your thoughts to another; how words, however eloquent, fall far short of your original intent. You are experiencing the difficulty in "stepping down" from one level of thought vibration to another, for such almost always results in a loss of fidelity. The same occurs between every other level of thought vibration—as we mentioned, for example, between dreams and your waking consciousness's interpretation of them.

The psyche, vibrating at its ultra high frequency, must "step down" in a series of steps such that it can fashion the physical body. It cannot make the leap all at once, from psyche to human form. There are two intermediate steps.

While the psyche's physical expression is tenuous, amorphous, and free-flowing, the two intermediate bodies begin to more firmly encase the physical body in a tight cocoon of vibration. The next step down from the psyche we will call the aura, a term with which you may be familiar. This is a body of vibration wrapped around the body anywhere from two to six feet, depending upon the area of the body and the physical and emotional health of the individual. Carving an organized, structured shape from the psyche's amorphous material, the aura emanates in two equal flows from the spine, swirling around the body to intersect before the sternum, flowing back into the spine. As mentioned before, the pattern of the aura's flow is etched into your ribs.

Stepping closer to the body, enveloping it more tightly, is what we will call the etheric body (again, a common metaphysical term). This body of vibration encases the skin anywhere from a fraction of an inch to three or four inches beyond the body's boundary. Because the etheric body is the last step away from physical corporal expression, it most closely assumes the qualities of bedrock vibration creating the physical world. It does not dance freely as does the psyche; it does not swirl and spin as does the aura; it remains a tight envelope of vibration, like a glove about a hand. You can think of it as your "fur," though the wind and rain may not respect it as such.

Finally, of course, is the physical body you know and recognize, wrapped in a field of skin. This body of vibration is the one your senses are tuned to perceive. It is the "slowest" of all your vibrational bodies, the one firmly anchored to earth, through which the themes and intent of your greater entity find physical expression. The body you know is the smallest, densest, and "slowest" of the four bodies of vibration constituting your expression in physical form.

There are several reasons why you carry four bodies—psyche, aura, etheric, physical—on your journey through life. For one thing, it is far too great a leap in vibrational terms from the psyche to your physical form. Vibration cannot instantly leap to a far slower frequency; it must squeeze itself down, step by step. Vibration must be organized, structured, along certain lines, and the psyche's physical expression—tenuous, hovering at the portal of the nonphysical realm—is too diffuse and amorphous to immediately step down into physical form. Each intermediate step brings the psyche's vibration closer to physical expression, more aligned with the qualities of bedrock. Each such step represents a more precise, finely focused organization of vibration into the patterns required to create and sustain the body.

You will recall that the purpose of a camouflage physical system such as yours is privacy, the freedom to think your thoughts and keep your counsel, sharing with others only what and when you choose. While you are each a unique spark of humanity, nevertheless you are never cut off from the greater source of your being. You are not cast adrift, but are forever bound to your fellows, and to the realms beyond physical existence. These unbreakable bonds are maintained by the three nonphysical bodies. Each operates at a different level of vibration, and perceives a different level of information. Thus, you are tuned into swarms of thought and information that your brain is not designed to routinely handle. As you might gather, the faster the vibration, the "loftier" the information available.

At the level of the psyche, the first physical step away from the greater entity, you are kept in constant contact with all of your greater entity's other earthly expressions—your reincarnational selves—and beyond the psyche's portal, through your greater entity, with the higher bodies of consciousness. The psyche is the level connecting you with the "collective unconscious" of the species, the level on which you are in contact with all others upon the planet, as you unconsciously draw into physical expression those mass events offering learning and growth. You collectively agree to experience certain themes and ideas, whether world war or a revolution in art or politics. This communal agreement will then be filtered through the individual psyches of those involved, determining the extent of personal participation. Every war ever fought was first conducted in the dream state, only later finding expression as blood spilled upon battlefield.

The next step down, that of the aura, is a level of vibration that keeps you in constant contact with earth conditions, planetary changes, and human events occurring around the globe. It is a more immediate source of information, apprising you of what *is* happening, rather than the psyche's pondering what *can* happen. While there is no need for you to be aware of every event occurring to every human being around the globe—indeed, your conscious mind is unequipped to handle such a flood—you are kept apprised of such information at the level of the aura. There are "information cells" which shoot about the globe at tremendous velocity, carrying information instantaneously to all of your species. This finds physical reflection in your global communication networks, where an event anywhere in the world is carried to you on radio or television waves within an hour. At the level of the aura's vibration, the time gap is negligible. An event occurs and you know it almost instantly; if not consciously, then at the level of the aura.

It is at this level that telepathy occurs. You have heard accounts of those who are suddenly seized with concern for a loved one, only to later be informed that at that very moment, the loved one died or was injured. The "information cells" carry such information to you instantly; and while such information normally never burrows down into conscious awareness, a tight, loving bond can pull it down into consciousness.

Each of you carries a unique identification, a matrix of vibration that is your "name" in the ledger of the universe. While your aura receives information regarding the events of all other lives upon the planet, most passes unrecognized, for the vibrational "names" mean nothing. If you share a strong, loving bond with another (particularly a family member, where reincarnational ties are also often involved), your aura recognizes the "name," and your love—itself a bundle of vibration—can latch onto the information cell carrying news of your loved one's demise, pulling it down into conscious awareness, slowing the vibrational information down to a frequency compatible with your brain's waking consciousness. This is your sudden "feeling" of concern for a loved one in his time of trouble.

The etheric body, that tight, form-fitting layer of vibration, alerts you to your immediate physical surroundings. It helps you navigate safely through the physical world. It stands between the cosmic and global levels of the psyche and aura, and the purely physical concerns of the body. It soaks in the vibrations of your immediate surroundings and feeds them to your conscious mind, alerting you to conditions which may not yet be physically apparent. You may have felt someone "watching you," felt a pair of eyes upon you, without knowing who was observing you, or where. You may have felt uncomfortable in certain locales, felt a sense of danger or threat, urging you to move on quickly, without any physically apparent reason. You know when someone is standing behind you, though your eyes and ears fail to detect his presence.

In all such cases, the etheric body—picking up levels of vibration beyond the physically perceivable—passes that information on to the conscious mind, which processes the information, decides which is pertinent to your well-being, and further "slows down" that vibration to conscious awareness and physical reaction. The etheric body is your "force field," your shield and navigator as you move through the physical world.

Finally, there is the human body, the slowest and densest of the four vibrational bodies, the one perceptible to your five senses. Here is where the intent of your greater entity to experience physical life finally meets the earth. Here is where all the dreams and themes and schemes of human consciousness find expression. Here is where you create your reality, squeezing intent and purpose down into physical objects and events.

Sixteen

The Senses

Now that we have observed the progression of the greater entity's intent squeezing into the physical world step by step through psyche, aura, etheric, and physical bodies, let us more closely examine the construction of your body; specifically, how your senses interpret vibration.

It is well understood that your senses perceive vibration. Light waves and sound waves are absorbed by the eyes and ears. These vibrations are then interpreted by the brain into a three-dimensional world of color and sound, tuned as it is to perceive vibration in a unique and specific way, particular to the human species. Other species absorbing identical vibration through their perceptive mechanisms would interpret that vibration far differently. Which is "correct"? Neither, and both. All is interpretation.

Remember that in a camouflage physical system such as yours, you never experience vibration directly; you only fashion it into symbol through your senses. Your senses perceive as they do because the purpose of the human species is best fulfilled that way. Other species, holding other purpose and intent, perceive the same vibration along the lines most conducive to their growth and fulfillment. None is any more valid or important than any other. The Source delights in the infinite variety of interpretation as the creatures of the earth perceive the world through their unique filters.

Let us first examine the sense of sight. You know that your eyes perceive color along a relatively narrow band of vibration, that there are frequencies on either end of the spectrum, from infra red to radio waves, that your eyes do not perceive. How is the purpose of the human species related to this specific band along the vibrational spectrum?

First, consider what will appear an eminently obvious quality of eyesight: you can perceive objects only when a light source illuminates your surroundings. While this is readily apparent, consider for a moment: does this quality also hold true for your other senses? Must the sun be shining for you to hear, to taste, to smell?

Ignoring for the moment your species' invented artificial light sources, you see that only when the sun is shining can you perceive the physical world with your eyes. This begs the question: Are the world's objects always emitting vibration, which your eyes require sunlight to perceive, or does the sun itself provoke the world's objects to emit vibration?

You know that as the sun sparks the play of resistance among the earth's bedrock objects, the resulting excess energy is released as heat. This "heat" is simply vibration emitted by the earth's objects; radiation, if you will. The spectrum of visible light is only a small fraction of the total spectrum of electromagnetic radiation emitted by the earth's objects. What is the nature of this small band of radiation, that it should be able to stimulate your retinas, while all the rest passes unnoticed?

To focus our definition specifically on the human species, your eyes are designed to perceive vibration from objects of a density such that they cannot pass undetected through your body. In other words, if you can feel an object against you—and it cannot pass through you without harm— then your eyes are designed to perceive the vibration emitted by the object, in order to alert you to its presence.

What would happen if your eyes could not perceive the vibration emitted by trees? You would all be walking around with smashed-in noses and bruised foreheads. What if you could not perceive a cactus's pointy bristles, or a boulder crouched in your path, or a saber-toothed tiger ready to pounce? What if your food sources were invisible to your eyes? Any object that can physically affect your body's health and well-being, for good or ill, emits vibration along the spectrum of visible light.

Of the three basic types of vibration, only bedrock objects are visible to you. Air is invisible to you. Water, clear and pure, is invisible to you. Air carries virtually no bedrock charge; its density is so fractional compared to yours that your body passes through it with no effect. Water is dense enough that you can feel it against your skin, yet it does not impede you or harm you merely for its presence. Only those objects primarily composed of bedrock can physically affect you—for you too are primarily composed of bedrock. As your eyes' purpose is to chart a clear and safe course through the physical world, it stands to reason that the spectrum of visible light for your species is those frequencies of vibration emitted by objects of sufficient density that they can affect your physical body.

Consider another feature of sight as you experience it. In broad daylight your eyes drink in a spectacular flood of color, a brilliant, exquisite, multihued world. Yet, in the dark of night, the palette of color is lost; you are reduced to line and shadow and contrast. You see in black and white in low light situations. And, in total darkness, you perceive nothing.

This relates not to any deficiency in your eyes' construction, but to the fact that in low light situations there is little vibration for your eyes to perceive. The sun is no longer sparking the play of resistance among the bedrock objects of the world; they are not emitting excess vibration for you to interpret as a riot of color. In soft, dim light, objects feel little pull of resistance; thus they emit only a wisp of vibration. This is sufficient for your eyes to perceive an object in its basic dimensions, but no more. It allows you to still chart a course, but with less security.

If you ask why you should be deprived of this all-important visible vibration at night, consider that your species is not constructed to remain conscious twenty-four hours a day. You must relinquish your hold on the physical world and return to the realms of the psyche. It is you who close your eyes to do so, sealing off any possibility of receiving visible vibration. Just as the physical world constantly blinks between physical and non-physical realms, so must you. As your species' purpose is to symbolically manipulate the physical earth, it stands to reason that your ability to do so is lessened or lost at night, when the earth itself is no longer manipulated by the pull of the sun. The earth returns to its bedrock state. So must your consciousness return to its primal home. Night and day, earth and sun, sleep and wakefulness: they all work in harmony to fulfill your private and communal purpose.

Consider the placement of your eyes. Other species, like the fishes, carry one eye on either side of the head; further, their eyes absorb a much wider field of information. Yet your eyes are planted side by side, facing forward. All visible vibration emitted by objects behind you and to your sides is lost. How does this quality of human eyesight relate to the species' purpose?

You exist to symbolically manipulate the physical world. Your implements for manipulating the world are your hands. They are hinged and jointed on your arms and elbows to work most effectively and efficiently when held before your chest and abdomen. As this is your purpose— manipulating the world with your hands—it stands to reason that your eyesight would be finely focused in that area where your hands most naturally work.

You have not the fishes' need for a constant, heightened awareness of all surrounding activity; you do not share their constant ballet of predator and prey. With your conscious mind you can fashion a safe and secure reality; once so established, you set about manipulating the world: building tools and instruments, painting and sculpting, murdering and embracing your brethren. All with your hands. So your eyes, drinking in the spectrum of vibration emitted by bedrock objects, focus on the field where your contact with the world fulfills human purpose.

All objects emit radiation that is never detected by your eyes. While some frequencies are detected by your other bodies—your etheric body can "sense" an object you cannot see if your eyes are engaged elsewhere—only those frequencies directly related to your species' purpose are visible. Your purpose is to symbolically manipulate the physical world; it is only the bedrock objects amenable to your touch that register on your retinas. All other vibration—extraneous, not related to your purpose—passes unseen through you.

The second primary sense is hearing. Notice that, in contrast to your eyes' fine focus before you, your ears absorb vibration from all directions. They provide a generalized background of information, a cocoon of sensation, keeping you apprised of your immediate environment.

As with the spectrum of visible light, there is a spectrum of audible sound. Sound waves below and above the frequencies audible to the human ear pass undetected. Knowing that your species was specifically designed to interpret a given band of audible vibration and disregard the rest, how is the audible spectrum related to your species' purpose?

Consider how sound, any sound, is formed. There must be movement. There must be friction. There must be resistance. When you speak, your tongue and lips and larynx move in certain ritual patterns, forcing pressure against the atmosphere, forming sound waves which travel—move—to another's ears. A musical instrument must be plucked or pounded or strummed or blown for there to be music—again, sound waves moving through atmosphere. A tree falling in the woods, to use the proverbial example, wrenches its roots against the resistance of soil, then hurls its bulk against the ground—movement, friction, resistance. This sets off vibration which your ears interpret as the crunch and crash of a tree meeting earth.

This is eminently obvious. When you seek peace and quiet, where do you go? To a place where there is no motion, no bustle. When the bedrock objects of the world are still, there can be no sound. Sound is created only when objects move, causing friction and resistance. The resulting cycles of vibration are interpreted by your ears as sound.

Given that your body is a bedrock object, and that its density allows it to be affected by other bedrock objects, it stands to reason that you need to be aware when another bedrock object is moving toward you, or around you, or behind you. If you sit in a forest clearing and all is still, you hear little. Your safety and security are not threatened. If you suddenly hear the crack and snarl of a tree's roots wrenching against soil, you know that a very large and dense object—a tree—may possibly be headed in your direction. It would behoove you to determine if this is the case, which you do by looking—focusing your primary sense of eyesight—to determine the tree's trajectory.

Dying of thirst, you may hear the babble of a brook—water rushing over bedrock—thus alerting you to the presence of an environmental condition you desperately seek, but which your finely focused eyes alone could not uncover.

Most fundamentally, then, your ears perceive those frequencies of vibration emitted by bedrock objects in motion which can affect your physical body. Those frequencies of vibration which cannot affect you physically—ranges audible to other species—you have no need for. Your purpose is to navigate safely and securely through the world, manipulating it as you go. Any time there is motion about you, movement among objects or animals that may affect you, the frequencies emitted by such movement are perceived by your finely tuned ear.

The ear itself cannot pass judgment on the sound waves it perceives; it can only pass this information on to the brain. And it is here where your species' setup is genetically programmed. The sound of a babbling brook behind you is cause for no alarm; how can it harm you? A low, guttural growl from five feet away instantly sends adrenalin cascading into the bloodstream.

Why the difference? Are both not simply sound waves passing into your ears? Yes—and it is your brain that interprets these sound waves according to the overall blueprint of your species. A babbling brook might strike terror in the heart of a butterfly, unable to swim and instantly drowned upon contact. The low, guttural, feline growl would mean nothing to it; cougars do not feast on butterflies. So each species carries an instinctive, genetically programmed series of responses to the sounds of the earth.

It is as if there were a "library" of all possible sounds, into which every earthly species is tuned. Hearing a given sound as it passes through the ears to the brain, the question is first: what is it? Matching the vibrational pattern of the sound with its twin in the "library," you determine the source and meaning of the sound. But when this information is transmitted to you, it will be interpreted along the parameters established for your species. Here is where the families of consciousness enter, fashioning unique experience from essentially neutral data. Sound waves are just sound waves. It is each species' interpretation that determines one's reaction, and this interpretation is genetically and culturally fashioned.

Just as your species has invented alphabets and art forms interpreted by your eyes, so do you manipulate the world through sound. Speech is a deliberate manipulation of the environment, in order to communicate with others. Music is profoundly evocative, as it flows from the unseen rhythms and vibrations forming your world. So while your ability to hear most fundamentally serves to ensure the safety of your body, your species builds on this quality (which you share with many other species) to deliberately and consciously enhance and ease your manipulation of the world.

You alone have complex languages, squeezing your dreams and hopes and fears into the symbol of speech. You alone have orchestras and barbershop quartets and blistering rock and roll. You alone can sit by a radio and hear others of your species speaking half a globe away. While you manipulate the world primarily through your hands guided by eyesight, the secondary sense of sound enhances your experience of a physical world, both keeping you safe and allowing you to deliberately fashion new and unique experience.

Taste and smell are senses not normally associated with perception of vibrational frequencies, as are sight and hearing. Yet, since all is vibration, these senses must also be perceiving and interpreting certain bands of vibration.

First, consider what portion of the earth's vibrational patterns you can taste and smell. As with sight and hearing, you taste and smell only bedrock. Pure, clean air has no taste or smell. Pure, clean water has no taste or smell. So we have narrowed the field of vibration perceived by taste buds and nose down to bedrock.

Just as sight provides a finely focused concentration in a narrow area of perception while hearing provides the larger, generalized field of sensation, so also do taste and smell work in tandem. To taste something, you must come in physical contact with it, upon your tongue. Yet smells waft to your nose without deliberate effort on your part, alerting you to conditions far removed from your immediate environment.

Most fundamentally, taste and smell work together to ensure that only objects of neutral or salutary effect come in contact with your body. Again, the purpose of your senses is twofold: First, to ensure a safe and secure reality; second, to use that safety as the basis for exploration and manipulation. The senses of taste and smell are distinguished from sight and hearing in that you cannot use them to manipulate the world. They are solely passive senses, absorbing information about your environment. You cannot create alphabets with your taste buds, nor sing with your nostrils. The senses aiding your manipulation of the world are sight, hearing, and touch. Taste and smell stand apart, finely focused on ensuring a safe and secure environmental field.

Inanimate objects carry little in the way of smell and taste. As long as they are stationary (meaning your ears do not perceive motion), they cannot harm you. You can sit upon a rock, upon the ground, upon a glacier, and your nose could be asleep, for all the information it can perceive about your environment. And your taste buds are scarcely provoked to ecstasy if you nibble a pebble. The inanimate bedrock objects of the world emit little vibration in the spectra of taste and smell.

Thus, you see it is organic matter, matter suffused with life, that stimulates taste and smell. Now, all matter is imbued with consciousness. There is no "dead" matter, anywhere in the universe. All pulsates with the beat of the primal pulse; all carries purpose; all seeks fulfillment through the physical medium. But the families of consciousness manifesting as the "inanimate" matter of the world—rocks and soil and ice—are so radically different from yours that for your purposes, you entirely disregard the notion of any "life" within such objects. There is nothing you can offer them, nor they to you. The fields of endeavor are so radically different that never the twain shall meet. You may physically meet at the twain— your posterior upon the ground—but you do not jabber with the rock that supports you.

It is those families of consciousness manifesting as "organic" or "animate" species that most concern you, for you are a member of such a family. There are hierarchies upon hierarchies of consciousness infusing the earth. Human consciousness is a subset of mammalian consciousness, which is a subset of animal consciousness, and so on. Because human consciousness belongs to the "organic" and "animate" fields of consciousness, it naturally follows that you are most interested in, and able to relate to, other species within that family.

More, as your body is an organic construction, you require a constant ingestion of organic materials to sustain its life. Air and water you require for reasons covered earlier. Food, bedrock materials suffused with organic consciousness, you also require. This keeps you apprised, on levels unseen, of information and knowledge carried by the substances you ingest, literally absorbed into your consciousness.

Since it is organic substances you must ingest, it is organic substances your senses of taste and smell are most attuned to. Again, the purpose is to keep you safe and secure.

If you have any doubt about the freshness of a food, what do you do? The prudent course is first to sniff it—to see if you can detect any evidence of decay through your nose. This permits you to judge a food's suitability before taking the risk of swallowing it. If it passes the nose test, you may take a small bite and consider the more sophisticated analysis of your taste buds, the last checkpoint before a substance is absorbed into the body. A rotten food will provoke a violent reaction, in which you spit out the food before it can be swallowed.

Now, what is the purpose of this? What is the danger in eating decayed food? Why should the body care?

We return to our discussion of the plants and animals of the world, and their connection with the earth pulse. Plants are constantly bathed directly by the earth pulse, as long as they remain rooted to the soil. Animals carry their own pulse generator, the heart, inside them. In both cases, the purpose is to keep the organism infused with a steady stream of vibrant energy. Any organic, living thing is the physical manifestation of a nonphysical grid of intent existing in the nonphysical twin universe, designed to create and sustain the organism. As the primal pulse is the portal between physical and nonphysical realms, all living things must be constantly bathed by a rhythmic pulse in order to sustain physical life.

In plants, imbued with a rudimentary form of consciousness, it is enough to bathe in the earth's pulse emanating from the soil. In animals, where a higher degree of consciousness requires mobility, the earth pulse is carried inside, its rate altering depending on the activity undertaken, thus granting you freedom to engage in both strenuous exertion and blissful relaxation.

This pulse acts as the "glue" which holds an organism together. In physical terms, the roots carry nutrients to the plant's stalk and leaves, while the heart circulates the blood. In deeper terms, this pulsing rhythm serves as a physical anchor to the consciousness infusing a plant or animal. It binds the Source's intent to Its physical expression. It serves as the nexus between body and soul.

When the bond between consciousness and physical form is broken, and the rhythmic pulse no longer suffuses the organism, it dies. An uprooted plant, or one whose roots have withered, no longer absorbs the earth's steady pulse. An animal whose heart has stopped ceases to live. Once the connection with the earth pulse is broken, the physical organism loses cohesive intent, and the individual elements of its form are no longer united in sustaining a larger organism. The "glue" is gone. The process of decay is simply this: The individual elements of an organism, no longer bound in an embrace of cohesion, now act independently, falling back on their fundamental characteristics rather than subjugating them to a greater purpose.

We have already discussed the four vibrational bodies you carry with you through life. In good health, they are unified fields of vibration, without gaps or holes, sealing you in a tight cocoon of energy. Suffused with purpose and consciousness, they hold your physical form together. The same holds true for every other organism; they too are surrounded by energy fields designed to create and sustain their physical bodies. As long as the connection with the earth pulse or heart pulse remains steady and true, these fields emit a steady, cohesive, salutary vibration.

This is the spectrum of vibration perceived by the nose and tongue. They are specifically tuned to organic matter, to judging the "health" of your surroundings by perceiving the vibrational energies of the organic beings in your environment. In the case of the substances you ingest, they ensure that what you eat still retains enough of a cohesive vibration that its ingestion will not harm you.

Consciousness does not evaporate instantly upon physical death. There is no "moment" of death for any organism. While you can uproot a plant, or detect that someone's heart has stopped, and declare that death has occurred, what you perceive is only the first step in the lengthy process of death. Once the organism is no longer able to sustain life, cut off from earth or heart pulse, the energy fields about the organism do not instantly evaporate. They continue to surround the organism. Gradually, only gradually, do they dissipate. As they do so, the cohesion imparted by the energy fields to the organism is lost. Here is where decay and rot begin, when the energy fields have gone and the basic chemical components of an organism are free to pursue their individual natures, rather than contribute to maintaining a greater whole.

What holds you together? The binding, the glue, is consciousness. This flows from realms infinitely far above the range of physical universes, showering and splintering down into increasingly fine focuses of intent, the smallest such division of consciousness being the human psyche. From the psyche flow your other vibrational bodies: aura, etheric, physical.

Now, at each level, the proportionate blend of consciousness to bedrock changes. The psyche is almost entirely consciousness, the qualities of bedrock having only the slightest effect. The aura is more influenced by the properties of bedrock, sculpting itself in a more distinct physical shape. The etheric body is a step closer to bedrock, slowing down the psyche and aura to a level just above the vibrational patterns of physical life. And the physical body is most closely aligned with the bedrock earth, composed of inorganic elements blended with consciousness, suffused with purpose.

As is true for the human species, so holds also for all other organisms. All are surrounded by energy fields "slowing down" the intent of their families of consciousness in a series of steps, down to the level of physical vibration, joining bedrock. It is these levels of vibration, these energy fields, that taste and smell are most attuned to. While sight and hearing perceive vibration directly emitted or caused by bedrock objects, smell and taste perceive the energy fields surrounding them.

The body does not benefit from ingesting inorganic substances, for such are suffused with little consciousness. It upsets the body's natural harmony to ingest decaying matter, for decay evidences that consciousness has departed, leaving the elements to revert to their fundamental natures. Like releasing a pack of unruly children in a china shop, the result is rarely to anyone's advantage. Your body, suffused with consciousness, can benefit only from ingesting other substances whose energy patterns, whose energy alignments, are similar to yours. You do not benefit from eating rocks and dirt, though they contain the same basic elements as flesh or plants. The difference is that organic materials are bound together by, and blended with, consciousness.

The more time has passed since an organism was first separated from its pulse source—earth or heart—the more its surrounding energy fields, the cocoon of consciousness, will have dissipated. The nose and taste buds, attuned to perceiving not the organic substances themselves but their surrounding energy fields, steer you toward "fresh" substances and away from "rotten" ones. They guide you toward those foods still imbued with consciousness, and away from those collapsing in a heap of inorganic elements.

Have you ever known the delight of trout or salmon fresh from the river and into the frying pan, how your tongue just shouts for joy? Have you crunched your teeth into corn on the cob, ten minutes off the stalk and sweet as creation's first morning? Or a salad of vegetables just picked from the garden? What are your tongue's messages as it luxuriates in such ambrosial delight?

Have you ever bitten into an apple and faced a brown, rotting pulp as a worm waves hello? And what telegram does your tongue send you?

Why the difference? The difference is the degree of consciousness surrounding the food, manifesting physically as electromagnetic radiation of a frequency no device can detect. This radiation, this vibration, is the earthly expression of consciousness blending with inorganic elements to create organic life. The more suffused with consciousness your food is, the more your tongue delights in its ingestion.

The nose offers a wider field of perception. It alerts you to environmental conditions, again on the level of radiation, or vibration, emitted by organic substances. To sit on a mountainside in the spring sun is to know the sweet smell of heaven itself as the flowers lustily chorus their joy, the grasses bursting in verdant hope from the earth. Your nose perceives the tumultuous cacophony of consciousness as the hard, quiescent winter soil surrenders to the sun's pull of resistance, of life, and swarms of consciousness burst into multitudes of shape and form. This exquisite symphony of life, of consciousness blending with earth's elements, emits swarms of harmonious vibration, overwhelming your nose just as an orchestra thunders in your ears.

Smell can also alert you to environmental conditions hazardous to your safety. Fire! cries the brain when the nose smells smoke. Smoke is the sudden release of an organism's inorganic elements under the intense stimulus of fire. Such a condition, such a furious sizzle of energy, overwhelms any attempt of consciousness to sustain the physical organism—yours as well, if you do not clear out! So smoke carries warnings of threat and danger to your nostrils, a level of vibration far higher than eyes and ears perceive, alerting you to a condition you may not yet see or hear. Realizing the situation, you engage your reason and manipulating senses—eyes and ears—to navigate a safe escape from the area of danger.

In summary, the nose and taste buds are designed to perceive the energy fields surrounding organic matter, organisms suffused with consciousness. They are designed to keep you safe and secure; again, an essential ingredient of a life dedicated to manipulating the earth. They ensure that the substances you ingest are suffused with sufficient consciousness that they can blend easily with the harmony of the body. They alert you to environmental conditions that carry hints of threat, or bundles of delight, to your experience. They are, in fact, the "highest" of your senses in that they perceive the highest level of vibration, of electromagnetic radiation. For they perceive not only the radiation, but the consciousness with which it is blended. They slow down such information to the point where your brain can perceive and act upon it, while you need not consciously consider the process. They are your private link with the fields and families of consciousness which inform and create your magnificent world as it teems and swarms with life.

The last of the five physical senses is touch. Unlike the others, fixed in place upon your head, touch is spread evenly upon the body's surface. Some areas are more sensitive than others, but all carry sensation to the brain.

Of all the senses, touch perceives the "slowest" level of vibration. As with every other sense, it is primarily tuned to vibration emitted by bedrock. Air, still and calm, offers no stimulation to the skin. Water's effect varies depending upon its temperature, but this is not a fundamental quality of water itself. You do feel water against the skin, since its matrix carries fields of resistance and attraction, stimulating the body's bedrock features. But it is bedrock objects, the physical earth, that have the greatest effect upon the sense of touch.

Let us return to the level of the primal cells for a moment. Their purpose is to sustain the three-dimensional universe, each primal cell holding its place in the matrix. They never move. Only vibration moves, jumping from primal cell to cell. The cells themselves remain fixed.

The cells exist to express vibration. The greater the vibration, the greater the area of the cell is filled with charge, with "bulk," although at this level there is no physical mass. There is a maximum amount of vibration that any cell can hold; in our simplified model, we have expressed the range from 0 to 10. No primal cell can carry a charge of 11. There is no more "space" inside the cell to carry a greater bulk, and they never expand or alter their shape.

Can a bedrock object and air occupy the same space? They do, constantly, for between the atoms and molecules of any object floats empty space. The degree of empty space determines how soft and spongy, or how hard and enduring, the object will be.

Can a bedrock object and water occupy the same space? Any fish in the sea will tell you they can, and do. For a fish, while displacing water as it swims, is also primarily composed of water, and the water molecules in its body are constantly replaced by those ingested in the mouth and absorbed through the flesh. You too are principally composed of water, carried upon a bedrock frame, while living in air. Neat trick!

Can two bedrock objects occupy the same space at the same time? Using the example of two dense objects like rock, you see they cannot. Two rocks cannot occupy the same space at the same time. Why not?

The vibrational patterns standing behind the two rocks cannot mesh. If each carries a fundamental charge of 9, for both to occupy the same space would result in primal cells holding a charge of 18. This is impossible. The cells cannot contain such bulk. Try as you might, you can never force them to share the same space.

The sense of touch is primarily designed to allow you to sense the presence of bedrock objects, those of sufficiently high charge that they cannot pass unnoticed through your body. Your body and a bedrock object cannot occupy the same space at the same time. One or the other must give. And your soft and pliable body, composed primarily of water, is generally the loser in any such confrontation!

You see the similarity with eyesight, which is the perception of vibration emitted by bedrock objects at a distance. Yet touch involves not so much an apprehension of vibration emitted by a bedrock object, as the direct contact with that object. You are not perceiving light waves bouncing off an object, nor hearing its movement around you, nor smelling its life force. You are butting up against the object, primal cell to primal cell, and meeting it directly, rather than interpreting its vibrational qualities at a distance.

As with all other senses, the fundamental purpose of touch is to keep you safe and secure. You must feel at ease in the world before you can set about consciously manipulating it, building cathedrals and painting canvas and composing symphonies. The rudimentary, physical needs must be taken care of first: shelter, hunger, thirst. With these needs satisfied, you can proceed to embrace the higher purpose of your species: manipulating the world with a rational mind.

Touch allows you to feel both great pleasure and great pain. As should be obvious, what brings you pleasure enhances your purpose on earth, while what causes pain impairs it. A warm bath, lying in the grass, making love, all bring you pleasure. They all affirm your existence, enhancing your attainment of a happy and fulfilling life. Being struck by a car, losing a limb to a chain saw, being dropped in hot oil, all bring you pain. They all impair your ability to move freely, to manipulate the world without restriction.

Your experience of pleasure and pain is, at base, your body's judgment of whether the vibrational fields in close contact with it aid or impair your life's purpose and fulfillment. Pleasure and pain help you navigate safely through the world, allowing you to seek out life-enhancing experience while avoiding threats to your freedom and mobility.

On a higher level, pleasure and pain are the "slowed down" versions of information transmitted through the vibrational bodies carried about the physical body. Anything you experience is transmitted through the etheric body to the aura, then to the psyche, across the primal pulse portal to the greater entity, and so on. You are never alone! Nor does the slightest occurrence in your life pass unnoticed, but is instead broadcast to the far reaches of the universe. For the three higher vibrational bodies exist for only one purpose: to create and sustain the physical body, and to steer it safely through life on its path to fulfillment.

An attack by another on your bodily integrity is interpreted as pain because it violates the intent of your higher vibrational bodies. When the intent of an attacker overrides that intent—and when you choose to draw such an event to yourself (as you must, however unconsciously)—the pain is the physically felt version of discordant vibration rippling through the higher bodies. Your purpose has been violated. The smooth harmony of your higher bodies has been disrupted. This disruption, this grinding, discordant vibration, you perceive as pain.

What brings you the greatest physical pleasure is contact with others. The higher their degree of consciousness, the closer it hums to yours, the greater the pleasure. A stone offers cold comfort. A field of grass—a step into organic life, suffused with consciousness—provides a tingling warmth. Petting a dog or a cat, having them curl up in your lap, offers a greater degree of pleasure. Finally, those closest to you in consciousness, your human companions, offer the greatest experience of pleasure. A touch, a caress, a massage, a loving sexual union, are the greatest pleasure you can know.

Remember that the purpose of ingesting air, water, and bedrock foods on a daily basis is to bring you information about the condition of the world, information that is processed on unconscious levels, necessary for your maintaining a healthy stance in the world. Yet nothing can match the exuberant flood of information exchanged when in close contact with another of your species.

Consider what happens during an embrace. Your psyches overlap. Your auras overlap. Your etheric bodies overlap. All levels of vibration, of information, are in direct contact, allowing the highest quality of information exchange. The closer you are to someone, the greater the fidelity with which you exchange information, psyche to psyche, aura to aura. Only those within a few inches exchange information at the level of the etheric body. And those up against you, skin to skin, offer the highest quality of information.

Much more is involved, of course. When you deeply love the person with whom you are in contact, your love—itself a sizzle of vibration—works to evaluate the beloved's health and physical condition. Great healing can take place, quite unconsciously, if an area of low energy, tending toward disease, is buttressed with a sudden warm infusion from a healthy body, particularly when carried on the bond of love. Statistics show that single people die earlier than those with life partners. Affection literally heals the body. Those bedding down alone every night, year after year, literally deprive themselves of the healing that a life partner can offer.

Touch is intrinsically involved in your species' primary purpose, manipulation of the physical world. This is why the tips of the fingers are so sensitive. As your hands are your tools of manipulation, their front line of contact—your fingertips—is exquisitely sensitive to the properties of the objects you touch. Hot and cold, smooth and rough, wet and dry, soft and hard, all are transmitted instantly to the brain with a touch of the fingertip. They alert you to the qualities of the material at hand, its suitability for further contact and manipulation.

Touch is your direct experience with the bedrock objects of the world, up against your body. Pain and pleasure are signals to your higher vibrational bodies of your condition, whether it eases your purpose or endangers it. Contact with others of your species in warmth and love brings news from afar, and offers strength and healing to the body. Your power to sense the qualities of bedrock enables you to chart a clear and secure course toward your private and communal purpose of manipulating the world.

You see how exquisitely your senses are designed and tuned to fulfill human purpose. Your species, alone on the earth, manipulates and investigates the earth through the use of symbol. Your senses perceive levels of vibration which, first and foremost, keep you safe in the world of physical objects; and second, allow you to fashion and mold the world's objects as expressions of your purpose.

Consider for a moment how the earth's other species differ from you in this regard. While other mammals share your five senses, they reshuffle them in hierarchies of sensitivity and importance, based upon each species' purpose. Most mammals are far more sensitive to smell than you, for instance. Smell is the "highest" of the senses in that it apprehends the vital life forces emanating from all living organisms. As animals are much more deeply rooted to the natural world than you, it follows that they would be more sensitive to these life force energies. A dog sniffing the tree trunks of the neighborhood can determine who of his species has been by recently, how long ago, and for what purpose. The vital life force imparted along with the bladder's telegram carries all such information; the stronger are the life forces surrounding the message, the more recently it was planted.

Dogs and cats also visually perceive the higher vibrational bodies around other creatures. They perceive your etheric body routinely and, on some occasions, your aura as well. You do not appear to them as you appear to each other; instead, they also perceive the flowing swirls of energy radiating from your body. You may walk into a room bristling with emotion, anger or fear, and find your cat or dog slinking away, without your saying a word or moving a muscle to indicate your fulminating feelings. Animals need wait for no such sign; they read it in the billowing clouds encircling your head and beat a hasty retreat.

Except for those who have chosen the expanded awareness of psychic ability, your species is deprived of such information. Why? Remember your purpose, specifically related to the camouflage system in which you live: freedom, free will, privacy of thought. If others could routinely read your mood by observing your etheric and auric bodies, your privacy of thought would be lost. Your power to conceal your true emotions—however damaging or mendacious it may be to do so—is nonetheless your right and privilege. It forces others to deal with you on the level of symbol—your emotions stepped down into symbolic speech. This ensures your privacy, while further enhancing your purpose of experiencing life through symbol. You cannot see the energy fields of others. You cannot hear their thoughts. Thus are privacy and free will ensured.

Understand that your senses do drink in vast ranges of vibrational information that you never consciously behold. It is in the brain that such information is lost, because it cannot be processed. Each frequency or wavelength of vibration must find a corresponding receptor in the brain for that vibration to be consciously perceived. If the receptor for a wavelength is missing or damaged, vibration along that wavelength cannot be processed and it dissipates, unnoticed. Each species' brain is specifically constructed to perceive vibration along the spectra of greatest value to it in fulfilling its purpose, with the hierarchy of importance "built in" to the sophistication of the receptors.

"Evolution," the notion that animals adapted their senses based on environmental conditions over the millennia, has no basis in reality. Each species was created and thrust into existence all at once, in your time terms. Each species has its brain configured specifically to perceive and process vibrational information along the wavelengths, and of the strength, most conducive to fulfilling its unique purpose.

You, O manipulator, carry eyesight to alert you to the presence of the earth-stuff from which you forge your experience; hearing to alert you to movement about you; smell and taste to perceive the life energies about you; and touch to judge the safety or danger of objects, and to share sensual pleasure with others. All senses lead to ensuring your safety, allowing your unhindered exploration and manipulation of the earth. For such have you chosen earthly existence.

Seventeen

The Coordinate

By now you should begin to have an inkling that what you perceive in your daily life is just the tip of the vibrational iceberg. Your senses perceive vibration along a few select bands of frequency, and then only in fairly attenuated strength. Eyesight alerts you to the presence of bedrock objects around you. Hearing alerts you to their movement. Touch registers their presence against you. Smell and taste absorb their life force. Yet these are just bits and pieces of al the vibration swirling around you. Air and water claim little pull on your senses, yet these too are swirling fields of vibration. And bedrock objects, which you perceive only along certain narrow bands of vibration, have a far greater and deeper reality than you can comprehend.

Begin to step back from your picture of a physical world spread with permanent and enduring rock and sea and sky. Understand that your experience of the world is just a sliver of the full reality standing behind your perception. Realize that what you perceive is *symbol*. You never perceive an object in its full dimensions; you reduce it to fragments, narrow bands of vibration, crumbs of truth. You never perceive absolute reality; you only interpret it in narrow, fragmented pieces. You reduce it to symbol. In truth, your world and universe are but vast, complex, swirling fields of energy and vibration suffused with consciousness. You pick and choose a few wavelengths—visible light here, audible sound there—and interpret the greater reality in fractional, symbolic form.

Step back also from your perception of your body. You see it as flesh and bone and blood, ending neatly at the skin. Again, your perception is but a symbol of the full reality. The physical body you perceive is but one of four you carry through life, the "slowest" of the four. In truth, your body is an impossibly complex swirl of vibration, organized and suffused with consciousness. Your body is light. Your body is sound. It carries sensors, complex constructions designed to absorb bands of vibration, interpreting and blending them in the brain into a cohesive picture of a physical world. See your body now as a glowing body of light, about which pulsate your three other vibrational bodies. This is your true reality.

The physical form you experience is a symbol, a symbol of the construction of the energy fields standing behind the body you know. You experience the flow of blood through your veins. So are there "carrier cells" shooting throughout your vibrational bodies, carrying information to and from all other cells, alerting the higher bodies of the precise condition of every molecule in your body. Nerve impulses travel through your spine, radiating throughout the body, carrying orders for movement and activity. So do you also carry, like all living things, an axis, nature's most efficient design, through which impulse and consciousness are dispersed from the higher bodies to the physical form. It is this axis, carved into spine, to which we now turn our attention.

While all living things carry an axis, as specifically applies to the human body we will refer to the axis as the "coordinate." This differentiates it from the far cruder construction of an apple core or stalk of celery. It also carries hints of its magnetic power in drawing in the events of your life.

If we consider the nervous system in toto, from the base of the spine to the top of the brain, what do we find? That the higher we go, the more complex is its construction, and the "higher" the information processed. The spinal cord deals with the immediate physical concerns of motor movements. The brain stem services the lower mental concerns like self-preservation and rudimentary thought. Moving higher in the brain we find the centers of symbolic manipulation: mathematical and verbal abilities. The higher portions of the brain carry the power of "higher" intelligence that makes your species unique. Here is where your dreams, hopes, and ideals sizzle and crackle across the synapses.

Thought is vibration. Your thoughts, your beliefs, your dreams, all have an electromagnetic reality, a vibrational frequency. The "higher" the thought, the faster the vibration on which it is carried. This is physically reflected in the components of the brain, the higher areas being home to higher levels of thought.

Remember that vibration must "step down" to a certain level in order for you to perceive it; you recall the examples of a dream being squashed down into visual imagery, and the difficulty in fully expressing lofty thoughts through speech. A step down in vibrational level always results in a loss of fidelity, of richness, of complexity and depth.

The nervous system's layout reflects the construction of the vibrational bodies surrounding it. Earth's bedrock vibrates at a far slower frequency than does any thought. As consciousness is seeded into the world from "above," it is increasingly "slowed down" the closer it approaches the earth. Vibration cannot leap great chasms, but must gradually step down through successive layers.

This explains why mythologies always place pantheons of gods, and Heaven, "above" you, while Hell and its miserable denizens are "below" you. Heaven, being the mythical realm of pure love and absolute peace, represents the highest possible level of vibration. Hell, that slime pit of murderers, child molesters, and used car salesmen, represents the very lowest of your species, the "lowest" possible vibration.

In some metaphysical circles it is common to posit the existence of "chakras," specific sites located along the spine, each of which focuses its energy on a specific feature of the body. The highest chakra, the "crown" chakra, leads to the spiritual realms, while the lowest, the "root" chakra, powers the sex organs. Such chakras are frequently assigned colors, with violet assigned to the crown chakra, on down to red at the root chakra. Further, chakras are often assigned musical notes, the root chakra grunting C while the crown chakra trills in B.

You see, in each case, how symbol is used to reflect increased vibration as one moves up the spine. The "C" note is the lowest, the fundamental, in the key of C, while each successive note is "higher," meaning it literally vibrates at a faster frequency. The slowest visible light wave is red, moving up through the rainbow to violet at the crown.

The concept of chakras certainly has validity, in the sense that the concerns of your spine's components change as one moves along its length. We wish to avoid any notion of discrete, distinct "spots" along the spine where vibration suddenly, radically, shifts. Instead, there is a smooth flow of gradually descending vibration from crown to base. For the sake of convenience this has been broken down into distinct "chakras," each assigned a specific function. In truth, there is constant flow along the spine, a perpetual give-and-take among all levels, as vibration gradually slows down toward the base.

We call the human spine a "coordinate" because it acts as a magnet. It draws some vibrations to it and repels others. On a daily basis, it balances and blends the cosmic radiation of the sun with the steady pulse of the earth. Just as your body is composed primarily of water—the child of sun and earth—so is your body a blend of the vibrations emitted by these two celestial bodies. The faster vibrations of the sun meet the slower pulse of earth; between them, you fashion their energies into the hybrid construction of the four vibrational bodies.

When you walk upright, you carry your brain away from the earth's energies, under the sway of the sun's pull. You are receptive to a higher level of vibration. Consider: what position do you assume to think deeply? Lying down, sitting, or standing? Almost all of your conscious deliberation occurs while you sit or stand. A person deep in thought may stand and pace the floor, but rarely would he lie on the floor to do his deepest thinking.

When you lie on the ground, every segment of your spine receives the full blast of the earth pulse, and in equal intensity. This is why lying in a grassy meadow is so relaxing; your head is "out of the clouds," has "come down to earth," and deep thought gives way to drifting daydreams and fancies, floating in loose fragments through your awareness. Bathed in the steady pulse of earth, your spine, housing the coordinate, relaxes its sharp, cogitative focus and surrenders to the free association of infancy.

Rising from the meadow, your coordinate stands perpendicular to the curve of the earth. It no longer absorbs earth energy equally along its length; now the head stands tall above the earth's pulse, influenced by the sun's higher frequency. Now, pacing through the meadow, or along the . beach, or through the woods, one conducts one's deepest and weightiest thought. With your coordinate pointing to the sun, magnetically pulling down its high frequency, you engage the higher portions of your mind.

Later we will return to the coordinate and its all-important role in the manufacture of your life's events. Come to appreciate that you carry in your spine a magnetic axis whose position relative to the earth and sun influences the type and quality of thought in which you engage. You too carry a north and south pole; you too live under the sway and pull of earth and sun playing upon the electromagnetic swirl that is your body.

Part Three

THE NATURE OF EVENTS

Eighteen

੭

Master Events and Probabilities

All time is simultaneous. Perhaps few of the metaphysical world's concepts so grate and grind against your conscious mind as this. For you must take a series of moments to read and process the words, while those words deny that the very process by which you comprehend them exists! To unravel this puzzle and assuage your mind's umbrage, we need to examine in depth the nature of events.

First, our definition of an "event" is any occurrence experienced in the physical world over a period of moments. You can break any experience down into an almost infinite number of simultaneous events. You hold this book in your hands, for instance. That is an event. The light source illuminating the book is an event. What you sit, stand, or lie upon as you read is an event. The temperature around you, indoors or outdoors, is an event. Extraneous noises about you are events. And so on and so on, ad infinitum. You can see that any experience, while you consider it to be a single "event," is in fact a thick and rich multiplicity of events layered together simultaneously.

The duration of an event can last anywhere from less than a nanosecond to a lifetime—and beyond. For your life itself, its sum total of experiences, can be considered an "event," as can each moment spanning the stretch from birth to death. There is no fixed duration to an event's expression in time, then.

Rather than say "all time is simultaneous," which your conscious mind fights and claws against accepting, consider now that all events are simultaneous. These events find expression in the medium of time, the flow of moments, while they originate in dimensions far beyond your earthly experience of them. To delve deeper into the realm and nature of events, we must now cross the portal of the primal pulse, back into the dimensions knowing no time and space.

Beyond the primal pulse, beating the universe to life in its fundamental dimensions of time and space, time cannot exist. These are the realms of the families of consciousness which seed your world with its infinitude of species, all as expressions of the Source's intent to experience earthly life in as rich and multifaceted a variety as possible. These families of consciousness divide and splinter into finer and finer focuses of intent, breaking the earth's fields of consciousness down into animate and inanimate life, then further dividing into plants and animals, further into avian, piscine, and mammalian species, and so on. Human consciousness is that unique focus of rational mammalian form dedicated to manipulation and exploration of the earth.

It is at this level that all events, from the tiniest casual flip of a newspaper to the blood-drenched horror of world war, find their genesis. All events of your life, of your world, spring from the realms beyond the primal pulse, in the realms of the families of consciousness. It is only later, in your time terms, that the events created in such realms find expression in the earth's flow of moments.

Remember that the first physical expression of human consciousness is the psyche, a unique spark of consciousness dedicated to sustaining a single human life from birth to death. This is where consciousness first crosses the primal pulse. Thus, because all events are created in the realms beyond time and space, we say that all events are simultaneous. They exist at once, every moment from the universe's birth to its end—as you experience them! For on the planes where all events are simultaneous, birth and death, beginnings and endings, have no validity. It is only you, with your consciousness gliding along the track of linear time, who perceive events in such a fashion.

If all events are simultaneous, how do you experience them in the world of space and time? How are they fed into the earthly system so magically, so seamlessly?

What unifies all corners of the physical universe system is the primal pulse. Its steady, sure, regular beat provides the underpinning beneath all physical experience. This beat pulses at a speed incomprehensible to your conscious mind. The fastest of your number-crunching computers is but a lumbering tortoise compared with the frenetic whir of the primal pulse. It is the fundamental beat of time, the archetypal rhythm, the pulsing heart of the universe.

Just as vibration increasingly slows as it nears the earth's bedrock, so too does the primal pulse slow its rhythm down to velocities consonant with physical universe construction. Just as your senses are designed to perceive certain narrow bands of vibrational frequencies, so also is your mind built to experience events in time only at a certain speed or velocity. The primal pulse must be "slowed down" to a rhythm compatible with your conscious mind, for you to experience an event in your life's flow of moments.

Just as your senses perceive bedrock objects as the symbolic expression of unseen, nonphysical grids of intent springing from the twin universe, so can you consider events to be blocks or grids of intent feeding themselves into the linear time flow. Each event of your life can be considered like a block of ice, slowly melting drop by drop. Each "drop" is a moment in time. You cannot expect the block of ice to disintegrate instantly into a puddle. It must release its form drop by drop. So must events drip into the river of time, drop by drop, moment by moment.

The larger and more tightly compacted is an event's grid or block, the longer will be its expression in time, its drip into the flow of moments. Events involving enormous human issues—like slavery versus freedom, for example—require centuries to play out, countless souls participating in the drama's flow, splintering the cosmic theme into an infinite variety of slants and focuses, the better to explore such issues from every conceivable angle. In contrast, events of little significance—your morning cup of coffee—carry no larger importance in the upper realms, meaning such an event can play itself out, drip by freshly-brewed drip, within a matter of minutes.

Your conscious mind is constructed to handle only so much information at one time. We have already seen how it selects a few narrow bands of vibration from all the electromagnetic radiation available to it, as a way of finely focusing your awareness toward your goal of manipulating the world. The same holds true as events are experienced in time. Your mind can process only "so much" at once. Only so many drops of intent, seeded into the world from the realms above, can be consciously perceived and interpreted at one time.

Just as there are frequencies of vibration your senses cannot detect, so are there velocities of events which entirely escape your notice. Events must be "slowed down" to a certain speed before your conscious mind can perceive them. So events, originating in the realms beyond space and time, must "step down" into the flow of world events just as vibration slows as it nears earth's bedrock. Only those events traveling at a certain speed will be perceptible to you.

The purpose, again, is to ensure your freedom and free will. For as we will see, events are not set in stone, shoved into your life against your will for you to experience them, like it or not. Instead, events are plastic. In their primal state they have no existence in time. It is you who break them down into a series of moments. And even then, your experience of events is highly subjective, and largely under the control of your conscious mind.

You are at the mercy of no event, then, but can through conscious choice alter the duration and intensity of any event. This ensures and enhances your free will. You are at the mercy of nothing. No event is thrust upon you. All of this will be explored in much more detail later. Our point now is merely to explain the purpose of your conscious mind's construction allowing events to reach awareness only at certain speeds, and only as a series of moments. The purpose is to guarantee your free will, the purpose of human life.

As a creature in a physical universe, you are biologically tied to the beat of the primal pulse. This pulse beats steady and sure throughout the universe, sparking every primal cell at the same instant, a cosmic metronome reverberating through the far reaches of space. Each beat of the primal pulse carries a "signature," a unique identification, which forever melds its imprint onto every event occurring at that specific pulse. In basic terms, you could conceive of this signature as a simple numerical progression: the first primal pulse at the dawn of time was 1, the next moment was 2, and so on.

Much more is involved, of course; the signature is not a numerical value but an energy matrix binding together all universal events occurring at each beat of the pulse. There is a pulse matrix indelibly binding all events occurring on January 24, 1940, at 2:33 in the morning. A consciousness properly attuned could step into that energy matrix and spend eternity exploring everything occurring in the universe at that moment.

This carries into our discussion of human experience in the universe. It means that each beat of the primal pulse is uniquely coded as a specific moment in time. Consider the flow of time, from the first hazy dawn to the stars' last flicker, as being broken down into a series of pulses, composing the master schedule of the universe. You do the same, with far cruder blocks of time, in your calendars listing year, month, day, and hour. The universal master schedule breaks these time units down to the tiniest fraction of time, the fundamental, the primal pulse. Each such pulse carries a unique code binding it to that "moment" in time.

This master calendar provides the structure into which events can feed. All events are simultaneous; all flow from the realms beyond space and time. Yet they are not randomly tossed into the flow of moments, to drop into your laps in random and chaotic incongruity. Instead, they are always inserted into the time continuum at the moment of optimum benefit for those participating in the event. By latching onto a given beat of the primal pulse as it holds its place in the master schedule, an event steps into the world of time. It descends from the realm of nontime and enters the flow of moments. By linking the first "drop" of temporal expression with a specific primal pulse, the event can play itself out over a stretch of time most beneficial to the participants.

On a larger scale, if you consider your entire life span as an event, you see now how your greater entity can pick and choose among the historical periods of earth in which to spark shoots of intent to life—you being one such shoot of intent. Now you see how we can claim that all your reincarnational lives are fundamentally simultaneous, while they also play out over the progression of time. It simply depends on what level of reality you view. From the level of temporal earthly life, reincarnation is a series of lives played out over a vast spread of historical periods. From the perspective of the greater entity, all such lives exist at once. It is by linking with specific beats of the pulse that the individual shoots of intent sprout over the centuries.

Just as your experience of a physical object is but the icing on the electromagnetic cake standing behind your perception, so is your experience of an event just a fraction of the event's full reality. You experience only one version of an event in time, yet an infinite number of variations or gradations of that event exist as well. An event is "set up" with all possible variations built in. In deepest terms, an event is the sum total of all possible versions, or outcomes, of itself. These gradations, these limitless variations, we will call "probabilities." Each potential outcome or experience of an event is a probable version of that event. There are "master events," the unified, infinite versions bound by common intent, and "probable events," each splintering off from the master event to express a unique variation on the central theme.

How is it determined which probable version of an event you will experience? Is the decision made in a random cosmic crap shoot, the result of fate or luck or chance? How does a master event narrow itself down to the single version you experience?

Just as the world's objects are created in the nonphysical universe and then thrust into physical existence, thereby assuming the qualities of electromagnetic vibration, so occurs also with events. Master events remain on the nontime side of the primal pulse. The splinters, the probable versions, are fed into the physical system. These probable events then manifest as electromagnetic swirls, fields of vibration. They are governed by the properties of electromagnetism.

A fundamental principle of electromagnetism is that like attracts like. We have already seen this in the formation of vibrational fields creating bedrock, water, and air. This is the property of attraction, in physical terms the search for vibration carrying similarly contoured pattern.

This principle holds also in the world of events. Each probable version of an event carries a unique electromagnetic pattern and frequency. Here is where your coordinate, the electromagnetic axis encased in your spine, comes into play. The coordinate will carry a unique electromagnetic flavor, based upon your life experiences, your thoughts and beliefs, your physical health, and so on. The combined energy of all such factors results in a unique electromagnetic swirl sizzling along the coordinate. When the infinite probable variations of a master event are seeded into your life's flow of moments, your coordinate will latch onto the version most closely aligned in electromagnetic terms. It is this version of an event you will then physically experience.

As we said above, events differ both in pattern and in frequency. Frequency is a measure of vibration, how many cycles or beats occur within a given unit of time. As a general rule, the slower the frequency of a probable event, the more "negative" a potential it carries. You are not cast adrift in a neutral universe; the fundamental energy of the universe is joy, leading toward growth and fulfillment. Joy carries a far higher frequency than sorrow. As an event approaches your life in all its probable potentials, the happier you are—the higher the frequency carried in your coordinate— the more "positive" will be the probable event you pull into experience.

As an example, when you are depressed, you may find that things seem to fall apart rapidly, your life crashing down upon your head. Your health deteriorates. Your relationships suffer. In every aspect of life you may find event after event of a negative nature plaguing you, pushing you even further down the spiral of depression. Depression is a low frequency. When depressed, you magnetically pull into your life the "negative" versions of events.

This leads up to what is the single most important statement in this book. *Nothing happens to you except what you draw to yourself.* You are at the mercy of nothing. Neither chance, nor fate, nor luck, nor an omniscient God, plays any part in the unfolding of your life's events. *You stand as the gatekeeper of your life, allowing entrance only to those events of your choice.* To consider that anything has been thrust upon you violates both electromagnetic reality and the purpose of human life. Fields of similar pattern attract, while disparate fields repel. So do you repel any event contrary to your coordinate's vibration. So do you attract only those events, those probable versions of events, carrying potential aligned with your life's condition as expressed in the coordinate.

In truth, there is another source of events beyond the control of your conscious mind. Events chosen before birth, as elements of karmic balancing and cleansing, may be set up ahead of time to slide into your life at the moment of optimum benefit. Such an event will be "coded" to match a given primal pulse occurring at some point after birth; and at the precise beat selected, the event begins its unfolding in time.

Still, you are at the mercy of nothing. For if you expand your view from your solitary life to the perspective of your greater entity, you see that all events are chosen to round out and balance its full experience of earthly life. There is no thought of retribution or punishment, only the determination to balance events with their opposites. And even when such an event is set up before birth, you still carry great power to ameliorate or diffuse it, given the condition of your coordinate at the time and the extent to which you understand karmic principles.

As is true on the individual level, so also applies to events of the larger society. You each contribute your personal energy, at the level of the psyche, to the overall human vibration of the planet. This mass vibration pulls into physical actuality those events most aligned with the condition of your species. The pull and force of this electromagnetic field is so great that your species is in large part responsible for unusual meteorological conditions and sudden planetary changes such as earthquakes.

In summary, nothing can happen to you except that which you draw to yourself. Such is true on the lofty level of consciousness, where human life was granted freedom and free will; and such carries over as consciousness seeds the physical universe at the levels of electromagnetism.

You create your own reality. There is no other rule.

Nineteen

〜

Thought, Experience, and Object

Our definition of events as being any occurrence manifesting in the physical world over a period of moments, is broader than you might initially think. For while the experiences of your private and communal existence are indeed events, they are only one class of events, one subset of the larger rubric of events. If an event is any occurrence manifesting in the temporal world, then a most significant aspect of events is this: *all objects are events.*

You are accustomed to thinking of objects as "things," the planet's profusion of basic elements molded into varieties of form, or those your species fashions from such raw materials. You draw a sharp distinction between such physical objects and your life's experiences, your emotions, your relationships, your daily flow through life. Yet, at base, both physical objects and life experiences are events. Let us explore this further.

Returning to our discussion of your perception of a physical world, you will recall that you perceive only a fraction of the total electromagnetic reality of any object. Its vibrations must emanate within a certain range, must "slow down" to the frequencies that your senses are tuned to perceive.

As briefly mentioned in the last chapter, the same holds true for events. They must "slow down" for your conscious mind to perceive them. As events are fed into the physical system at the portal of the primal pulse, they vibrate at far too rapid a frequency for your conscious mind to latch onto them and immediately pull them into your life's experience. They must slow down their vibrational frequency, in a series of steps, to a level compatible with the mind's operational frequencies.

The fundamental difference between life-experience events and physical-object events is that objects carry charge, sculpted by pattern, while experienced events carry only pattern and no charge. The difference flows from the frequency of the energy swirl creating the event.

The primal pulse gradually slows as it forms the physical system, down to the earth pulse allowing creation of bedrock. A primal cell can contain a burst of charge only when there is sufficient "time" between pulses to allow for the charge to sprout from the filament, fill the cell with bulk, then reabsorb the vibration into the filament before the next beat of the pulse, shooting the charge back to the nonphysical universe.

A primal cell pulsing too fast to allow this expansion and contraction of charge can never carry a burst of vibration. Each beat of the pulse can therefore stimulate only the walls of the cell, while allowing no vibrational bulk within.

To expand our earlier model, the primal cell's wall, its envelope, will assume a unique pattern with each beat of the primal pulse. Obviously, the cell wall cannot carry any charge. Yet the cell wall is itself a grid of vibration, and carries highly specialized codes of information, patterns of vibration, as fed to it by its twin cell in the nonphysical universe.

So a primal cell pulsing too rapidly to contain any charge is still capable of transmitting vibrational information, of assuming unique configurations and contributing to the larger structure of which it is a part.

You can see now the basic difference between experience and object: Objects must carry bedrock charge for any of your senses to perceive them. Only bedrock frequencies stimulate your senses. Those swirls of vibration carrying no charge you cannot physically perceive.

There is still a finer distinction into two main types of nonphysical events. Life experience events are those that seem to "happen" to you in the world of objects. Walking down the street, driving a car, buying groceries: these are all experiences in the temporal world, events "stepped down" into the physical plane while not solidifying into bedrock.

The other main type of nonphysical event is thought. Your dreams, loves, ambitions, plans, schemes, resentments, jealousies, fears, wonders, affections, apprehensions, decisions, designs, plots, and hopes—all the components of your mind's stream of consciousness as you navigate your course through life—these exist in the realm of thought. Thought is the highest level, or frequency, of events as experienced by your conscious mind.

So the three main types of events are thought, experience, and object. Thoughts whir the fastest, shooting through your mind at tremendous velocity. Life experience is the next "slowest" level of event, slowing down thought's frequency to a vibration compatible with temporal expression in the physical world. And as vibration slows even further it allows the expression of charge within the primal cells, charge creating bedrock objects perceptible to your senses. At base, thought, experience, and object are fundamentally identical: swirls of vibration, slowing their frequencies down in steps such that your experience of them leaps from private thought to experience in the physical world to bedrock objects.

Once again, the aim is to fulfill your purpose: to manipulate the physical world while enjoying freedom of thought. If your thoughts were instantly projected onto the world at large, like a projector flashing onto a movie screen, your privacy of thought would be lost. It is you who choose which thoughts to share with others, by reducing them to speech—stepping them down in frequency to sound waves or words upon a page, wrestling them down into physical symbol.

Your power of volition extends far beyond merely deciding which thoughts to share with others. For the point of earthly life is to experience the effects of your thoughts projected onto the physical world; to literally sculpt your life's events through the power of belief and thought. You do so by slowing the frequencies of the events you attract down to rhythms manifesting as experience and object. The life you know is simply the projection of your thoughts. Yours is the ultimate power: to create your own reality.

Thought, experience, and object are the three basic levels of events as experienced by your conscious mind. Yet these are actually the three "slowest" versions of events. They are those events vibrating at frequencies compatible with the electrical impulses in your brain, which, we hesitate to point out, do not travel at the speed of light.

Yet events exist on many higher levels of frequency, beyond the reach of your conscious mind's perception. Again, events always slow down in a series of steps, moving toward expression in the physical realm. Those events fresh from crossing the primal pulse into physical existence whir at the fastest frequency, gradually slowing down in increments.

Each step down in frequency represents a loss of fidelity from the original intent of the master event lying beyond the primal pulse. Each step down reduces the event to crude, fragmented, diffuse expression, bled of its original richness.

Many artists will agree that their finished works never come close to the original vision, the initial inspiration which provoked them to creation. That spark of inspiration, bursting in refulgent glory from the far reaches of divine potential, must be "slowed down" by the artist to become a creation perceptible to the human senses—meaning that it has reached the slowest frequency in the hierarchy of events. As such, reduced to bedrock symbol, there must necessarily be a loss of intent, of richness, of inspiration. This is the artist's agony and ecstasy, the struggle to render in the physical world bursts of inspiration no ear can hear, no eye can view, no hand can touch.

Overcome with emotion for a loved one, you may say, "Words can't begin to express how I feel about you." Again, your love—the inexpressible appreciation for the divine spark in another—must be stepped down into the hollow trinket of "I love you," a mere symbolic wrapping on a far richer truth.

Upon awaking, you struggle to make sense of your dreams. Even those experienced at dream interpretation are stumped from time to time by a seemingly chaotic jumble of fragmented images. What in the world was that all about? you wonder. Dreams—explorations into realms far beyond the physical, where your psyche soars once released from concern for the body's safety—must squeeze their thick, rich meaning down many levels of frequency, down to a series of physical symbols painted on the brain's conscious awareness. The loss of fidelity, of truth, is enormous. Dreams are better *felt* and *absorbed* than consciously interpreted. Squashed down into symbol, they fade into crude caricatures of the profound experience giving them birth.

In these few examples, you see how a step down to a lower frequency of event always results in a loss of fidelity and richness. You never experience the pure, unfiltered, undiluted strength of an event. Your conscious mind could not endure it. It is not designed to perceive absolute truth, only fragments and symbols. Realize that just as physical objects are symbols of the deeper reality lying behind them, so are all your life experiences symbols of their deeper and richer source.

As always, there is no sense of deprivation involved in your experiencing symbol rather than absolute reality. That is what you chose earthly life for. Does your world appear as a pale, drab, mind-numbing penitentiary to you? Or as an infinitely rich, impossibly diverse crucible of creation? And knowing that your world and experiences upon it are but a fraction of the greater truth and reality lying behind it, what fear have you of death, when such brings you closer and deeper into such realms? Death, where is that sting of yours now!

Twenty

ᕉ

Space-Time

If all objects are events, slowed down to a frequency allowing expression of vibration in the primal cells and perceptible to the senses, this leads us to a fundamental understanding of the nature of the universe. Space and time are two facets of one reality. They are one and the same.

We have said that the primal pulse beats the universe to life in its fundamental parameters of space and time. To raise our discussion to the next level of sophistication, we state now that the primal pulse creates the universe through the single fundamental element of space-time.

This understanding should flow easily from the preceding material. Objects—what you perceive as constructs and elements of a physical universe—are merely your senses' perception of swirls of vibration, perceptible along narrow bands of frequency. Further, you also understand objects to be the "slowest" level of event, their vibration of sufficient slowness that charge can burst to life within the primal cells.

An object exists in space—filling a certain matrix of primal cells with its bulk—and in time—lasting a certain duration of moments. In both cases, it is your conscious mind, tuned to its narrow perception of vibration, that perceives the object and its existence in time. Fundamentally, both attributes of an object spring from the single swirl of energy lying behind your perception. Your senses work in tandem with your conscious mind's tread along a flow of moments, and you divide your apprehension of an object into the fundamentals of space and time. Yet, at base, they are identical. Their source is the same basic energy. Your mind is simply tuned into two different frequencies, two different bands of perception, at the same time, labeling one space and the other time.

By crossing the primal pulse into physical expression, a grid of intent assumes the quality of physical life. This fundamental quality is space-time, the expression of intent as energy. This energy matrix swirls at differing velocities. Some slow sufficiently that your conscious mind can feed them into its linear flow of moments as thought. Some slow further into life experience. Some slow further, assuming the vibrational expression of charge, perceptible to your senses. These become the objects, the matter, of your physical universe.

An object exists in time because once a grid of intent has slowed its frequency to a level perceptible to your senses, it remains locked into that frequency until the grid of intent is fully dissipated. No grid of intent lasts forever. They are created for the purpose of seeding your world, your universe, with a constant evolution of experience. Each is born to dissipate, scattering its energy through the universe, to be picked up and refashioned into the next evolutionary step. A grid of intent vibrating slowly enough to be perceptible to your senses has chosen to dissipate slowly—so slowly that you perceive it as an object enduring through time. Nothing, no creation of God or man, lasts forever, you will grant. All have their point of final disintegration locked into their structure at the moment of genesis.

"Time" is a much higher frequency than "space." For time, the ticking of moments, exists in the realm of thought. Physical matter exists in the realm of objects. The fastest frequency your mind can perceive—thought—and the slowest—object—work in tandem to create a picture of an enduring physical universe. Yet behind your experience, creating it, are swirls of energy and intent carrying the unified quality of space-time. It is you, with your conscious mind, who split space from time and experience a temporal world of matter.

All objects are events. All experiences are events. All thoughts are events. All events originate in the nonphysical realms of consciousness, beat to physical life by the primal pulse. As events squeeze past the primal pulse, they are imbued with energy, the energy of space-time, then cast free to manifest according to their intent and the subconsciously broadcast desires of those who stand to benefit from experiencing their expression. Some you perceive as thoughts. Some you perceive as experiences. Some you perceive as objects. Many you experience as blends, hybrid constructions bridging levels of physical expression.

At base, in its primal state, the physical universe and its flow of moments spring from the single quality of space-time, the archetypal energy of existence.

Twenty-One

୨ଡ଼

The Event-Body Link

Perhaps you begin to see a connection between the nature of events and the construction of the four vibrational bodies you carry through life. Each of your bodies vibrates at a different frequency, each step away from the physical body representing a jump to a higher frequency. Events also step up in frequency as they find expression as object, experience, and thought. These two fundamental parameters of earthly life are inextricably linked.

The physical body is the slowest of your four vibrational bodies. It alone vibrates slowly enough to allow the expression of charge within its primal cells. It assumes the qualities of bedrock, to varying degrees depending on the corporal structure involved. While principally composed of water—which also vibrates slowly enough to carry charge—your body is configured principally as a bedrock entity.

Matching the body's slow vibration, manifesting as bedrock, is the slowest level of event, bedrock objects. Because the swirling clouds of energy standing behind your body and the earth's bedrock objects vibrate within sympathetic frequencies, you can perceive objects, and they can affect your body.

In deepest terms, of course, there is no distinction between your body and an object, for your body falls into the category of objects, itself a subset of the larger rubric of events. The difference is that we are distinguishing the unique human family of consciousness from the earth's bedrock objects, holding you apart as suffused with a distinct and private purpose. While your body assumes the qualities of bedrock objects, it is suffused with human consciousness, for which the body acts simply as the vehicle.

The next step up from the physical body is the etheric body, that cloak of vibration tightly encasing your body in a cocoon of protective sensors. Its purpose is to help you navigate a safe course through the physical world. It is privy to information not normally available to your conscious awareness. It perceives vibration on the next step "up" from the physical body.

The etheric body's vibration is sympathetic with the next step up in events, to those categorized as life experience. Life experience is the first nonphysical level of events, a step up from bedrock objects. Since this is the level of vibration where things "happen" to you in the physical world without solidifying into bedrock, it naturally follows that the etheric body's purpose is to aid you in charting a smooth course through the world of experience. It apprises you of immediate environmental conditions, as a way of alerting you to potential danger, or potential pleasure. As such, it helps you select those experiences most beneficial to your learning and growth, ensuring your free will.

The next vibrational body is the auric body, extending as far as six feet from the physical body. At this level, the auric body vibrates with sufficient intensity that it is able to tap into the network of global consciousness carried by the "information cells" whirling about the earth. This represents a step away from the purely physical concerns of your body in its place and time, moving into the larger realms of mass consciousness and events. This level of vibrational frequency is linked to the next highest step of events, your mind's conscious thought processes.

Your conscious mind acts as a filter for all the information disseminated to it by the auric body. The vast majority is dismissed from conscious awareness as it bears no relation to the immediate physical concerns of your body's stance. Yet there are some elements of the auric body's information which do reach consciousness—in the example given before, if sudden injury or death befalls a loved one, you may become aware of a strong feeling of concern and worry. This is the auric body's information squeezing into consciousness, pulled into awareness by your bond of love. Just as you could never read every newspaper, magazine, and book published, for most of the information is of no value to you, so too does the conscious mind filter the auric body's comprehensive world overview down to information of immediate concern.

The next highest vibrational body—and the last step in the physical system—is the psyche. The psyche rides the portal of the primal pulse, drinking deeply from the families of consciousness giving it birth, but casting an observant eye on the flow of worldly events, particularly those holding potential impact on you.

We have not yet explored in depth the realms of events higher than your conscious mind's thought processes. The next step up is what we will call the "superconscious" level of events. These are events still swirling in latent potential, as probabilities, not yet linking with private or communal human consciousness. They have not yet found their "home." It may not yet be the best "time" for them to begin unraveling in the flow of moments. They are potentials, literally the events of the future descending from the nonphysical realms to search out the times and places where they can find the most beneficial expression.

This superconscious level of events is linked with the human psyche as a way of joining, at the very portal of the primal pulse, the world's potential events with human consciousness. This begins the sorting and sifting process, allowing events to be magnetically drawn to those individuals and communities where they can offer the greatest benefit from their expression. This occurs on levels far above your normal waking consciousness. You become aware of such material, and participate in decisions and choices as to which events you will privately and globally experience, in the dream state every night.

Incidentally, you will notice that we never use the word "subconscious" to describe any level of mind. For the word implies that there is awareness beneath your earthly experience. In fact, the levels of thought, experience, and object represent the three slowest levels of events. There is none lower. There is nothing "lower" than what you experience consciously, sorry to say!

Briefly we have outlined how the four vibrational bodies you carry link with the four levels of events. Your bedrock body perceives bedrock objects. Your etheric body navigates you safely through the world of experience. Your auric body feeds a stream of global information to your conscious mind's thought processes. Your psyche links with superconscious events, fresh from the nonphysical realms, providing the initial filtering and direction of events seeking temporal expression.

As events are fed into the physical system, they acquire the quality of space-time. This means that from the moment of their inception to their physical expression, a gap of moments, a stretch of time, must intervene. No event falls straight from the nonphysical realms into your laps.

Each event you experience is only one version, one probable facet, of the larger master event giving it birth. Which version you experience depends upon your beliefs, thoughts, and health, encoded in the coordinate, acting as a magnet to probable events of similar configuration. All of this takes time.

This carries several implications. First, you are precognitively aware of every event occurring to you, well before its actual expression in time. The first hesitant link is made at the level of the psyche. Here, a cluster of probable events will ride the psyche's intent down to the next vibrational level. In other words, while a master event seeds all possible variations of itself into the physical system, your psyche carries the stamp of your coordinate, representing the electromagnetic version of your thoughts and beliefs. Therefore, out of all probable potentials of an event, only those relatively sympathetic to the vibration of your coordinate will link with the psyche. A certain narrow band, or cluster, of potential events joins the psyche's intent at this level.

This is the level of superconscious thought, and it is only rarely that you consciously become aware of the process occurring "above" you between psyche and superconscious events. Your mind could never endure the vibrational intensity, for one thing. For another, there is no purpose to your consciously being aware of every possible occurrence in your life. Such awareness, in fact, would override your purpose. So the process most often occurs without dropping into consciousness.

In rare instances, you are aware of such a process. Since at this point the event in question is not a single version, but a cluster of probabilities, you will most likely not feel directed toward a specific action, nor feel that any specific event is bound to occur. Instead, you may feel an inexplicable unease, a vague feeling of danger or warning bearing no relation to your immediate physical surroundings. Because the "event" is so amorphous and unformed at this point, you rarely receive specific information about its potential expression. You are left with vague, unformed, diffuse feelings.

If the bond between psyche and superconscious event confirms that you would benefit from the experience of the event, it will "step down" into the next slowest vibrational frequency. This is the level of the auric body, feeding information to your conscious mind. Again, most such information is never brought to full conscious awareness. At this level, the aura is in contact with global events, and is sifting and sorting events based on both mass and private benefit. In other words, an "event" may be clearly about to manifest physically, and the auric body determines if you would personally benefit from sharing in the experience. If so, your participation is "arranged." If not, the auric body severs the link between your vibrational bodies and the probable events, leaving others to experience the physical version.

This is the level where precognition is more concrete and specific. And while you may consciously feel no trace of an impending event, your aura, thoughts, and coordinate act together to prevent your participation in events not to your benefit. For example, you may be driving to the airport to catch an airplane when a tire blows, forcing a lengthy repair and causing you to miss the plane. Damn! you cry, why did this have to happen to me! You later learn that the plane exploded in mid-flight, killing all on board. Thank God! you cry.

You have blamed cruel fate for your misfortune, then thanked God for being spared, in both cases demonstrating your ignorance of the nature of events. Those choosing to suddenly exit physical life often participate in a communal experience like an airplane crash. If all passengers holding reservations for a specific flight have decided to participate in this event, and you too hold a reservation for that flight, your auric body is aware that the flight is being used as a vehicle for exiting physical life. If it would not suit your purpose to leave physical life at the time, you must not board the airplane. The need for you to miss the flight is so urgent that the auric body will arrange whatever events are necessary to prevent your timely arrival. These events are "pushed down" to the vibrational level of experience and object—like a tire blowing on the road to the airport.

Were you consciously attuned to precognitive information as a matter of course, you need not experience such an event of hindrance. Allowing the urgent warnings from the aura to ease into consciousness, you might feel a strong message not to take that flight. You might decide you would rather fly another day. In any number of ways can this information impress itself upon your conscious mind. If your habit is to respect feelings and impulses as they glide into consciousness, you spare yourself much trauma—and the cost of a new tire.

This example was meant to demonstrate the connection between your auric body and events at the level of thought. While the psyche may have tentatively linked with a superconscious event, the finer focus of your auric body may determine that there would be no benefit to your participation. The link is severed. You will not participate in the event's physical expression.

If, on the other hand, the auric body confirms that such an experience is to your benefit—and it does this by examining the electromagnetic condition of your coordinate and the event's probable versions to determine the degree of sympathy—then the cluster of probable events will be narrowed to a discrete, specific "version." From the fairly broad range of potentials, a more precise focus is selected, that probability most aligned with your beliefs, thoughts, and health. This information is fed to your conscious mind, registering at the level of thought.

Again, at this level, most such information is never consciously perceived. Your free will always reigns supreme. You may receive dire warnings from your auric body; but if you choose to ignore them, that is your privilege—a privilege with a price. You may have had "gut feelings" warning you against a certain course of action, ignored the feelings, proceeded with your course, and wound up wishing you had paid closer attention to those unspoken warnings. You are under no obligation to respect the steady flow of guidance from your auric body. You are perfectly free to stagger from disaster to disaster, blaming fate and chance and luck and God as you bandage yourself up before sallying forth to again face the cold, cruel world.

Your culture's rejection of any "nonrational" thought reduces you to the mentality of robots, stumbling around helter-skelter, prey to any breeze that blows your way. From our perspective, nothing could be more *irrational* than denying yourself the steady flow of wisdom from the auric body as it guides your path through life. That is its purpose. That is why it exists. You are never cast adrift. No event falls upon you without warning. You might cast a glance about your society and consider whether your exclusive emphasis on "rational" thought has brought you contentment, a healthy environment, food and shelter for all, and a world at peace.

The next linked level of vibrational body and event is the etheric body's awareness of life experience events. Here is where thought is stepped down into your experiences in the physical world. Here is where the events first drawn by the psyche, and fine-tuned by the auric body, find their physical expression. This is the level of event in which things "happen" to you, and where you make things happen.

Your etheric body's purpose is to aid you in navigating through the world of objects. It does so by becoming aware of vibrational energies not perceptible to your senses. The field of information perceived by the etheric body is restricted to your immediate environment. Keeping you safe and secure in that environment ensures your freedom to manipulate and explore.

Most "events" on this level carry little significance. If you think of each act you commit during the course of a day, how many are dripping with truth, thundering with cosmic significance? Most such "events" are designed simply to transport your body through the physical world as you pursue higher purpose. Many such events occur on levels entirely unconscious—every beat of your heart, crackling synapse in your brain, urge to draw a breath—all these are regulated beyond your conscious mind's awareness. As long as your body is functioning well, there is no need for conscious awareness of its condition. Great pleasure and pain, carrying messages of salubrious and harmful corporal experience, focus your attention directly on the body. Otherwise, the events of its homeostatic processes and circadian rhythms never ride into consciousness.

Events at the level of life experience fall into two categories: those that seem to "happen" to you, and those you deliberately make happen. For while you magnetically draw to your life all of its experiences, you carry always the free will to imprint your unique reaction back upon the world. An event seeming to "happen" to you would be losing your job. That event, though chosen on levels unconscious, nevertheless seems to be imposed from without. Your area of volition is your reaction—anger, suicide, shrugged shoulders, relief. And you carry the freedom to keep your reaction to yourself—maintaining the privacy of thought—or to share it with others, through speech or deed. It is your choice, always, whether to "step down" your thoughts into experience in the physical world.

The final linked level of vibrational body and event is your physical body and its relationship with the bedrock objects of the world. This is the realm of the senses, those sensors feeding you slivers of truth along narrow bands of vibration. As a bedrock object, your body is influenced by other bedrock objects. In order to maintain your secure stance in the world, you need to know when objects impinge upon you—what they are, when they move, how they feel. These parameters your senses bring to you, as the "slowest" level of information necessary to ensure your safety and ability to manipulate the earth.

While it may seem that this arrangement leaves the body and its senses the poor, neglected cousins of the cosmos, in fact they are the ultimate purpose and aim of your existence. You exist to explore and manipulate the earth. You do so at the level of body and bedrock. All other levels of consciousness exist solely to sustain your freedom to pursue your fulfillment in the physical medium. They have no other purpose. Each step "down" in frequency more finely focuses your field of perception, and further narrows the potential events of your life to those specific events most closely aligned with your intent and condition, as carried in the coordinate.

Your body and its experience in the world of space and time are not the second-hand, leftover end products of the higher levels of consciousness and event. They represent the very purpose of your existence, the final step in the delicate and complex process of weaving events into the fabric of your life. There is nothing "crude" about your experience. It is precisely what it was meant to be: the expression of divine potential in the physical realm. You are the final, indivisible, eternal spark of your greater entity's intent, else you would not be here. You are not cast adrift in a cold universe; you *are* the universe, the child of infinite realms of energy and intent whose sole purpose is to sustain the life path of your divine, unique potential.

Twenty-Two

Event Gravity

Events travel on cycles. You can imagine them bouncing in a circular pattern, at each bounce dipping closer and closer to the world of physically experienced events. If you think of linear time running along a straight line, visualize events bouncing on their cycles above the track of linear time, with each bounce stepping closer and closer as they follow the forward flow. At the point of intersection, where the event links with the track of time, the event is physically experienced.

Imagine that our main classes of events—objects, experiences, thoughts, and superconscious thoughts—are stationary layers beginning at the earth's surface, gradually rising toward the sky. The lowest level, of course, would be the bedrock objects, and the earth itself. The next step up would span the distance from your feet to your head, for here is where most life experiences occur. The level of thought begins at the head and rises above it, reaching toward the superconscious events which encircle the globe like the stratosphere.

Now, into this model of stationary layers are seeded sprouts of events, fresh from creation in the nonphysical realms, dropped into the world of space-time. As they bounce closer to earth on their cycles, these events slow their vibrational frequencies. You know that a space capsule dropping from the far reaches of exosphere to splashdown encounters tremendous friction along the way as the earth's atmosphere thickens, squeezing the capsule with increased resistance. This, quite literally, is what happens to events. As they drop lower toward the world of objects, they encounter increased resistance from the thickened layers of vibration.

What pulls the space capsule to earth? Gravity. At base, gravity is the tendency of objects of similar charge and pattern to attract. Because a space capsule and planet earth are composed of bedrock, they attract. The enormous bedrock globe exerts a fierce pull on the minuscule capsule, so it is the capsule that plummets to earth, not the other way around. In truth, the earth does pull, however slightly, toward the capsule. But the greater bulk of the earth makes it appear stationary as the capsule is pulled magnetically toward the earth's core.

The same occurs with events. Although they encounter resistance from the increasingly thick vibrational layers, they are magnetically pulled down to earth to the extent that their electromagnetic qualities are sympathetic with those who stand to experience each event. This is "event gravity." The principle is the same. Because events carry no charge, except when manifesting as objects, "event gravity" operates solely on sympathies of pattern, electromagnetic configurations.

At each nadir of its cycle, as an event steps closer to physical expression, the cluster of probabilities is increasingly winnowed to the one, or few, most aligned with the coordinates of those experiencing the event. In other words, each probable version of an event rides its own cycle. These travel in clusters, essentially as a "package," as they approach the world of experience. With each drop in vibrational frequency, at the nadir of each cycle, the configuration of the coordinate becomes more clearly defined. Those probable versions least sympathetic to the coordinate will then drop away; they can descend no further. There is no "event gravity" to pull them through the thickening layers of events. So they bounce forever latent, meaning they will not find expression in the world of events.

Each drop closer to the level of experience will further narrow the field of probabilities. The coordinate acts as a magnet, pulling down the probable version(s) most aligned with its configuration. At the moment just before a cycle intersects the linear time line, the final link is made between coordinate and event. This single probable version is then pulled into expression as thought, or experience, or object.

"Event gravity" is how you create your reality in the world of physical experience.

Because all events originate in the nonphysical realm, we state that all events are simultaneous. Further, any event that is seeded into the physical system is not then forever lost to the nonphysical realm. Instead, any seeded event is a "copy" of its nonphysical original. Just as the physical universe blinks back into its nonphysical twin universe, so also does every physically experienced event spring from a nonphysical master event.

The result, quite obviously, is that not only are all events simultaneous, they are also eternal. No event is ever finished. There is no end, and no beginning, in the nonphysical realm. Every event plays forever. What you experience is one tiny sliver of a master event, and that master event swirls forever in all its potentials. You choose to experience one facet of the event. The master event experiences all facets, and does so throughout all eternity.

No event is ever finished. While events seem to sprout and die in your experience, wrapped in precise births and deaths, no such overtures and final curtains play in the realm of master events. It is you who present events upon the world's stage as a series of finite acts.

This carries many implications. For one thing, no "past" event is ever finished. You may well have seen its probable version dissipate in the linear flow of moments. Yet the master event is eternal, beyond the pull of time. So nothing is ever finished, dead and buried.

One result is your power to dip into your reincarnational lifetimes through hypnosis. Under the trained guidance of a hypnotist, you can relive significant events of past lifetimes, as a way of understanding their influence on you now. For those lifetimes are just as vibrant, on the level of master events, as yours is to you now. Those individuals still live.

Consider the process of hypnosis. To reach the deepest hypnotic state, the primary concern is to ensure your physical safety. You cannot enter hypnosis while walking down the street; your attention must be focused then on the world of objects. But with your safety secured, you are able to relinquish your intense focus on the physical world. This means that the higher vibrational bodies can relax their concern for your physical safety, and direct their energy outward and upward. As they do so, you can directly and consciously plug into the information carried at the level of auric body, psyche, and even beyond.

In deep hypnotic regression, you can cross the portal of the primal pulse, rejoin your greater entity and cast glances down at any historical period of earth, and your experiences at that time. These are then relayed to you in full strength. By reversing the normal flow of energy from the physical body to the upper reaches of consciousness, you have access to the unlimited realms where all events occur simultaneously.

By the same token, you can become aware of events before their physical occurrence. We have already seen how this information is fed to you by the psyche and auric body, before "stepping down" into the world of experience. Since most such information is of no value, it is never brought to conscious awareness.

Animals, firmly rooted to the natural order and not blocking their awareness by a nonsensical emphasis on "rational" thought, are routinely aware of such information. Barnyard animals are well known for sensing a storm, an earthquake, a tornado, well before the event finds full physical expression. This is no miracle, no stupefying act of precognition. Any event manifesting in bedrock—like an earthquake—must "step down" to that level through the higher vibrational fields. Because consciousness, animal consciousness, is attuned to these higher frequencies, they literally experience the event before it physically occurs.

You see, at this level and from this perspective, the event is not broken into fragments—the mental awareness followed by the physical earthquake—but is instead seen as a continuous flow, all of which is intrinsic to every event. First you sense it, then you see it. This is how events work; the physical expression is always the last step. The distress evinced by animals aware of impending disaster represents their awareness that the event's physical expression carries the potential for bodily harm. This is why animals seek shelter, to whatever degree they can. Their bodies, bedrock objects, stand to be affected by the bedrock wrenching of an earthquake. This information is also available to the human race, if it ever chooses to engage all levels of mind and chart a healthier course through the world of events.

All "future" events exist now. While most members of a society carry no awareness of the approach of potential events, you have several classes of individuals who do routinely perceive such information. These are the artists and inventors.

Artists soar past the world of object, experience, and thought, to the realm of the superconscious. Here is where latent potentials and trends encircle the globe, carrying pregnant hints of the future. Artists, those who have chosen before birth to contribute to the world in this way, can plug directly into the superconscious realm, absorb the latent potentials of the planet, and return to earth, sculpting their knowledge into song and sonnet and statue.

The artist's great frustration is to render in bedrock what can never find full, rich expression in the world of objects. For the "event" the artist has tapped into bounces still as a potential. Its "time" for expression has not arrived. It cannot suddenly drop to earth; it would burn you with its intensity. So the artist crafts fragments of his vision, morsels of truth, struggling to reduce his vision to bedrock.

The cutting edge of art often repulses mainstream society. They can find nothing of value in it. Mainstream society always rests securely in the world of object and experience, never venturing into the uncharted realms of the psyche and superconscious. They allow themselves no awareness of the potential events looming over their heads. And so cutting-edge art, fragments of potential, means nothing to the mainstream as it cannot fit into the existing conceptual framework of society. Society has not yet evolved to the point where it can appreciate the meaning and truth behind cutting-edge art.

So often you read of artists who struggled, unknown, neglected, scorned by their cultures, left to die miserable deaths, tossed like Mozart into a pauper's grave. You shake your heads in wonder and disgust: Those philistines! Didn't they recognize genius when they saw it?

Of course not; they couldn't. The artist was saying, "Here is your future," and mainstream society could make no sense of these fragments of promise, these symbols of tomorrow. So the artist, and his works, was dismissed as one more starry-eyed dreamer in his starry night.

You have such among you now, artists working in innovative media and producing works that mainstream society can make no sense of. So they struggle in obscurity, driven to wrestle into symbol the world of tomorrow, struggling to apprise you of your own future, while many scoff at and scorn their works.

Future generations will look back in wonder at your generation's rejection of these artists and their art. Philistines! they will sneer. Didn't they recognize genius when they saw it? And so the cycle continues. The artist's ecstasy is to float in the realms of the psyche and potential events, privy to information most never even dream of perceiving. The artist's agony is to wrench truth into symbol, only to face the jeers and guffaws of those unable to peel away the symbolic wrapping and behold the naked truth within.

While the artist struggles to render the future in symbolic wrapping, the inventor leads the march of technology. For your species' purpose is to manipulate the environment, fashioning it into devices and processes which both allow further technological growth and ease the physical circumstances of life. Inventors, those on the cutting edge of technological innovation, tap into the same plane of knowledge as do artists, but their intent is different and the information they gather differs accordingly.

Human life has two main evolutionary currents: one is to manipulate the physical world, the other is to progress spiritually, to pursue higher and higher realms of truth. In a healthy society, these twin strands march hand in hand, technology aiding the spiritual progress, and vice versa. It is the banks of spiritual progress that the artist taps into. The inventor concerns himself with the march of technology, at base an increasing sophistication in understanding the properties of matter and the laws by which it operates.

Since all events are simultaneous, the future exists now. Most in a society carry no awareness of the future potentials hanging above them.

Yet inventors (and we would include brilliant theoretical scientists in the category of inventors, though they may fashion no physical objects) are able to tap into the higher realms, the level of the psyche and its broad overview of human evolution. They tap into the potentials. This is the realm of "What if..." After months or years of struggle, "What if" becomes "Here it is."

All technologies exist now. Inventions and processes you consider far off in the future, they exist now. Those too distant to light the imagination of even the most inspired inventor, they exist now. Do you imagine you will be burning fossil fuels forever? Sheer logic tells you that you cannot; their finite limits will one day be reached, the last oil well squeaking dry. Do you wring your hands, gnash your teeth, and rend your garments at the prospect? Or do you realize that light is energy, sound is energy, and that there exist *now* technologies through which light and sound can be converted to power every device your species can create? Do you look forward, or do you plant your feet in the primordial swamps from which you now draw petroleum, bemoaning your fate? Where do you wish to direct your energy and intent?

Inventors often state, with some wonder, that their inventions suddenly appeared to them in the dream state, or while engaged in an unrelated pastime, especially one bringing pleasure and a dissociated state. By now you should recognize the process and realize that no wonder is called for. In the dream state you travel up through the level of the psyche and beyond, to the realms where space and time do not exist, where all inventions hover in full, ripe potential, there for the plucking. An inventor, whose waking consciousness vibrates at a higher level than most of his mainstream brethren, is able to pull this dream material down into symbolic image with less distortion and loss of fidelity than others could. There is more "truth" contained in the remembered dream, because it has been crunched down less far. It retains more vitality and richness. This allows the waking consciousness to recognize the connections and processes others have missed—and to set about fashioning them into bedrock.

Artists and inventors—spiritual evolution and mastery of the world—in a healthy society they work in tandem, each complementing the other, rolling the society forward on its twin tracks of human purpose. They float above the realm of mainstream society, tapping into future potentials hovering at the level of the superconscious, struggling to pull events down into the flow of time. Art and science, the wings of your species, on which you soar to ever greater heights of spirit and mastery.

Twenty-Three

Evolution of the Species

Our discussion of artists and inventors has raised an issue of fundamental importance relating to the purpose and progress of the human species. Let us examine this further.

You see, you have not been cast adrift in a cold, hostile universe, to eke out a miserable existence, cut off from your Source. Your species was not plunked into its first primordial cave and left to stumble as best it could through the ensuing Ages of Bronze and Enlightenment and Space.

Artists and inventors tap into the same level of precognitive information, perceiving it according to their unique slants and intents, and urging the society forward in both spiritual and technological terms. The two must walk hand in hand in a healthy society.

While "evolution" in the Darwinian sense of natural selection and animals mutating to form other species is creative nonsense, there is an "evolutionary" path to the human species, but only in spiritual terms. Your basic form and purpose do not change. What changes over time is the level of your spiritual and technological sophistication.

Imagine a spectrum of spiritual progress, in which one end is marked Absolute Ignorance, while the other shines as Absolute Truth. No human being mired in Absolute Ignorance can survive for long; some basic understanding of how the world works is necessary to sustain the rudiments of life. And no human consciousness can perceive Absolute Truth, for you have deliberately chosen the facade of physical existence as a means of exploring fragments of truth, slivers of enlightenment.

And yet, there is a steady progression along the spectrum of spiritual progress. This is not accidental; you are not randomly stumbling forward, constructing pantheons of gods and demons, then discarding them when something better falls into your laps. There is a steady, deliberate progression of spiritual understanding, aided and abetted by technological sophistication.

You can superimpose the linear time line atop the spectrum of enlightenment. They mesh; they overlap. As time marches forward, as you experience it, so does your spiritual and technological sophistication.

Tying this process in with the nature of events, and the vibrational layers events pass through before being physically experienced, you can see that, at base, the progress of spiritual evolution means that each successive event is experienced less as symbol and more as truth. There is a blend of symbol and truth in any event you experience. You never perceive the full strength and truth of an event, just a sliver. You experience one symbolic version, and claim that to be the entire event. So there is a blend of symbol and truth in all that you experience.

Over time, as you progress, each event carries more unvarnished truth and less symbolic wrapping. Your consciousness is able to reach higher into the world of events, meaning events must step down through fewer layers of density to meet you. Since each step down in vibrational frequency means a loss of fidelity, and an increase in symbol, the higher your consciousness can reach, the closer you approach truth.

This is accomplished by a gradual acceleration of the "core vibration" of the human species. You are tuned to perceive vibration along certain narrow bands: these are your physical senses. You are also tuned to perceive truth, to pursue wisdom and spiritual understanding, along certain parameters. The level of such understanding attainable by you individually and as a society is determined by your core vibration.

This core vibration is implanted at birth. Remember that each beat of the primal pulse carries a "signature" binding together all events transpiring anywhere in the universe at that precise moment, as a means of maintaining a universal master schedule. All babies born at a certain time, a certain minute, will have forever imprinted on their consciousness the core vibration of the species at that precise time. This grants a consistent worldview to all those born in a given culture, at a given time. It would serve no purpose to have some born Neanderthals while others are walking on water. A species as gregarious as yours must share a certain common understanding, a similar level of perceivable truth, in order to build and sustain community.

Unless overridden by later experience, this core vibration carried within each individual determines the level of spiritual and technological progress that the individual may attain throughout life. It links each individual with the members of his generation in a common bond of understanding, a mutual worldview.

You notice the resistance of the elderly to technological change. Many fear the advent of the computer and its rapid spread through your society.

Yet their grandchildren can manipulate a joystick before they can walk. The younger generation is literally tuned to a higher level of spiritual and technological understanding; the computer poses no threat to today's Space Age toddlers.

At the same time, many in the younger generations find their parents' religions to be sterile and bereft of any application to today's world. Are mind-numbing sermons larded with obscure references to millennia past truly the highest form of spiritual truth? The younger generations, feeling the upwelling spiritual revolution approaching the planet, turn their backs on the deathbed dogmas of yesteryear.

In technical terms, human progress in spiritual and technological growth is accomplished by accelerating the core vibration of the coordinate, the vibrational axis each person carries within the spine. This means, first, that events of a "higher" nature can be pulled into physical expression. It also means that the mind is equipped to perceive higher levels of truth, less smothered under symbolic wrapping.

Further, this accelerated core vibration means that a given event will require less time to play itself out. Remember that events are born in realms beyond space and time; there is no given time span built into any event. Its duration is eminently malleable, as we will later explore in depth. A human consciousness tuned to a higher frequency can literally experience an event in its entirety in less time than a consciousness tuned to a slower frequency.

As an example, imagine that a given event contains 100 "event units" which must be dissipated for the event to fully play itself out. A consciousness vibrating at a frequency of 20 "event units" per minute would require five minutes to perceive and experience the event. A consciousness operating at a frequency of 50 "event units" per minute would require only two minutes to experience the event. The same event, carrying the same vibrational swirl of "stuff" to be dissipated, is expressed in two radically different durations. The difference is determined by the core vibration of the individuals involved.

On an individual level, this is the basis of intelligence. How much time is required for an event—a fact, a date, a mathematical equation, a law of science—to be absorbed into the memory, ready for recall? Smarter children are referred to as "quick," while their struggling classmates are labeled "slow." This principle is readily apparent in any classroom; the smartest find the answer fastest, while the others struggle longer. The time required for an event, a unit of data, to be absorbed into the mind's mastery is the basis of intelligence.

This principle holds also on mass levels. The time a society requires to experience an event will depend upon the core vibration of the society's populace.

Consider for a moment the explosion in technological growth experienced in your century. Has anything ever equaled it? Has any culture ever evinced such accelerated learning and sophistication?

Since all events exist now, and all technologies exist now, you can deduce that a society such as yours, gobbling up technological events at such a furious pace, is one whose core vibration is accelerating. You are able to leap in one year what would take prior cultures five years, or ten, or a hundred. The time required to create and master a new technology has accelerated to a feverish pitch.

The great crisis in your society, and the source of all your problems, is that your spiritual understanding has not kept pace. Your technology gallops by leaps and bounds, while your spiritual understanding shuffles with bound feet on the flanks of Mount Olympus and Mount Sinai. This schism, this gap between technology and spirituality, is literally ripping the society apart. You can create all kinds of marvels, but you have no basis for making ethical or moral decisions about how to use them. You split the atom, a heinous violation of the natural order, because your spiritual understanding lags so far behind your technological prowess. Science can create wonders and marvels, but it cannot balance them with moral and spiritual truth illuminating you as to which paths you should pursue and which you should not.

Consider for a moment some of the moral and social battles raging in your society regarding the worth of human life. Should abortion be permitted, ever? Should we make exceptions for rape victims? What if the fetus carries genetic defects? If it is born without a brain, can we "harvest" its organs to benefit others, or should it be left to die? And what of capital punishment? Is it ever morally justifiable to terminate the life of another, no matter how heinous the crime? Should it apply only to those who murder police officers? children? innocent bystanders? Should mitigating circumstances enter the determination whether to end the life of the perpetrator?

Some oppose abortion and capital punishment in all cases. Some oppose abortion and embrace capital punishment. Some support both. Some go further, advocating euthanasia for the elderly and "defective." Do you see where this leads you? *You cannot even agree on the worth of human life.* You cannot even decide when it is morally justifiable to terminate the lives of your own species. Your spiritual understanding lags so far behind your technological growth that you stagger about from dilemma to crisis to catastrophe. Before abortion was technologically possible, no thought need be given to its morality. Before you were able to "harvest" the organs of anencephalic infants, no ethical questions could be raised. Yet as technology rockets forward, and your spiritual understanding wallows in the primordial muck of yesterday's mythology, you are left with a world in crisis, unable to chart a clear and consistent course.

As events are fed into your system, they carry spirit and technology forward, hand in hand. They are meant to work in tandem. They must, for society to retain its health and cohesion.

The fact that your technologies are accelerating at such a phenomenal rate clues you that this is no ordinary time, no ordinary century, in which you live. Just as a hurdler builds up speed and momentum before leaping the hurdle, so now is your society accelerating toward a period of unprecedented growth and understanding, a "New Age" of enlightenment. Yet the schism between science and spirit must be healed before your society can step into the New Age. If your society refuses to face and heal the schism, the ripping fabric of your culture will ultimately be torn asunder, the society collapsing in an amoral, anarchic, unprincipled, radioactive rubble.

Understanding the nature of events as you now do, you can see that the "events" of your gradual spiritual progress have been fed into your system all along. You simply have not tapped into them, as your beliefs would not permit the link to be made. Yet you suffered no similar hindrance in technological progress, so those "events" have fallen neatly into your temporal experience.

It is not necessary for you to run back to the starting line and dash through every "event" of spiritual progress between Mount Olympus and the present day. Since science and spirit tap into the same realm of the superconscious, by simply altering your core vibration, altering your beliefs, you can plunge headfirst into the same level of spiritual sophistication that science now enjoys in the technological realm. You can leapfrog the last eight hundred years of spiritual progress all at once, diving into the "events" awaiting you on the superconscious level.

Just as cutting-edge art confuses and repulses much of mainstream society, so will any sudden, wrenching leap into new spiritual understanding be cause for deep concern and ridicule. Mainstream society, those attuned only to the play of events immediately upon them, lacks the framework into which to place the precognitive traces of the future held in art, and in the burgeoning spiritual movements.

This explains the schism between traditional religions—in your culture, Christianity and Judaism—and the New Age philosophies. Those tapping into the superconscious realm of spiritual truth cannot help but reject the ancient traditional dogmas, as such bear little relevance to today; were meant to speak to their own time, not yours. Those clinging to traditional religious dogma will necessarily fear any step away toward a higher understanding, both because of the discomfort any change in the status quo entails, and because it carries the threatening hint that perhaps—just perhaps—traditional dogma has outlived its purpose.

So the rise of New Age spiritual thought is furiously resisted by the mainstream. Those leapfrogging centuries of spiritual growth in the space of months and years threaten to crumble the foundations of those clinging to their ancient dogmas. The vibrational frequencies evinced by old and new levels of spiritual understanding are so discordant that there is little confluence, little overlap where the two bodies of thought can meet and share. The break is clean, and sharp, and irrevocable.

Had you evolved spiritually as you have evolved technologically, there would be no such schism. Each gradual step would have been taken by everyone at once—save the usual conservative slowpokes, stumbling over their shoelaces and whining for everyone to slow down—and each "event" of spiritual growth would have been experienced by the society at large. Having stunted that easy, gradual growth, you are now squared off, with some standing firm in their tracks, unwilling to consider their dogma in light of present-day understanding, while others leap and bound into new realms of consciousness.

As an analogy, apply the current state of spirituality to the realm of technology. Imagine that yesterday your neighbor on the left invented the first horse-and-buggy and set out for a ride. Marvelous! you exclaim, what speed, what comfort! This morning, you discover your neighbor on the right has built a gleaming spaceship. He checks in with Houston Space Control, hops into the cabin, and blasts off for the moon. Most likely this would set the neighborhood tongues to wagging. You see, the technological leap is too great for mainstream society to assimilate all at once. The leap from horse-and-buggy to spaceship must proceed gradually, through a series of progressive steps, as has taken centuries to play out in your experience.

Such is occurring now in the spiritual realm, where horse-and-buggy dogma squares off against the interstellar trajectory of cosmic comprehension. The gap is too great for the average mind to leap. The intervening steps are missing. The smooth flow of events has been broken, gradual steps replaced with galloping leaps of faith and understanding.

Incidentally, had your society spiritually progressed at an even, gradual pace, there would be no need for the phenomenon of channeling. On vibrational terms, channeling is where the everyday waking consciousness of the channel can "step aside" to allow the inflow of higher spiritual knowledge. The guiding entity, existing on the nonphysical realm above the superconscious level, can descend the vibrational levels and link with the coordinate, or intrinsic energy pattern, of the channel. This circuit bypasses the channel's normal consciousness, his waking level of spiritual understanding.

Such is necessary in your time because you lag so far behind in spiritual understanding that you quite literally face the prospect of world collapse, world destruction. The danger is that too few persons can achieve spiritual progress on their own in time to alter the communal human vibration and avoid pulling into experience the "event" of world collapse. So channels have agreed to participate by serving as the vehicle for a level of spiritual understanding they do not normally possess.

In the case of this book's production, we employ the Space Age development of a home computer to express our New Age spiritual knowledge. While the inner mechanics of the computer and the deepest levels of our understanding may escape our host, he can repress his waking consciousness and allow spirit and technology to link—"user friendly" computer with "user friendly" spiritual understanding. Such is the age in which you live!

Spiritual and technological progress are meant to work in tandem, easing the society forward toward greater levels of mastery and truth. While your technology has proceeded on a relatively even keel, your spirituality has lagged far behind. As a result, the "events" of New Age spirituality seem so foreign and threatening to many, for they represent a great leap forward, a leapfrog through the centuries, rather than a steady, even progress.

Let us affirm that we do not wish to endorse every philosophy, product, and belief espoused under the "New Age" rubric. A snake oil vendor is still a snake oil vendor, no matter how many layers of saffron robes he cloaks his mendacity behind. In the end, truth will out. The truly valuable, the truly spiritual, will persist and flourish.

Free will always reigns supreme as your inviolate right. Facing you now are two stark choices: a harmonious, happy, free, peaceful world; or a charred cinder floating through space. Both exist *now*. Both are there for the taking. Which "event" of the planet's future do you wish to pull into physical expression? This is the challenge of your age.

Twenty-Four

ॐ

The Space-Time Seesaw

Events vary in intensity. Some thunder with deep purpose and meaning, while others pass as vaporous wisps. Some require centuries to play out, while others dissipate in milliseconds. Some are suffused with profound issues of spirit and meaning, while others focus on quiescent banalities.

An event's intensity is "built into" its structure on the nonphysical realm. The deeper and higher its purpose, the more individuals involved in its expression, the greater its intensity. As mentioned before, you can conceive of each event as consisting of "event units," each unit expressing a given quantity of "event stuff" which must be dissipated on the earth plane.

Each probable variation of an event will carry a different intensity. The master event, in creating all possible variations of itself, does so by altering the intensity, the concentration of "event units," within each probable version.

As events are seeded into the physical realm, they acquire the quality of space-time. This is how events manifest in your world, as episodes of temporal duration in the world of objects. At base, space and time are the same root energy, expressed along different frequencies, interpreted by your mind as two distinct qualities of space and time.

So an event's intensity will be expressed, or defined, by the parameters of space and time. Yet, how is it determined how much *space* will be taken up by an event, and how much *time* for it to play itself out?

Here we begin to delve into the plasticity of events. For there is no set law rigidly cementing an event's expression into space and time. A constant flow between space and time adjusts the event's expression. Finally, and most important, is the involvement of the individual experiencing the event. Here is where freedom and free will are guaranteed, in your ultimate power to determine the nature and expression of your life's events.

First, consider that any event you experience is one version, one probable version, of its master event. Which probable version you experience is determined by your coordinate, magnetically pulling into experience the event most aligned with its intrinsic configuration. Since each probable version of an event carries a different intensity, your coordinate—your thoughts and beliefs—determines how "intense" an event you will experience. This is the first level of power and control over the events of your life.

Consider that every event occurring in your life also has a probable version in which the event *never* finds physical expression. Every time you go skiing, there is a chance that you will break your leg. So the decision to go skiing will trigger a "master event" of your breaking a leg on the slopes. That potential hangs there, waiting to be activated if drawn to earth by your thoughts, beliefs, and desires at the time.

If, for some reason, you would benefit from the incapacitation and trauma of the event (however difficult it is for you to perceive any such "benefit"), then your coordinate pulls down into expression the "event" of your broken leg. Yet, if there would be no purpose served by the inconvenience, expense, and pain of a broken leg, your coordinate will never link with any version of the broken-leg event. The master event still exists—in all of its potential outcomes—and you choose *not* to experience the event. This is in itself a "version" of the event, the determination not to draw it into your life's experience. Such a version has just as much validity as the version sending you screaming to the hospital and laid up in traction.

So any event carries within its potentials a "nonevent" version in which you never physically experience the event in the world of space and time.

The conclusion drawn from this is that any event you do experience has been drawn into your life by the power of your coordinate. Since there is always a version in which you do not experience the event, any experienced event must have been drawn into expression. You see how freedom and responsibility are inextricably intertwined! You carry the ultimate freedom, to create your own reality, and carry with it the ultimate responsibility, of knowing that nothing happens to you but what you draw to yourself.

Between the "nonevent" version and its most intense expression lie infinite gradations. Moving on to another cheery example, that of a car accident, consider how many different possibilities there are. You may spot the potential catastrophe in time to swerve and avoid hitting the other car. You may graze each other. You may smack each other broadside. You may crunch head on. You may escape unhurt. You may be injured. You may be killed.

All these gradations are probable versions of the "event" of an automobile accident. Which version you experience depends principally on how *intense* is your intent to experience the event. For intensity is expressed in space and time. The horror and trauma of a major automobile crash, two vehicles destroyed and two drivers in the hospital, play out over a huge span of time—the pain and suffering and recovery—and space—the destroyed and useless vehicles. A less intense version, in which you graze each other, results in an exchange of insurance company information, a day in the repair shop, and then it is put behind you. Less space, less time—less intensity.

An event's intensity is determined by which version your coordinate magnetically pulls into your life. The more intense an event, the greater will be its expression over space and time, for such are the fundamental parameters of your system.

A crucial understanding is that you are never "locked into" experiencing a single probable version of an event. Since the version you experience is pulled into expression by your coordinate, which is itself a reflection of your thoughts, you can change the version of an event experienced, even in mid-event, by changing your thoughts. You can do so either to intensify the experience or to lessen its intensity. In fact, this occurs in almost all situations; almost all experienced events are blends of various probable versions. You are locked into nothing, then; even when you pull an event into your life, you can alter its expression in mid-event.

You know, for example, that in a traumatic incident, the more distraught or angry you are, the less clearheaded your thinking, the more "negative" the event will likely be—meaning you prolong its intensity to your detriment. By deliberately taking deep breaths, telling yourself to calm down, you instantly alter your coordinate from the intense vibration of anger and panic to a more quiescent calm and rational thought. Instantly, the intensity of the event will dissipate. Whatever "negative" effects you experience will find expression over less space and time.

You are at the mercy of nothing, then, even when you find yourself drawing "negative" events into your life. At any moment, yours is the power to alter an event's intensity by altering your coordinate's magnetic attraction to the event's probable variations.

You can imagine events perched in the middle of a seesaw. On one side sits time; on the other, space. The higher one side rides, the lower the other falls. The more space an event fills, the less time it will last. The longer an event's duration, the less space it will fill.

Consider again our analogy of event units, particles built into every event at its genesis. These event units are imbued with the quality of space-time. They can be dissipated either in space or in time; to them there is no difference. The number of event units carried in a probable event determines its intensity.

An event carrying 100 event units can be expressed as a 50-50 split between space and time. Or it could alter to 80-20 or 30-70. The balance is determined both by the individual's initial intent in pulling the event into expression and by the individual's reaction while the event is occurring.

Let us move from the theoretical to the prosaic. Take an event which results in anger on your part. This reaction, this burst of anger, is in itself an event. Whatever the cause of the anger—a stubbed toe, a fight with a spouse, a loss in sports—the "event" of your anger is determined by the condition of your coordinate, which carries your beliefs, thoughts, and experiences. Some would react by exploding with volcanic rage; others merely shrug their shoulders. You see the difference in intensity here, which "version" of anger is pulled into expression based on an individual's makeup and personality, as carried in electromagnetic terms within the coordinate.

Whatever the cause, you now feel anger. The anger will be of a certain intensity. Because you have pulled it into physical existence, it must be expressed. It "clogs up the works" until it is released and you can move beyond it. So you now face a wide range of optional expressions—but *they must be expressed in space and time.* You cannot tell yourself, "No, I'm not really angry, I refuse to express it," and expect the anger to dissipate. Having pulled the event into physical expression, stepped down to the level of thought, it must now be released by stepping down further, to the levels of experience and object.

If you choose to express the anger mostly in space rather than time, you may shriek, "I'M MAD AS HELL!" What are you doing? You are squeezing your anger into sound waves—in themselves an impression upon the physical world. You make those sounds by forcing air through your larynx, which vibrates in response to the intensity of the air's force. Ah, intensity! The more intensely you force air into speech, the more intense are the sound waves emitted, the more intense is the reaction upon the physical world, and the more intense is the volume heard by others. Surely, those within earshot will have no confusion divining your mood at the moment. So they too are drawn into the event—further enlarging the spatial scope of the event, thus dissipating it more quickly.

Another "space" reaction would be to kick something, smash something, destroy something. In basic terms, such manipulations involve a radical and sudden reordering of the elements creating an object. While normally these elements will disintegrate of their own accord over time, you can hurry the process by active manipulation—*intensive* manipulation—which hastens the process. You express intensity by altering an object's expression in space—the angrier you are, the greater the damage, the more intensive the alteration of elements.

If you have been taught that anger is a "negative" emotion and must be repressed at all costs, you cannot dissipate the event of your anger in space. So now it shifts to the other side of the seesaw and expresses itself in time. Oh, what a great, delicious stretch of time awaits the event's expression as the martyr silently nails himself to the cross and holds his tongue! Me, angry? Of course not! So the anger stews and stews and stews, stretching out over minutes, hours, days, weeks, months, lifetimes, dissipating its event units solely through time, never as space.

Of course, an event may grow tired of being dragged out so long and it will seek its own physical expression. An ulcer! Oh, rapture! Here is an event which causes daily discomfort and worry. Its owner feels better about discussing it with his wife and doctor than he ever could admit to feelings of anger. So the event finds expression in space after all—the hole in the stomach, the verbal complaints to spouse and physician. For the denial of one's anger is in itself an event, a swirl of energy, compounding the initial energy of the anger. Linked, anger and denial, they find expression over a more intensive field of space and time—the painful ulcer and visits to the doctor—than the original anger would find alone, if expressed and dissipated immediately.

Later we will explore the world of emotions in more depth. This small example was meant as one demonstration of how events *will always manifest.* Your power and responsibility lie in owning up to what you have drawn into your experience and seeking the healthiest possible expression, juggling the elements of space and time to find the most salubrious mix.

Moving from an example of an emotional event experienced by one individual to larger communal events, the same principle holds. An event's intensity is first determined by the communal vibration, the mix of all coordinates involved in the event's expression. Once an event of a given intensity has been pulled down into the world of experience and object, it is eminently malleable and mutable, seesawing back and forth over time and space, as determined by the actions and reactions of those involved.

An example of such a communal event would be the actions of a neighborhood after a tornado strikes. Perhaps three houses are damaged, and one destroyed, while the others remain untouched. Even those living in the intact houses are participating in the "event" of the tornado, as they cannot help but notice the devastation wrought on their neighbors, and to the extent there are emotional ties involved, the tornado's wake will tie them to their neighbors in their time of need.

If the character of the neighborhood is such that each jealously guards his own turf and cares nothing for his neighbor, then those whose houses were damaged or destroyed must face their problems alone. They must rebuild solely on their own resources. They may lack the money (a concept expressed spatially) to immediately rebuild, so the repairs must proceed over a longer period of time.

Because the event's expression is focused on those individuals directly involved, it requires more space and more time to play out, heaped upon the unfortunates' shoulders. Theirs alone is the expense; theirs alone is the time spent in recovery. Their aloof neighbors, meanwhile, will also experience the event over a longer period of time, watching the repairs proceeding slowly, as money allows, grumbling about lowered property values. Because the event's intensity is narrowed to a few individuals, it plays out in those individuals' lives in intensified time and space—money and weeks spent in repair.

Had the same neighborhood enjoyed a familial warmth and compassion among neighbors, the event's intensity would be splintered among many, reducing the intensity of any one individual's experience. Even those directly devastated would be less burdened by the event, for others would come to share the load. "Tell me what happened," says the compassionate neighbor, and as the owner of the devastated house spills out his story—air pressure across the larynx, impressing sound waves upon the ears of listeners—his pain lessens. He feels better; his body has dissipated the energy of his sorrow and loss. As neighbors embrace their unfortunate fellows, bedrock body meets bedrock body, etheric to etheric, aura to aura, psyche to psyche, the compassionate neighbor literally absorbing chunks of grief expelled from the unfortunate's body in waves of energy—reducing his pain's expression in time.

The community may chip in to buy materials for new houses, then throw a house-raising party and rebuild them by themselves in a week's time. The more energy expressed in physical, spatial actions—hammers pounding nails, saws slicing plywood—the less time is required to achieve the event of a completed new house.

You see, then, that on a communal level, an event's intensity will again be expressed through the fundamentals of space and time. How much space, how long a time, before the event is "finished" in your experience, its event units fully dissipated, is determined by the reactions of those choosing involvement.

Some events require centuries to play out. Some themes and issues regarding human worth and dignity are so profound, so evocative, so thick and rich, that even if they fill the very globe with their expression, they still must stretch out over generations to fully dissipate.

Consider the issue of slavery, slavery versus freedom and dignity. In your culture, you can look back to the Jews enslaved by Pharaoh to see how very long this issue has been playing itself out in Western culture. Its variations are endless: the czar and his serfs, the plantation owner and his African slaves, royalty and peasants, the Afrikaners and the black townships. All over the globe this theme plays itself out, generation after generation, as your culture wrestles with issues of human dignity and worth. Are some born to serve others at the lash of a whip? Or are all born to seek their own fulfillment?

You can see how the "events" of slavery's expression have progressed over the millennia. Again, you are not staggering haphazardly forward, but riding atop an undercurrent of spiritual evolution carrying you toward deeper and higher spiritual truth. You may look back in disbelief and disgust at cultures past, where human beings were chattels, and scorn them for their backwardness. Yet, remember, all individuals born in such eras carried a given worldview implanted at birth, defining the upper reaches of spiritual truth each generation could realize. When all in a culture—religious, political, and social realms—believed without question the moral rightness of their cultural worldview—and such is almost always the case—the issue of human dignity never arose. It was manifestly obvious that some were born to serve others; this was God's plan, confirmed by the church.

Slowly, over centuries, as each succeeding generation was born carrying a slightly higher level of spiritual understanding, such an issue had to be openly faced. In your country, this manifested as the abolition movement. To buy and sell human beings was fundamentally immoral. What a shocking thought this was to the ears first hearing it! For, again, progressives are by nature urging mainstream society forward, toward the future, when the mainstream prefers to squat in the present and be left alone. Thus the furious battle between abolitionists and those who held the black race to be born for no other purpose than to pick cotton and raise white babies.

In large part, such an issue plays itself out over so long a stretch of time because your spiritual understanding is mired in outdated and irrelevant dogmas. Your spirituality has not kept pace with your technology. There are still many who carry the psychic vestiges of the slave owner's worldview, that those of dark races are inherently inferior. For so long the church validated and blessed this arrangement, this worldview, slamming on the brakes of spiritual growth.

Remember that as time progresses, and the core vibration of the earth and its inhabitants accelerates, less time will be required to express a given event. An event is gobbled up faster by a higher tuned consciousness than by its backward compatriot. So the effect of the church's deliberate retardation of spiritual evolution was to guarantee that events such as slavery, involving questions of human dignity, would require much longer to play themselves out. As long as the church, the site of spiritual truth, validated the extant worldview rather than pulling it forward, it guaranteed that such events would require a greater span of time to dissipate.

As we have seen before, because your spiritual evolution has not proceeded on an even, gradual course, it must stagger forward in great fits and starts. The point arrives where the schism between where you *are* spiritually and where you *ought to be* is so great that the society threatens to disintegrate. At such times, the prescient and enlightened can yank the society forward in huge leaps, compensating for all those incremental steps not taken.

In America, you experienced such a leap as the abolition movement culminating in the Civil War. A full century later, the civil rights movement exploded into consciousness, yanking the society kicking and screaming into the twentieth-century level of spiritual truth. Not only were blacks not to be bought and sold like cattle, they were also not to be denied full rights and equal participation in the society.

You see how the civil rights movement accomplished its goals: by spreading itself over a vast spatial area, it healed in a decade the societal wounds that festered for a century. Strikes, boycotts, speeches, rallies, protests, sit-ins—all spatial events, drawing in huge numbers of participants on both sides of the issue, dissipating the event's energy through the medium of space.

If the civil rights movement had limited itself to politely declining to sit in the back of the bus when ordered, you would still be drinking from separate water fountains. Because the movement splashed its energy and spiritual truth over the entire nation, great leaps and bounds could be taken where before the mainstream society had taken only spiritual baby steps.

The civil rights movement was but one element of the explosive sixties, when every repressed group rose up in anger and defiance, challenging the power structures that so long denied them equal status and opportunity. In your century, as your technology shows, the core vibration of the planet and its peoples is accelerating exponentially. Your spirituality lagged so far behind, was so backward, that the time for delicacy was long past. Only a furious explosion of energy, the wholesale rejection of mainstream values, could right the society's wobbling course. The Sixties was a time of sudden acceleration of spiritual energy approaching the planet; and as your society stood mired in the mythologies of millennia past, it was torn asunder by the wrenching spiritual leaps of the decade's civil rights, feminist, environmental, and other movements.

In three brief examples we have seen how an event's intensity is expressed in the fundamental parameters of space and time. A master event seeds all possible variations of itself, all probable versions, into the physical system. As they approach the world of experience, they acquire the quality of space-time, twin funnels through which they pour their expression into the world of events. Each individual, each community, each society, each world, holds ultimate power as to how it will experience events. First, the event's intensity is determined by the private or communal thoughts and beliefs of those involved. Then, space and time ride the seesaw of expression, with you grabbing a hold on either end and tilting it back and forth as you please, determining the mix of space and time through which the event finds expression.

You choose the events of your life. You choose their intensity, their duration, their spatial expression. Yours is the ultimate power, and the ultimate freedom. You create your own reality.

Part Four

THE POWER OF MIND

Twenty-Five

༄

The Electric Belief Screen

We have maintained throughout that you create your reality through the force of your thoughts and beliefs, and that these levels of mind are electromagnetically encoded in the coordinate, the energy swirl encased in your spine. In this section we will delve further and more explicitly into the realm of belief and thought, how they are created and manifested, how they attain electromagnetic configuration, and how they combine with the thoughts of others to create your shared world.

First, let us define "belief." A belief is a mental framework which organizes and stores your experience in the world of events. A belief is a filter through which all incoming perceptual data flows. A belief allows connections to be made between objects and events, organizing sense data into patterns and relationships. A belief structures your experience. A belief categorizes, labels, interprets, judges, and defines your life's flow of events.

You never perceive absolute truth. You never perceive vibration directly. Each of your senses feeds you fragments, slivers, crumbs. These symbolic fragments are fashioned in your mind into a coherent, three-dimensional world. It is your beliefs that organize incoming sense data into a cohesive, comprehensible, stable world picture.

Each unit of vibration absorbed by your senses passes through two stages. First, what is it? The senses relay their data to the brain, where a given vibration is linked with the universal patterns stored there, allowing instant identification of the vibration's meaning. This determines the "what"—the comprehension of a vibrational unit's origin.

Someone walks toward you. He waves a hand and offers hello. He smiles. Each of the uncountable waves of vibration given off by the person's approach is perceived by the senses—in this case, the eyes and ears. His bedrock body gives off electromagnetic radiation within the spectrum of visible light. Each primal cell containing his body's bulk will emit a unique vibration. Your eyes are not designed to perceive discrete units of vibration at this level; instead, the picture blurs, washes together, so that you see a cohesive body instead of a matrix of blinking primal cells. Each primal cell gives off vibration sparking different portions of your rods and cones, painting the body's bulk with color—a red shirt, blue pants, black hair, pink skin.

The body is moving; as it does so, the number of primal cells filled with its bulk expands—he is moving toward you. He waves. He smiles. When the person offers "hello," your ears vibrate with the sound waves created by his larynx; the ears pass this information to the brain, where the complex series of air pressure variations is linked with its corresponding meaning, then blurred and blended into a cohesive whole: "hello."

This is the "what." Your senses relay vibrational information to the brain, where it is blurred, blended, and rendered intelligible to the waking consciousness.

The next stage of any experienced event is interpretation. The raw sense data must be organized and interpreted. This is the function of belief. Your beliefs act as sorters, organizers, categorizers, absorbing sense data and sifting it through their framework. These beliefs have been implanted from earliest infancy through the present moment; they act as the filters or screens through which sense data is organized into coherence.

You never experience vibration directly. You perceive fragments, symbolic remnants of deepest truth. The only way you can navigate through the world of events is by carrying with you at all times a framework through which sense data is organized and interpreted. It is not enough to know, "What is it?" You must also know, "What does it mean?" For only after such interpretations are made can you chart a course ensuring your safety, seeking out pleasure, avoiding pain, manipulating the world to your advantage, and so on.

This level of interpretation, this organization of sense data, is the purpose of belief. The sum total of all your beliefs—most of them hidden from conscious awareness—can be considered a screen, a filter. Your belief screen acts like a computer, sifting and sorting incoming data into recognizable, manageable chunks of understanding.

In the example given above, simply knowing that a man is walking toward you, waving and offering "hello," is insufficient data on which to base judgment of his potential effects on you. This data must be interpreted. If this man is your father, and you recognize that special wave as meaning he has brought you a present, your interpretation will be delight. If the man is the neighborhood sadist, who always waves and offers hello before zapping you with a cattle prod, your interpretation is panic. If he is a stranger, you may stand your ground and respond demurely until you ascertain his purpose. In all such cases, the raw data is virtually identical—

a man approaching, smiling, waving. It is your interpretation, filtered through your belief screen, that determines your reaction, that fills out the raw sense data with emotional richness.

When we say that you create your reality through your beliefs, you can see how the process begins at the very perception of the world around you, its first impression upon your consciousness. You are not drinking in raw, neutral data. You are interpreting symbol. How you interpret these symbolic fragments of vibration is determined by your beliefs.

If you were attacked by a dog as a young child, you may carry a fear of dogs throughout life. As soon as your eyes say "dog," you register fear of attack. This is a belief, built into your belief screen: all dogs are dangerous.

If you are a boy raised in a family of calculating, cold, shrewish women, domineering and henpecking their husbands, your belief screen will register "shrew" every time your senses perceive "woman."

If your time at the beach always brings you pleasure, days in the warm sun, swimming in the surf, good friends and good times, whenever your senses register "beach," your belief screen will say, "good time."

If you are punished every time you open your mouth in school to protest against mindless, bullying authority, as an adult when your senses say "authority figure," your belief screen will say, "bully."

Now, reverse all of the above examples. Your senses drink in the identical vibration, interpreted by your brain into a coherent picture of the world about you. Now, what does your belief screen say? "Dog" means "faithful friend." "Woman" means "warm-hearted lover." "Beach" means "bad time." "Authority figure" means "benevolent protector."

Each of you carries a belief screen, formed by your experiences from the first moments of life. You carry it with you at all times. It organizes and interprets your senses' perceptual data. It determines how you judge your life's experiences. It is the first level of "creating your reality," because you have not yet responded to any event in the world; you are simply drinking in the scene. As you do so, the "what" is converted into "what does it mean?" This belief screen, this structure of interpretation, transforms symbolic, vibrational fragments into a full, rich, coherent world.

It is impossible to overestimate the importance of the belief screen you carry through life. It colors and interprets every bit of data your senses perceive. Since you never perceive absolute truth, and never perceive vibration directly, yours is an experience of symbol. Symbols, as you know, are constructs that stand for, or represent, deeper truth, while never fully carrying that deeper truth. The cross and the Star of David are symbols; each word you speak is a symbol; every nation's flag is a symbol; a musical note is a symbol; a photograph is a symbol; geographical boundaries are symbols. In all such cases, you can readily see, the symbol is a crude representation of a deeper truth; a manageable, easily recognizable, reduction of a greater reality.

To move our understanding to the next level of sophistication, understand now that *every experience of your life is symbol.* Never, ever, can the human consciousness perceive pure, undistorted truth. Never can your senses drink in the full range of vibration about you. Never do you perceive blinking primal cells; you blur and blend them in your mind. Every object you see, every experience you have, every emotion and thought you feel—all these are symbols, deeper realities stepping down into the world of object and event.

Returning to our field of easily recognizable symbols, consider your reaction upon viewing the cross, the Star of David, the stars and stripes, the hammer and sickle. Each such symbol triggers a reaction within you, based upon your upbringing and life experiences. The symbol itself is neutral. It is just a design brought to your attention by your senses. It is your beliefs that determine your interpretation of symbol.

Expanding our awareness to understand that all experiences are symbols, you realize that all of life, every moment, is filtered and interpreted through your belief screen. "Objectivity" is impossible. "Impartiality" is impossible. All is interpretation. Interpretations are made at the belief screen, organizing your experience into a coherent, manageable flow of events.

If every experience is symbol, and symbol is interpreted through belief, then experience is interpreted by belief. You do not perceive absolute reality. You create your reality through your beliefs. They fashion your experience, every moment of it.

The belief screen has a physical, electromagnetic reality. Your brain stores its experiences in memory. While most of what happens to you is forever lost to conscious memory, every instant is forever stored in the brain's memory banks. Each experience will be classified and stored based upon the various attributes of the experience. First, when did it happen? Who was with you? What was your body's reaction? What was your emotional reaction? What did you learn? And so on, virtually ad infinitum.

Each experience is cross-indexed, in a way, allowing access from a variety of triggers. If someone asks, "Remember that day when you were seven years old," your mind begins the search chronologically. If the question is phrased, "Remember when you and your mother were visiting Florida," the search begins by association—your mother—and geographically—

Florida. And so on, and so on. Each experience is filed in all its parameters, building webworks of associations connecting and cross-indexing your life's experiences.

At the level of the brain, these associations manifest as impulses, electrical impulses leaping synapses. In this sense, the brain is a highly sophisticated computer, organizing and retrieving data along its network of electrical pathways.

Each experience carries not only the raw physical data of what occurred, but also your interpretation of it. This interpretation further contributes to your belief screen. So a given bundle of sense data—one experience—will have tied to it your emotional reactions and associations. These two levels of experience are stored in different parts of the brain. One level is pure sense data, while the realm of emotions and beliefs is carried "higher" in the brain. Yet, while these two components of every experience—sense data and interpretation—are stored separately, they are inextricably linked. To recall an experience in its physical parameters is to also draw up the emotions you felt at the time. The two are inseparable. Whenever one aspect is triggered, the brain immediately links it with its partner.

If you find yourself free associating sometime, just follow the flow of your thoughts and see if you cannot pick up the process described here. If you think "anger," for instance, you may view a flashing series of events in your life during which you felt anger. The events, the physically experienced moments, may be completely disconnected in terms of locale, your age, others with you, and so on. The connective link is your emotional state, anger. All those disparate experiences are organized under the rubric "anger," and when anger is triggered, all sense data linked with it will float to awareness.

Similarly, if you consider a long-term relationship with another, holding that person firmly in mind, a flood of diverse emotions may flow through you. Anger at those harsh words, delight in that gentle caress, humor in that expression, pride at that achievement, and so on. In this case, you hold the sense data component steady—one individual—and allow all of its associative emotional triggers to flow.

Since the brain operates on electrical impulse, and since the two components of an experience—sense data and interpretation—are stored in separate portions of the brain, it naturally follows that there must be substantial networks built up between the two, in order to allow instantaneous recall of any experience in all its richness.

Each experience throughout life, as it is filed in its two separate brain compartments, further contributes to the networks of impulse running between the brain's components. If an experience seems to confirm your extant belief structure—"all police officers are bullies," for example—then it strengthens the network running between the visual apprehension of a police officer and the emotional expectation of being bullied. If, on the other hand, you experience a warm, kindly officer going out of his way to help you, then the experience cannot be filed away along the existing network. For that network leads only to the interpretation of "police officer" as "bully." So a new associative network must be built, between "police officer" and "friend."

Each subsequent experience you have with police officers will confirm either one or the other interpretation. Bullies or friends? Each such experience will further strengthen the network, the connective strand, between sense data and its various interpretations.

Over time, if all future experiences with police officers are positive and happy, the network connecting "police officer" to "bully" will atrophy. Now, when the brain perceives sense data reading "police officer," the connective strand runs to the emotional reaction of "friend."

Because this all occurs on a physical level of electrical impulse, discharging across synapses, and because electricity is governed by the laws of electromagnetism, it is literally true that your belief screen has an electromagnetic reality. The connective strands binding sense data to interpretation are electrically etched into the brain. The triggers, the connections, the associations, all find electrical expression.

The impossibly complex series of connective networks and associations summarizing your entire life's experience to this point can be considered one gigantic electromagnetic grid. Through this grid, through this belief screen, every experienced moment is split into its two essential components of sense data and interpretation. Some existing networks will be strengthened; others will be weakened; new connective strands may be forged where there was none before. Your belief screen is never locked rigidly into place, but is eminently malleable, altering instantly based upon the never-ending stream of fresh experience each new day brings.

Of course, any physically experienced event is a reflection of a deeper reality. The brain's network of electrical impulses is a vastly slowed down version of the communications taking place at the levels of psyche, auric, and etheric bodies. Thoughts and beliefs, crackling across synapses, are a "slower" version of the information exchange and retrieval systems available to the higher vibrational bodies. The purpose of stepping this material down into physical terms in the brain is to align your thoughts and beliefs to a level of vibration where they can interpret physical reality while remaining one step above the level of object and experience. Your brain's impulses are perceptible to no one's senses, ensuring your freedom. At the same time, they are stepped down enough to focus and align with the vibrational frequencies of the lower levels of experience and object.

Further, the brain's impulses, manifesting as electricity and imbued with the qualities of electromagnetism, literally pull into expression the events of your life. To this process we now turn our attention.

Twenty-Six

The Event Magnet

We have seen how events are seeded into the physical system, originating in the nonphysical realm and acquiring the quality of space-time as they approach physical expression. At base, any event is simply *intent*, thrust into the physical sphere. Your universe exists because the Source intends that it exist. You exist because your greater entity intends that you exist. Just as all realms of creation flow from the Source's intent to explore Itself in all possible manifestations, so is that initial intent splintered and fractured among uncountable realms of activity. This intent, to explore and to grow, trickles down through your family of consciousness, through your greater entity, down to you, where you stand as the final spark of intent, one human life.

Your physical system is set up with certain fundamental principles. Both camouflage and direct physical systems operate with vibration as their fundamental, irreducible unit of creation. Those in direct physical systems perceive vibration directly and fashion it according to their intent and desire. Those in camouflage systems such as yours perceive symbolic fragments of vibration, interpreted by the senses and brain into the fiction of a three-dimensional, physical world.

While all events spring from the womb of intent, they must acquire the properties of the physical system in order to manifest within that system. They must be governed by the same rules and principles governing every other element of physical creation.

As events are seeded into the physical system, at the portal of the primal pulse blinking from physical to nonphysical realms, they acquire the quality of space-time. Space-time is the fundamental energy of the physical system, from which all other elements and structures spring. At the most basic level, space-time is one indivisible field of energy. As it approaches expression perceptible to your senses it differentiates into different wavelengths, one band of which you interpret as space, the other as time.

Space-time is how nonphysical events, grids of intent, acquire the properties of electromagnetism which govern your system. Let us review these fundamental parameters of physical universe construction.

Vibration travels most efficiently in a straight line. The smallest possible "straight line" in the universe is a single row of primal cells, joined end to end by a filament stringing the cells together. Vibration travels far more readily along the filament than it can through the lateral walls of the cells, though this is possible.

Each primal cell carries charge, an electrical burst, when sparked to life with sufficient intensity. It is the nature of a primal cell carrying charge to induce its neighbors to raise their charge to a similar high level of vibration. There is no urge in the opposite direction, to reduce charge. The impetus is always toward higher charge, meaning greater bulk filling the cell.

The primal cell's charge is further sculpted by pattern, unique configurations carved into the charge's expression. Those cells carrying high charge will induce their lower-charged neighbors to raise their charge; as the cells of lower charge tend to "resist" these entreaties, the process of resistance is born. Pattern causes attraction, while charge sparks resistance. These are the fundamental "processes" of the physical system.

"Electromagnetism" can be broken into "electro" and "magnetism" for this discussion. As you know, electricity is pulsations of charge flowing in a straight line. This represents, on an immensely vaster scale, the properties of vibration pulsing through a string of primal cells. The urge is to pulsate, and to travel in one direction.

Magnetism reflects the processes of attraction and resistance. Observe what occurs if you experiment with two bar magnets, placing them end to end in various ways. A north-north pairing repels. A south-south pairing repels. Only when the north pole of one magnet is brought near the south pole of another magnet do they attract.

This may, on the surface, appear to contradict the fundamental principle that like attracts like, but view the larger picture. When the two bar magnets attract, north to south, they pull together and form one continuous north-south magnet. They are no longer two separate magnets, but act now as one. Thus they fulfill the quality of vibration that it flows most efficiently in a single direction, along a single axis. To place two magnets north end to north end is to ask vibration to flow in contradicting directions in the same space. This is impossible. They resist being joined in such a fashion. The urge is always to create the most efficient design, of vibration flowing steadily along an axis.

Thus, "electricity" and "magnetism" flow from the same fundamental principles. Electricity is the "simpler" version, as it expresses the basic nature of vibration in flowing most efficiently along an axis. Magnetism colors the process with the qualities of attraction and resistance, born of charge and pattern sculpted into the primal cells.

Incidentally, you can see how gravity flows from the same processes. "Gravity" occurs when bedrock objects attract. Since bedrock objects, by definition, carry high charge of similar pattern, meaning they spark little resistance, their urge is to attract. High charge attracts high charge; if their patterns are similar, the bind is that much tighter. Gravity in your world is simply the enormous bedrock earth exerting its magnetic pull on the bedrock objects upon its surface, or above it. The denser an object is, the more its matrix is filled with high charge, the greater a pull the earth can exert, and the "heavier" the object seems.

When you travel to the moon, which is smaller than the earth and therefore exerts a weaker magnetic attraction, your bodies can leap and bounce over the peaks and valleys in a way they could never achieve at home on earth. Essentially, then, gravity is magnetism, the bedrock earth pulling toward its core the objects and creatures upon it—the denser the bedrock elements, the stronger the pull.

We have mentioned before that while gravity governs the attraction of bedrock objects, the underlying principle, of attraction, also governs other levels of events. Objects are the slowest level of events. All other levels—experience, thought, superconscious thought—are governed by the same principle. "Event gravity" is every bit as real as the apple falling on Newton's head.

In the case of events, trickling to earth from the nonphysical realm, they have not yet slowed their vibrational frequencies down to the point where their matrices can sustain charge. They are not "slow" enough to allow the time for charge to fill a primal cell, so they are not governed by the attraction and resistance of bedrock objects. Yet events do imbue primal cells with pattern, carried in the cells' outer walls. This manifests as attraction and nonattraction (as distinct from resistance) between potential events and the coordinates of those standing to experience the events. The principles of "gravity" still apply. You see, the physical gravity you experience is just one subset of the fundamental forces of the universe, the principles of attraction and resistance.

Just as an object's density, its bulk, is determined by the number of primal cells it fills, so is an event's intensity expressed in the matrix of primal cells it fills. We have posited the existence of "event units" before; now you see they are simply primal cells, carrying pattern in the walls and no charge within. The greater the intensity imparted to an event upon its creation, the larger the matrix of primal cells it carries en route to expression.

Fresh from the nonphysical realm, nascent events begin to acquire the qualities of electromagnetism. At this stage, only attraction comes into play, as the events have not yet slowed sufficiently to allow expression of charge, from which resistance springs. At this amorphous, diffuse level, still so far from expression as object or experience, the energy contained in each event's matrix has not yet differentiated into the disparate wavelengths manifesting as space and time. This is the realm of space-time, the fundamental unit of energy as expressed in the physical system.

It is the nature of events, matrices of vibration, to express themselves physically. Just as bedrock earth pulls objects toward it, so do potential events feel a pull toward the slower levels of object and experience. This urge is electromagnetically encoded in the process of attraction. Where a similar field of vibration is detected, the event will be pulled closer to physical expression. Where no such attraction tugs on an event's amorphous swirl, it must remain forever latent, bouncing unexpressed.

What attracts these events down to earth? Your coordinate. The axis encased in spine acts as a magnet, pulling into expression your life's events.

Your brain sifts and sorts an extraordinary amount of data in every moment. While absorbing and interpreting sense data, it also juggles your thoughts. And your thoughts may be contradictory, canceling each other out, as you debate and deliberate which course to take, which path to follow, which action to commit. Your range of thought is infinite, while the range of actions you actually commit is far more limited. And how are these infinite realms of possibility expressed in the world of physical action? By sending impulses down the spine, barking commands through the nervous system.

Only those impulses deliberately sent down through the spine can result in your manipulation of the world. Your thoughts remain private; a decision to act requires that thought be stepped down to the level of bedrock body.

If events were constructed to magnetically latch onto every thought in your head, imagine the result. If someone angers you, think of the range of options confronting you, all of which you may consciously consider: say nothing, say something, say something very loud and rude, strike out, strike out with intent to harm, strike out with intent to kill. If each of these "events" instantly dropped into your life, merely for your thinking them, your freedom would be lost. Your freedom is to keep your thoughts private, expressing only a limited range at the level of object and experience.

So it is the spine, the nervous system's central column, that carries your decisions to the world of experience. Thus it is the spine, not the brain, which serves as the magnet for the events of your life. Notice also that the brain is a sphere, while the spine is an axis. Which is the more efficient design?

While your brain can consider an infinite spectrum of action, it is the spine that carries *those acts you actually commit in the physical world*. Your decisions to act, expressed as speech and movement, are reduced to electrical impulses traveling down the spine and along the neuronal pathways. All decisions become electrical impulses, assuming the qualities of charge and pattern.

Since events seeded into the physical world have acquired the same qualities, they are magnetically attracted to the coordinate, to the extent there is sympathy. An event's pattern is etched into the walls of the primal cells carrying it through the physical realm. These patterns link with similar patterns carried in the coordinate. You literally, magnetically, draw to yourself the events of your life.

Remember that the brain splits your experiences into two components of sense data and interpretation. These pathways are electrically etched into the brain, associative links between what you perceive and how you interpret it. Over time, if you link given sense data with the same interpretation, the pathway between data and interpretation will be strengthened. This makes it more likely that all subsequent sensual perceptions of the same data will be interpreted in the same manner, will fall more easily into the deep groove leading toward the established interpretation.

Since it is the nature of your species to share its thoughts with others, over time you are likely to verbally or physically express the associative pathways linking perception and interpretation. Any time you are with someone and you spy a police officer, you may say, "All cops are bullies." Even when alone, you may well speak your belief aloud. In order to reach verbal expression, the thought—"all cops are bullies"—must be translated, stepped down into a series of electrical impulses, sparking the muscles of your mouth and larynx to give them physical expression. The thought—"all cops are bullies"—therefore assumes an electromagnetic reality, a matrix of energy, fed into the nervous system.

This electromagnetic matrix must be slowed down to a gradual series of impulses, in order to be spoken aloud. The original thought crackles at far faster frequency than your verbal expression. Your thought must be stepped down, fed as a series of impulses to your body.

As it travels to the appropriate musculature, this electromagnetic matrix is carried in the spine. It is here, while still a preverbal bundle of energy, that the impending act becomes perceptible to the swirling clouds of probable events above you. You are no longer merely thinking about taking action; you are acting. You would not be doing so if you did not believe the course was proper. An impulse to action carries not only the appropriate instructions to the musculature, but also the "why?"—the belief that this course is proper and necessary.

While sense data and interpretation are split in the brain, they are rejoined in the spine, in the impulse to action. You act because you believe it proper to do so; this belief is carried along with the electrical impulse. So the electromagnetic swirl of every potential act, as it is carried through the spine, signals to potential events the content and flavor of your beliefs. Your beliefs acquire the qualities of electromagnetism.

Carried in the spine, the axis held perpendicular to earth and pointing toward the stars, your beliefs magnetically pull toward you the probable events of your life. These experienced events will then seem to confirm the initial beliefs that drew them into expression. As an example, if over time you announce that "all cops are bullies," you will find daily confirmation of this belief everywhere you turn. Every newspaper article describing police brutality will be slavishly pored over; those citing officers for heroism and bravery will pass unnoticed; your eyes do not perceive them. Countless brushes with the police where their acts are neutral or benign will also pass unnoticed. There are no neuronal pathways to carry the thought "all cops are friends," so the event cannot be stored. The second step of perception, interpretation, is blocked. The sense data is discarded, or stored solely as raw data without the associative emotional component. Thus it plays no part in shaping your worldview.

The first step in belief creating reality is in interpretation, how you judge the raw physical data entering your senses. The second step is in your actions, the physical impressions you make upon the world based upon your belief that you are taking the proper course. Each such act carries the belief fueling it within its electromagnetic matrix. These matrices of belief magnetically attract events of similar contour from the realms of probability. These potential events, once physically expressed, will confirm the initial worldview, those connective associations between sense data and interpretation, that sparked the act's genesis.

Do you see the self-perpetuating cycle here? And do you see how it operates on the properties of electromagnetism? Belief creates interpretation, which creates neuronal pathways in the brain, which sparks you to action in line with those neuronally etched beliefs, which magnetically attracts potential events confirming your original belief. An exquisitely sensitive and precise feedback system.

You create your reality through your beliefs. This is not metaphysical hash dredged up from the voodoo swamps of superstition. This is fact.

Twenty-Seven

۶

The Belief Screen Quiz

When you hear the phrase "United States of America," what images spring to mind? A militaristic fortress of imperialism, running roughshod over the smaller, weaker nations of the world, enforcing its capitalist Manifest Destiny at the point of a gun? A nation of drug addicts, stoned out, turned on, an insatiable junkie for the world's supply of heroin and cocaine, mendaciously accusing Third World nations of not doing enough to stop the flow of drugs its citizens demand? A nation of burnt-out youth, dropping out, shiftless, apathetic, listening to ear-shattering, head-banging music while thumbing their noses at parents and teachers? A nation handed over lock, stock, and barrel to Big Oil, Big Developers, Big Corporations, chewing up what few wild places remain in their insatiable lust for profit?

Or do you see a nation of hardworking, industrious, vibrant, vital people, the refugees of the world, thriving in the heady atmosphere of economic and personal liberty? A nation of boundless generosity any time disaster strikes within or without its borders? A nation dedicated to fair and open political discourse, without threat of censure or violence against those opposing the status quo, however strident? A nation of incomparable natural beauty, and the determination to preserve it for generations to come? A nation that stands as a symbol, a beacon, burning brightly through the noxious clouds of repression and terror under which so many of the world's peoples live?

Was the universe created by God in a span of six days? Was it created by a Big Bang, an explosion of hydrogen, spilling out into the vast reaches of space and solidifying into the vast dance of planets, moons, meteors, galaxies—all by chance?

Are environmentalists elite snobs who want to lock up wild lands and prevent others from enjoying them? Do they resent the wealth and success of others, slamming on the brakes of progress, hindering the economic development of the nation?

Or are they the prophets and saviors of your age, urging a halt to the mindless money lust that sweeps like a prairie fire through your natural resources, leaving you bereft, on a sick and dying planet? Do they act from love, giving their time and energy selflessly for the benefit of all, even generations unborn?

Is homosexuality an abomination in the eyes of God, a crime against nature, a mortal sin? Is it a psychiatric disorder caused by a cold father and domineering mother? Is it a choice made before birth as a way of experiencing a unique and refreshing facet of human sexuality?

Are politicians all two-faced liars, lining their pockets with campaign contributions from fat cats, jetting around the world on "fact-finding missions" to invariably exotic locales, puppets in the hands of industrial interests, spewing endless streams of mendacious verbiage to retain power, scorning the constituents who elected them?

Or are they hardworking, dedicated public servants, juggling the impossible demands of diverse constituents while struggling to keep on top of the flood of decisions required in an increasingly complex society? Do they sacrifice time with spouses and children on behalf of those who elected them? Do they work crushing hours for far lower pay than they could earn in the private sector? Do they balance the endless demands for more government services, while the taxpayers balk at footing the bill for what they demand?

Has God fated every moment of your life? Are you living out your inescapable role in His grand design? Or has He set you free to experience life on your own? Does He continue to care about you? If you suffer, why doesn't He intervene? If God becomes angry, will He punish you, your nation, your world? Will there be a Judgment Day?

If there is no God, what is the meaning of life? Are you just accidents evolved from sea slugs, staggering around in pointless confusion for your meaningless span of years? Are you all alone in the universe? Does everything that happens result from luck, chance, and accident?

Do you have any responsibility toward the unfortunate? Should you feed them, clothe them, shelter them? How much are you required to sacrifice on their behalf? Is it the government's role to care for them? Should it be left to the private sector, to charity? What of those in other nations—are you responsible for them as well? Must you feed the world?

Are Jews the chosen people of God? Are they engaged in a conspiracy to take over the world? Does God hear their prayers? Can Jews get into Heaven? Are Jews the only denizens of Heaven? Is their ancient claim to the land of Israel still valid in your day? Should they share their territory with the Palestinians?

Is capitalism the economic system offering the highest standard of living and greatest personal and economic liberty? Is it worth the cost of polarized upper and lower classes? Should this gap by ameliorated through taxation and government-sponsored welfare programs? Should the system be gutted and replaced with the Marxist model, guaranteeing health care, education, and housing for all, eliminating great disparities of wealth, at the cost of personal freedom?

Are women as smart as men? Are they as strong? Are they as talented? Are there times in the month when they cannot be trusted with important decisions? Should they stay home with their young children, or should they be free to pursue careers? Do young children suffer emotionally when deprived of their mothers' care? Is this the mothers' fault, or society's?

Has God given humanity dominion over the beasts of the earth? Are the world's creatures here for the pleasure and use of humans, or have they their own unique purposes? Is it acceptable to use oxen and horses as beasts of burden? Is it acceptable to eat animals? Is it acceptable to beat in the brains of harp seal pups to make fur coats? Is it acceptable to kill animals in experiments leading to human benefit? Can animals feel? Can they love?

Are men all little boys in big bodies, using and discarding women like cans of beer, afraid of commitment, insensitive louts, unable to feel or touch or genuinely love? Or are they God's gift to woman?

Are women all calculating little shrews, whining endlessly about marriage and children, scheming to marry rich, divorce quick, and live high on the hog the rest of their lives? Or are they God's gift to man?

Are children irrational little monsters, deliberately disobedient for the sole purpose of infuriating their elders, impossible bundles of energy and motion, wreaking havoc wherever they go, babbling nonsense about ghosts and goblins while they smear peanut butter on the Picasso? Or are they sparks of divinity, bearing the gifts of laughter and light and play, offering bottomless love and trust in their elders, showing you new ways of seeing the smallest iota of creation, singing divine songs of magic and mystery to make the angels weep?

Is rock and roll the century's greatest musical form, a political, social, spiritual blast of three-chord jubilation, a volcanic flow of red hot rhythm carrying its generation to ever greater heights of protest and party? Is it the execrable static produced by the talentless and tone deaf? Or is it the devil's music?

Is the world doing fine? Is everything going to hell? Is everything getting better? Do you fear the future? Do you embrace it? Do you not care?

Is the earth a hunk of molten rock encased in a hardened shell, a minor asteroid in the cosmic sweep? Is it a wondrous crucible of life, created and blessed by God? Does the earth possess its own consciousness? Is the earth alive?

What happens after you die? Is that the end, the grand finale, the universe's last cruel joke? Does your personality survive death? Does it remain "you" throughout all eternity? Is there a Heaven, a Hell, and a purgatory? Do you continue to learn and grow after death? Can the discarnate communicate with those in flesh?

Which of these truths do you hold to be self-evident?

What color is your belief screen?

Twenty-Eight

༄

Belief Hierarchies

Beliefs are built in hierarchies. A new experience, resulting in a new comprehension of the world, will spark a new or altered belief. This new belief is not randomly tossed on the heap of belief you carry about with you. Beliefs are organized into categories, fields of experience, layered one atop another as fresh experience adds to the accretion.

The fundamental belief in any given hierarchy we will call the "core belief." This is a broad, all-encompassing belief about reality. On top of it are layered derivative beliefs, all carrying the imprint of the core belief, while addressing themselves to smaller, more discrete areas of reality. The higher a belief is in the hierarchy, the smaller the area it applies to, and the more consciously available it will be. A hierarchy of belief is constructed like an inverted pyramid, with a single, irrefutable belief at the bottom while additional layers spread out into more superficial, and more conscious, beliefs about reality.

As an example, we can look at the realm of food. What is the final, irreducible belief in this area? "I must eat to stay alive." That is the purpose of food; that is why you eat. There is no "higher" or "deeper" purpose than that; you eat to sustain the life of your body. You eat because you must. So, "I must eat to stay alive" is the core belief in the realm of food.

Building from that belief, every culture holds differing beliefs about what foods must be ingested, must not be ingested, are acceptable on special occasions, are to be withheld from children, and so on. Hierarchies of belief build from the core belief, rounding out a culture's belief hierarchy regarding food.

Just observe the evolution of belief regarding food in your culture over the last century. You believed it necessary to ingest a large quantity of protein every day, preferably from red meat. You believed it important to eat several servings of dairy products every day to maintain bone strength. You believed, at least unconsciously, that the highly processed and preservative-laden foods in your supermarkets were to your benefit, or at least not harmful. If you thought otherwise you would not buy them, because to do so would be to contradict the core belief of food: to keep your body alive.

Notice the sea change in beliefs about food over the last few decades. Where red meat was once a healthy source of protein, now it is seen as laden with pesticides, antibiotics, hormones, and cholesterol. Where milk, cream, and eggs were considered healthful sources of calcium and protein, now they are spurned as brimming with fat and cholesterol. Where once a bread made of bleached flour, white sugar, and laden with preservatives, helped your body grow strong twelve different ways, now you look at the same loaf and expect to mutate twelve different ways from a single slice. A healthy diet is now one rich in whole, natural foods, avoiding sugar, caffeine, and red meat. So you believe.

The core belief has never changed. You must eat to stay alive. What changes is your perception of the relative value of the various foods available to you, which combinations are healthiest and most dangerous, which cause disease and which prevent it.

As with food, so with every other realm of belief. A fundamental core belief provides the nest on which other beliefs roost. These surface beliefs can shift with every blowing breeze of sentiment and never disturb the core belief.

This process is important because, so often, an individual seeking to change his reality through changing beliefs does not dig deeply enough. A few surface beliefs may be uprooted, but the core belief lies untouched beneath the soil. There, it will attract to itself new sprouts of belief, superficially different from the old surface beliefs, yet carrying the same core imprint.

Remember that each experience you have in the physical world is split into two components of sense data and interpretation. It is easiest for fresh sense data to be linked with interpretation along the existing channels. While new interpretations may sprout, they still ride on the unseen core belief, thus confirming it. Because vibration travels most efficiently along a straight line, any attempt to uproot the core belief and rewire the circuitry between sense data and interpretation will be resisted.

This you experience, on the physical level, as people resisting any new information which would cause them to fundamentally alter their worldview. There is comfort in the status quo; it is the most efficient place to be! A radically new way of viewing reality requires a massive rewiring of the brain's circuitry.

This process is, of course, itself influenced by belief. If you believe without question that the values imparted to you in childhood are eternal truths, not open to question, then that belief will in itself strengthen the resistance to any contradictory experience. If, on the other hand, you are determined to keep an open mind, to reconsider your values based on fresh experience, because you believe that to be the healthiest way to live, then that belief will aid the rewiring, allowing it to proceed more efficiently, thus meeting less resistance.

A core belief will, therefore, allow easiest assimilation of data along the existing circuitry. You are far more likely to find yourself experiencing events confirming your worldview than those challenging your values. You see what you want to see; you hear what you want to hear. All incoming perception will be funneled along the existing circuitry; any data too radically divergent from the core belief will be dismissed—"it didn't happen"—or will require a massive rewiring of circuitry.

A scientist working late in the lab may look up from his microscope to see his long-dead father standing before him. His father speaks to him about how proud he is of the work his son is doing, and he wanted to communicate this before moving on in the spiritual realm. The father then evaporates.

The scientist first experiences a moment of shock and panic. The existing circuitry of his brain simply cannot handle the incoming sense data; there are no neuronal pathways to connect "father" with "ghost." The sense data cannot be married to interpretation, so the impulses bottle up in the sensory lobe, sparking physiological reactions felt as shock. Ghosts do not exist. Consciousness does not survive death. These are the scientist's core beliefs. No circuitry exists to allow for the existence of ghosts.

The sense data, rummaging through the existing neuronal pathways for an associative link, will find other channels: The scientist mutters to himself, "I've been working too hard. I'm tired. I'm hallucinating. I need sleep." All these mutterings flow from the belief that an overworked body and mind can begin to lose its fine, sharp focus in physical reality and manufacture illusions. This is an acceptable belief to the scientist; the neuronal pathways are in place. So that is how the event is stored.

Now, if the scientist's ectoplasmic father says, "By the way, I left a chest of gold coins buried under the cellar stairs," and then evaporates, the scientist may still initially store the experience along the existing pathways. Being a proper skeptical scientist, however, he will go home and check under the cellar stairs. If he uncovers a chest of gold coins, once again panic and shock set in. This cannot be explained by the core beliefs carried by a proper scientist.

Before entirely new neuronal pathways are forged, the sense data seeks associative links along existing, parallel pathways. The scientist may tell himself that as a child, his father told him about the buried coins, and under the mental strain of his work, that memory was sprung from its neuronal grave into awareness. He may tell himself the whole incident was a coincidence. Both explanations can be assimilated along existing neuronal pathways.

But if the scientist declares, "No, this cannot be a coincidence and he never told me about any gold coins; something more is involved," then again panic sets in, for the brain's urgent need to instantly split sense data into interpretation is stymied. The sense data roams around its lobe, unable to find rest and peace until it is linked with an appropriate interpretation. In this case, the scientist may uproot his core belief that consciousness cannot survive death and replace it with its opposite: "Consciousness must survive death. I have proof." Once this belief is installed, a sense of relief descends, for the sense data can ride the new belief to link with an acceptable interpretation. The incident can then be left behind—with our scientist tiptoeing to Mass behind his colleagues' backs.

Fresh experience will always try to assimilate itself along the existing neuronal networks. Vibration travels most efficiently that way. It is easier to confirm one's worldview than to confront it. Yet, if experience warrants, and the existing networks cannot provide an adequate link between sense data and interpretation, new core beliefs must replace the old. You see now the hidden truth of the expressions "close-minded" and "open-minded." Those open to fresh experience, willing to evaluate the verity of their core beliefs, maintain open channels upon which new networks of belief can build. Those whose minds are shuttered against all incoming data contradicting their beloved core beliefs are like three-foot children declaring, "I refuse to grow another inch."

In the case of our scientist, after the contact with his ghost father, he may begin a search for evidence of other such experiences. A trip to the library will bear fruit in the form of books on poltergeist phenomena, near-death experiences, haunted houses, and so on. Should he choose to dig deeper, the scientist will find reams of such volumes. A whole new world opens up to him. A segment of society, and of life, that he was not even aware of before—because any brush with it could find no interpretative link and was dismissed—now consumes his life as he finds hundreds of volumes and case histories documenting that consciousness indeed survives death. This flood of new knowledge strengthens the nascent channel allowing for the belief that consciousness survives death. With the channel in place, the scientist finds daily confirmation of what before never even registered in his awareness.

You see what you want to see. You hear what you want to hear. Fresh experience will always try to find interpretation along existing pathways of belief. A radically divergent piece of intelligence will either be dismissed from awareness or will force a new level of understanding, a new pathway. Ideally, this process continues throughout life, as maturity brings a broader appreciation for the immensity of the universe and the limits of your knowledge about it.

In an open-minded individual, this perpetually expanding network of interpretation allows each successive event to be experienced less as symbol and more as truth. Each event you experience is a blend of symbol and truth, with the mix determined by your level of spiritual awareness. The "higher" the awareness, the more truth is beheld in every event, and the less symbol.

Reducing this process to electromagnetism, since your beliefs are carried within the spine, magnetically pulling in the events of your life, an experienced event will not only reflect your present spiritual level, but will also urge you to an even higher level, if you are open to it. Every event urges you to experience it more as truth and less as symbol. The choice, always, is yours.

In the case of our scientist, the core belief he shares with those of his profession is that only the physically perceivable world is valid, and that all of its processes can be understood by the rational mind. You see what a misguided lot such persons are. For the physically experienced world is the very slowest level of vibration, the lowest order of event, cloaked in symbol and reflecting only pale glimmers of truth. And this they hold to be the ultimate reality!

Our scientist, spurred by his dead father's appearance to investigate further, finds evidence everywhere he turns that consciousness survives death. He couldn't see it before; his core beliefs would not allow the information to be processed. Now, moving to a higher level of spiritual truth, he perceives what was invisible before. He perceives more truth, and less symbol, in every passing event.

Your level of understanding, your ability to divine kernels of truth behind symbolic wrapping, is determined by the nature of your core beliefs.

Twenty-Nine

Emotion

Because your society holds only the physically perceivable to be "rational," and all other levels of thought—dreams, emotions, artistic fire—to be "irrational," you rob yourselves of understanding the true significance of emotions. Indeed, you split "reason" and "emotion" into two opposing camps, and any time reason is "tainted" with emotion, you react with scorn.

In a healthy, integrated individual, there is no divorce between reason and emotion. They work in tandem. Both aid you in charting a clear, safe course through the world of events. To understand how this works, we must explore the origin and meaning of emotion.

You will grant that any emotion exists first as thought. Emotions spring up in reaction to perceived events. You hear something, see something, feel something, and the perceived event is split into its two components of sense data and interpretation. It is in the interpretation that your reaction springs to life: Do you believe the event to be beneficial? harmful? ridiculous? divine? Your belief network will interpret the event in line with its extant structure, and thus spark a reaction.

Now, this emotional reaction is almost always expressed physically within the body, is it not? You *feel* jealousy; you *feel* anger; you *feel* happiness; you *feel* love; you *feel* pride; you *feel* satisfaction. Pondering each of these emotional states, you can connect them with corresponding physiological states. A broken heart literally aches. Anger makes your pulse race. Happiness inspires you to jump for joy.

This is the fundamental difference between so-called "rational thought," which remains on a cerebral level, and the world of emotion, which spills into the body and provokes it to action. "Rational thought," remaining on an unemotional plane, generally deals with sense data manipulations of the world. "Rational thought" is your brain's computer, its efficient, ever-vigilant navigator through the world of events. It commands the body as you drive a car, solve a crossword puzzle, work with your hands, master a musical piece, pore over a textbook, wash the dishes, pilot an airplane, sculpt art from clay, fix your breakfast. What you call "rational thought" is the processes of your sensory lobe manipulating the physical world, steering the body's course safely through it.

Every creature upon the earth, whatever its size, engages in "rational thought." Each perceives sense data and manipulates its body accordingly, steering a clear and secure course through the world.

Emotions make you human. They provide the richness, the depth, the meaning to life. They round out your mere manipulation of the world with purpose. *Why* do you manipulate the world? To achieve satisfaction? love? happiness? triumph? revenge? fulfillment?

In a healthy individual and society, rational thought and emotions work in tandem. They are partners, leading you through the world of experience, both navigating a clear and secure course and providing meaning to what you do.

Emotions spring from the interpretation side of experienced events. After the senses perceive the raw data, filed away in the sensory lobe, that data is shipped along the neuronal pathways to find interpretation: what does it mean? And it is here that a given event is evaluated, along the lines of your beliefs, in light of its effect upon you, your body, and your life's course.

The realm of emotion is actually far more "rational" than that of the data assimilated by the sensory lobe. For the sensory lobe makes no interpretation; it simply stores data, and sends orders through the nervous system as it is commanded by the higher levels of the brain. The sensory lobe alone can make no evaluations as to the wisdom or folly of a given course. It strictly focuses on the manipulation of the body and world, but receives its instructions from elsewhere. This "elsewhere" is the realm of emotion, those belief structures interpreting incoming sense data and comparing them with your body's desire to chart a clear and secure course. Emotions, most fundamentally, are your brain's interpretations of sense data, along the lines of its beliefs, for the purpose of ensuring your safety in the physical world.

If someone approaches you with a red hot bar of iron and announces he is going to tattoo you with it, what do you do? Calmly ponder the situation as the iron nears? That would be the response of the sensory lobe, the site of "reason," knowing nothing of belief-fueled interpretation. Most likely, unless you find tattoo graffiti of interest, you will scream and fight your way from the sadist's presence. The incoming sense data has been interpreted along the lines of your beliefs—you do not believe tattoo graffiti is of interest or benefit, thank you—and the threat to you so severe that it must express itself in urgent physical action.

If, on Christmas morning, your child announces, "I didn't have the money to buy you anything, but I made you this," and you unwrap a laboriously constructed card of sequins and string and crayon, each little squiggle screaming love and devotion, hours of patient work squeezing your child's inexpressible feelings into a symphony of color and beauty, embroidered with the words "I love you," how do you react? The "rational" response is to announce in a robot voice: "You made a card. It is not as good as Rembrandt could do." Is that how you react? Or do you drop the card from trembling hands, reach out for your child and squeeze the very life out of the precious little lungs as tears spring from your eyes? Why such a reaction over a Christmas card?

Because, first, love is an expression of appreciation for the divinity in another, a recognition of the unknowable depths from which the soul of the beloved springs. An expression of love from a child is doubly touching because you recognize that children make no evaluations based on the meaningless trinkets of interest to the adult world—wealth, status, fame— but that children judge solely from the heart. To have such an affirmation from a child, particularly your own, is to confirm that *your life has value.* Your life has meaning. It has purpose. You are here for a reason.

You know all these things unconsciously, but often forget them in the day-to-day crush of responsibilities. An expression of love from a child touches you so deeply because it leapfrogs the sensory lobe and burrows directly in your most sacrosanct belief: my life has meaning. And because this belief is so crucial, so fundamental, so all-important, any time that it is stimulated to awareness by the soft-spoken judgment of an angel in flesh, the "event" of your response is too enormous to dissipate entirely within the brain. It must "step down" to the level of the body, the world of space and time, as tears and hugs and exclamations of love and gratitude.

In both cases, the sadist and the child, your responses spring from your beliefs. You believe the sadist's approach to portend danger. You believe your life has meaning, and embrace the bearer of the message. In both cases, the "event" of your belief's interpretation is so strong, contains so much "event stuff," that it cannot simply evaporate among the synapses of the brain. It must "step down" into the world of events, expressed as physical action.

The more strongly you believe an event to carry an effect on you, the greater the physiological reaction. Some incoming sense data carries such a slight potential effect that, although the data will be interpreted in line with your beliefs, it can remain on the level of thought. You balance your checkbook to the penny. Do you alert the media? No, you feel a slight inner satisfaction and move on. That "satisfaction," the security that comes from knowing that you and the bank believe you to possess the same amount of money, carries so little significance to your immediate physical circumstances that its emotional component—satisfaction—is dissipated easily within the realm of thought.

The greater the potential effect upon you and your body, however, and the more imminent that effect, the stronger the emotional reaction will be. Here is where emotions find physiological release, stepped down into the realms of experience and object. Someone telling you over the telephone, "I'm going to kill you," will certainly be cause for concern, but you are in no immediate danger, so the fear will be slight. If you hear those same words after a gunman has slaughtered a roomful of people, with you the sole survivor, your reaction will be commensurately stronger, for the danger is immediate.

The strength of your emotional reactions depends upon the severity of an event's potential effect upon you and the imminence of its occurrence.

We need not concentrate solely on negative events, of course. For the realm of happiness spreads from mild contentment to utter, unspeakable ecstasy. Again, the same principle applies. The greater an event's potential effect on you, and the imminence of its expression, determines the extent of your happiness. Being told that you have won a trip around the world, launching six months from now, will be cause for joy. Hearing the same news, but with the date of departure being tomorrow, will likely bring a far more jubilant response. Again, notice how your body expresses your reaction, from the smile of contentment to the frenzied leaping up and down and embracing of strangers of one in the throes of ecstasy. The greater an event's effect upon you, the more imminent its effect, the more "stuff" must be stepped down into physical expression, released through the seesaw of time and space.

Perhaps you can see the cycle of emotion. First, an "event" occurs in the exterior world which you drink in through your senses. Reduced to electrical impulses in the brain, it is split into sense data—what is it?—and interpretation—what does it mean? If an event's meaning stands to affect you deeply and imminently, your reaction—itself an event—must be stepped down to the world of experience and object to find full, healthy release. So the cycle is complete: an event occurs in the world of experience, and your reaction is expressed also in the world of experience. In between, your brain processes the triggering event into sense data and interpretation.

Notice how your privacy is ensured. Your thought processes, the hum of your interpretative evaluations of events, are entirely blocked from others. Your beliefs, your interpretation of events, are yours and yours alone. Yours is the power to deliberately fashion your physical reaction as you see fit. Though bursting with joy or sorrow, you may maintain a blank poker face. Though an event inspires no deep emotion in you, you may feign great anger or excitement, if it suits your purposes to do so. Thus is your privacy ensured; thus do you maintain your unique stance, revealing yourself to the world through your actions only to the extent of your choice.

Emotions are nothing more than belief finding physiological expression. You evaluate an event's effect on you, along the lines of your beliefs, and express yourself physically. The greater the event's effect, the stronger your reaction.

You can see how patently *irrational* it is to deny yourself the validity of your emotions, and their full expression in the physical world. For thought and emotion are meant to work in tandem. One cannot replace the other. Thought merely tells you what is happening; your beliefs interpret the raw data and trigger physiological responses enabling you to maintain security, and to impress upon others the nature of your thoughts. To deny the realm of emotions, to consider them "irrational," to hold them as being lower than your pure cognitive processes, is to shoot yourself in the foot and declare the highest form of ambulation to be hopping on one leg.

In your culture, the opposing camps of "rational thought" and emotions have been assigned exclusively to the two sexes. Women are emotional. Men are rational. The genesis of this division lies in the fundamental perspectives of the sexes. Man is the material keeper of the earth. Woman is the spiritual keeper of the earth. Man, focusing on physical mastery and manipulation, employs his dominant sensory lobe. Woman, steeped in the deeper realm of mystery and spirit, views the world more as interpretation, digging under the "what" to find the "why."

You see now how the two elements of thought and emotion work together in the healthiest individual. It is not enough to know "what." You must know "why," and you must have the courage to express your emotional reactions to others, for otherwise you rob them and yourself of true connection.

We have placed the phrase "rational thought" in quotes throughout because your definition and ours differ markedly. To you, "rational thought" restricts itself to the cogitations of the sensory lobe. From our perspective, rational thought is the integration of thought and emotional processes, through which you chart a clear and secure course, enabling you to truly understand and connect with others as you search together for deeper truth. That, friends, is true rational thought.

There is a greater danger in dismissing and ignoring the realm of emotion, beyond simply cheating yourself and others of true connection, and sprouting ulcers and cancers right and left as repressed emotions seek physical release within the body.

Remember that events never fall unannounced into your laps. As they approach physical expression, drawn into your life by the magnetic pull of your coordinate, they step down through the levels of thought, through your vibrational bodies. The first link is between psyche and superconscious thought; the next, between aura and thought; the next, between etheric body and experience; the last, between bedrock body and object.

One way for you to experience events is to pull them into physical expression, perceive them through your senses, interpret the vibrational data in line with your beliefs, and express a physical reaction. That is the "lowest" level of event, those finding physical expression. Events exist first in the superconscious realm, far above expression in space and time.

It is at this level that you may first become precognitively aware of an event as it nears physical expression. Your psyche, which stands between your body-mind and your greater entity, feeds information to you as to the events it is linking with on its level of activity. You are always aware of events before they physically occur. Yet, because such information is never perceived through the physical senses, it is often dismissed, ignored, or never brought to consciousness. It is not valid, in your eyes.

Superconscious events flow through the same networks and channels of interpretation as physical events. A potential event will be fed to the sensory lobe, where its likely physical expression will be determined—"what is it?"—and then sent to the interpretative lobe for evaluation—"what does it mean?" A potential event portending danger can trigger the same emotional response as a physical event carrying danger. Your interpretive lobe carries an identical reaction.

The problem, particularly in your culture, is that you grant no validity to anything not first perceived through the physical senses. So an event precognitively planting its traces in your awareness, and triggering an appropriate response, carries no weight with you. You find yourself with vague, diffuse, uneasy feelings, and no physical explanation. You dismiss the feelings. You do not evaluate them. You do not know how.

In such a situation, because you will not allow yourself to evaluate the potential event and physiologically react to an event not yet physically occurring, you cannot dismiss the event, cannot release it physically. So the event has not been dissipated, and it drops ever closer to physical expression. Ultimately, the event will find physical expression, and then your vague, diffuse, uneasy feelings become screeches of terror.

Events work both ways, you see. They can occur in the physical world, stepping "up" to evaluation and interpretation in the brain, or they can remain on the nonphysical level of superconscious thought, stepping "down" to the same processes in the brain. In either case, you can fully and completely experience the meaning of an event and release it from your life through an emotional, physical reaction.

Further, remember that all events you experience have first been pulled into expression by your coordinate, magnetically encoding your beliefs and thoughts. Nothing is thrust upon you; you draw everything to yourself. What level of vibration do you wish to experience events on? On the superconscious level, releasing them through understanding and emotional reactions, or stepped down further into the levels of object and experience? Not only do you draw every event of your life to yourself, but which level you experience that event on is also entirely your free choice. The self-perpetuating cycle of event-reaction-event is simply a way of talking out loud, thrusting your thoughts into physical expression. You create your own reality.

Here we must express a crucial understanding which we have not mentioned before. From the perspective of your greater entity, there are no "good" or "bad" experiences. There are no such judgments on the planes above the physical. Your purpose is to experience physical life with the absolute freedom to pull into expression any and all events of your choosing. For your greater entity to block some events from expression, because of their perceived deleterious effects, would be to rob you of your freedom. No such interference occurs. Whatever disasters and calamities you wish to draw to yourself, you may freely do so. For from all such experiences, you learn, and you grow. You learn that spending life in a wheelchair, or dying at age twenty of cancer, or being beaten by a spouse, do not lead to your highest fulfillment. These are lessons. These spark growth. "Good" and "bad" are entirely on the level of interpretation— which goes no higher than your thought processes.

At the same time, your greater entity grants you freedom to avoid experiencing any potential event you perceive to be of detrimental effect. This is the purpose of setting up the expression of events as trickling from superconscious thought to thought, to experience, to object. You are precognitively aware of any event before it finds physical expression. If, in your judgment—your interpretation of "good" and "bad"—you believe it against your best interest to experience an event, yours is the power to release the event from potential expression. How? By altering the magnet pulling it toward you—changing your beliefs and thoughts.

So while your greater entity passes no judgment on the events of your life, leaving you free to experience all the joy and trauma you can attract, you nonetheless have the power to evaluate events before their physical expression, and to avoid those you deem detrimental.

Naturally, women are more perceptive to potential events, since they have not been taught to block all such precognitive awareness. You call this "women's intuition," stuffing it into the Pandora's box of unwelcome reminders of the limits of "rational thought."

What could be more irrational than denying yourself the power to evaluate events before they find physical expression, and to release them while still at the superconscious level? What could be more irrational than stumbling through life as the hapless victim of luck, fate, chance, accident, disease—all because you have dismissed as invalid all data not perceived first through the physical senses? What could be more irrational than deliberately steering through life with a robot's mentality, refusing any upgrades to more comprehensive perspectives?

Emotions are judgments, evaluations of incoming sense data along the networks of belief. Events to your benefit spark reactions of happiness, joy, love, laughter. Events to your detriment evoke fear, anger, jealousy, despondency. The greater an event's effect, the greater your reaction's expression in space and time. The healthy individual expresses emotional reactions fully, releasing them from their cogitative cage, sharing his inner truth with others while freely moving on to the next experience.

Prephysical sense data is absorbed from the superconscious thought level. Potential events are evaluated for their potential effects, and the same process of interpretation and emotional reaction is triggered. This allows you the freedom to avoid physical expression of events you find to your detriment.

Whether sparked by physical sense data or superconscious thought, your emotional reactions flow from interpretation, interpretation springing from belief. Your beliefs determine your emotions. And if you believe that emotions and thought are meant to work in tandem, steering a secure course through the world, then yours shall be a charmed and precognitively blissful life, a life in which nothing sneaks up from behind or falls from the ceiling. A conscious life.

Thirty

༺

Human Vibrations

The novice metaphysician may latch onto the New Age rallying cry of "You create your own reality," and, in the first heady rush of liberation, declare, "Nothing can affect me! I am invincible! I create my own reality!"

If our young pupil were to stand naked in a snowstorm and defiantly cry, "You can't hurt me! I create my own reality!", what would the likely outcome be? Enlightenment or frostbite?

In theory, it is possible for the mind to so govern the body that one could stand in a howling storm and feel no effect. If you are capable of such mental control, we suggest that you leave this volume aside and levitate to the library for a weightier tome more in line with your understanding.

To say "you create your own reality" is not to free you from influence by others—persons, objects, events—outside yourself. In fact, a genuine understanding of how your world is created, and how you fit into the overall scheme, should lead to an appreciation of the extent to which outside events, objects, and persons can affect you. The consciously created life is one in which you deliberately design the environment and events of your life in order to enhance your happiness and fulfillment, free from the noxious influences of those who would hinder your progress.

Remember the purpose of the vibrational bodies you carry about your physical body: to alert you to immediate environmental conditions (etheric), alert you to planetary events and conditions (auric), and apprise you of events being pulled toward physical expression (psyche). These vibrational bodies all aid you in steering a healthy course through life. They have been granted you in recognition of how others can and do affect you, and how enhanced awareness of the energies of others assists you in consciously creating your life.

Let us take an everyday example. If you are looking for a new job, both you and your potential employer will agree that a personal interview is the best way to "get to know each other" while each evaluates the potential working relationship. Why can't such an interview take place on the phone? The employer wants to meet you in person. You want to meet your potential boss, and the other co-workers, in person. Why?

Because, consciously or not, you understand that only when you are in direct proximity to others can your vibrational bodies exchange information. While an interview may remain on the mundane level of qualifications and experience, your bodies are involved in far deeper levels of communication. You may leave an interview feeling inexplicably positive, feeling that the employer and you will mesh, that he projected "good vibes." Similarly, while your potential employer may seem pleasant and welcoming, you may be left with vague, diffuse feelings of negativity, "bad vibes."

A walk through the office will offer reams of raw material from which you consciously and unconsciously evaluate its emotional climate. Are people friendly, laughing, hardworking, courteous? Or are the employees all sulking at their desks, morose, uncommunicative, offering a pale and unconvincing "hello"? While these physical clues carry much weight in your evaluation, you are also sweeping up volumes of nonphysical information about the office and its workers. These may crystallize into uneasy feelings, a sense that this office would be an unlikely base from which to pursue happiness and fulfillment.

Two processes are at work here: the "vibrational matrix" of each individual you meet; and the office's overall atmosphere, which we will term an "energy vortex." Let us examine these in detail.

Each person carries a "vibrational matrix" blended into the coordinate. This, as you know, is encased in the spine, and serves as the magnet pulling toward physical expression the potential events of one's life.

A primary ingredient of one's coordinate is the time of one's birth. All persons born at the same time carry a common core vibration. As time progresses and the spiritual evolution of the species advances, each successive moment raises the race's core vibration a notch "higher" in spiritual understanding.

When we speak of the spiritual evolution of the human species, we are not referring exclusively to the religious mythologies of the day. Instead, it is the broader "worldview" to which we refer, this worldview influencing the state of political, religious, social, and artistic realms. This worldview is the glue that binds together the members of a generation in a common understanding, an established consensus as to the nature of reality. This worldview, this consensual outlook, is what we refer to as the core vibration of a generation.

Building upon an individual's core vibration, at birth one also carries latent potentials bearing karmic material. You are never born a blank slate, but always come into life carrying certain lessons to be learned, relationships to be healed. The time and place, the political structure, one's parents, are all carefully selected to provide the appropriate background for one to play out one's karmic material.

A comprehensive discussion of this process is beyond the scope of this book. But your coordinate can be imprinted at birth with certain "lessons," timed to unravel and manifest at certain points in your life. Because the primal pulse provides a master calendar for the universe, it is possible at birth to implant an event and time its release to the second, even an event not finding expression for fifty years. In other words, the coordinate will suddenly unravel the latent potential at the moment encoded at birth, and this potential exerts a strong magnetic pull toward a certain event; this event, existing on the superconscious level, will then slide into expression.

Karmic material may also carry more generalized influences on personality and behavior, above and beyond single, discrete events planned ahead of time. The purpose is balance and healing, leading toward fresh growth. A life of great opulence will be balanced with a life of poverty, in which no amount of struggle seems to lift one above the scraping and clawing of subsistence. This can be implanted at birth by "tuning" the coordinate to strongly pull toward expression events of poverty and to block any events of wealth.

Again, a more detailed discussion must await another volume. Our point now is that you always carry through life a karmic background which colors and flavors the events of your life. You are not here for a free ride, nor were you born a blank slate. There was a specific purpose to the time and place and circumstances of your birth. While these karmic influences may never reach conscious awareness throughout the entire span of life, still they flavor its every moment. Riding atop the core vibration implanted at birth, this karmic material carries a unique vibration of its own. This differentiates you from others at the moment of birth; it makes you utterly unique.

The combined flavor of core vibration and karmic material will be unconsciously available to anyone who meets you. Again, this can lie behind any inexplicable good or bad "vibes" you feel while interviewing with your prospective employer. You may unconsciously sense that the karmic material carried by your potential boss conflicts so severely with your own that a happy match would be impossible. You may find instant sympathy, and the sudden rush of warm feelings is a signal that together, you can work through karmic material that each would otherwise struggle through alone. Or, quite possibly, you and your potential boss have known each other in a past life and have some mopping up to do. In such a case, you might well feel torn by the seemingly contradictory push and pull of conflicting emotions: "He seems like a jerk but I really want to work with him!"

Layered upon the worldview and the karmic material will be a record of every event experienced by an individual from the moment of birth on. No event, however insignificant, is ever lost. Every act you commit, every thought you think, is indelibly written in the ledger of the universe. While you live in physical form, the electromagnetic swirl of the coordinate carries a literal record of your every past experience. Each successive event of your life will alter your coordinate's composition. You may fully release certain karmic material, freeing energy for other experiences. A burst of enlightenment may ignite your core vibration to a higher pitch, that of those born ten years after your birth. Most important, of course, will be the nature of your beliefs. What do you believe? For what you believe is what you will experience. The "higher" your beliefs, the more truth they carry, the "higher" the level on which you live your life.

Every moment of your life, every belief and thought you hold, is carried in the coordinate's energy swirl. This information is available to anyone within close proximity; the closer together you are, the greater the fidelity with which this information can be transmitted.

While you and your potential employer prattle on about the mundane banalities extolled in your résumé, far more important levels of information are being exchanged. What is this person's worldview? What karmic material has been carried forward? What are the inner beliefs and thoughts? What have been the life experiences so far? All of this material is unconsciously exchanged.

What happened to the precious privacy we assured you was yours for being human? It is still yours, for none of this information is exchanged consciously. You do not receive a computerized printout of every moment of a person's life, the karmic carry-over, and the core vibration implanted at birth. Instead, you are left with hazy, vague feelings: your potential employer was pleasant, or cold, or impulsive, or hostile, or bland, or beyond redemption.

You cannot always ascribe your feelings to anything spoken. Instead, you are left with an overall emotional impression, as the information gathered by your higher vibrational bodies trickles into conscious awareness, losing fidelity and richness as it steps down to the level of conscious awareness. Your privacy is assured, as is your employer's. You may carry an overall impression from your meeting, but you cannot pinpoint it to any specific causes, beyond what was openly spoken. No conscious invasion of each other's private lives has occurred.

Once the unconscious information has been exchanged, a judgment is made as to the merits of your joining in a working relationship. Is there sufficient sympathy of worldview, karmic material, and beliefs that you can work harmoniously together? Or do the vibrations and life purposes clash so severely that only miscommunication and trauma would ensue?

Unless there is a specific (usually karmic) purpose to joining in a relationship with one whose vibrational matrix is radically divergent from your own, you will tend to be repelled by the difference. Like attracts like. Grossly disparate vibrations grind and grate against each other. The events each is pulling toward expression can serve no benefit to the other. The life purposes, the methods of growth, stand at cross-purposes. In such a case, you will likely feel strongly repelled by an individual, often without any physical reason, and leave the interview thinking, "I could never work for that person!" Consciously, you cannot name the reason why. Unconsciously, you recognize that the drummers to which you march are flailing away in discordant rhythms, and you could never match each other's stride step by step.

It should be apparent that this process, of unconsciously exchanging information with those you meet, is meant to steer you toward those carrying sympathetic purpose and away from those with whom a relationship would serve no benefit. When fundamental life purpose is grossly divergent, there is little opportunity for growth and connection. Your coordinate acts as a magnet, pulling you toward those carrying similar life purpose and repelling you from those whose life potentials offer you no growth.

Consider what occurs when you travel to foreign lands. You may find native cultures to be exotic, fascinating, threatening, incomprehensible, harmless, or ignorant. What is this Dreamtime business, anyway? The world's geography reflects the electromagnetic fields from which the earth is formed. Disparate energy fields serve as vortexes of unique purpose, playing host to specific strands of human and animal life. The variety of human cultures provides an infinite range of home fields in which to plant oneself and seek one's private fulfillment.

Because those in foreign cultures carry a vibrational matrix so strikingly different from yours, there is little potential for genuine, abiding, heart-to-heart contact. You may admire a foreign culture; you may adore it; you may choose to live with it the rest of your life. But can you ever truly become a member of that nation, that tribe, indistinguishable in outlook and worldview from the natives?

In your own country, what common reference point have a millionaire businessman and a minority inner city youth? What can they talk about that will be of interest and value to both? They may pledge allegiance to the same flag, but the overlapping strands of life purpose are so few and slender that virtually no genuine communication can take place.

All such life purpose material is carried in the coordinate. It steers you toward those of your own "kind," those with whom you share sympathetic purpose, and away from those so radically divergent that there can be little growth in a relationship. If this seems to limit you to one narrow band of human experience, remember that no such limits exist on the level of your greater entity, who can pick and choose among the entire spectrum when planning your reincarnational progress. Each tribe, each culture, offers a unique focus on human life, a slant found nowhere else, covering the globe with wildly divergent home fields into which you plant yourself, sprouting to fulfillment in the rich and fertile soil of human diversity.

We have now touched on the second main element of human energy, moving beyond the discrete exchange between two individuals to encompass a broader wealth of individuals. Returning to our example of the job interview, you will want to tour the office and get a "feel" for its "atmosphere." These words carry more literal meaning than you might expect. For any combined group, whether a family, a tribe, an office, or a neighborhood, will carry a communal vibration. This we term the "energy vortex" of a group. The combined coordinates of those involved will create an overall energy field, blending their disparate private energies into a unique "atmosphere" which all entering the vortex will feel.

While you do create your own reality, you are influenced by the energy of those around you, and influenced by any energy vortex you step into. A highly positive vortex will stimulate your coordinate to accelerate your vibrational matrix, enabling you to draw more positive, uplifting events into your life. A negative vortex will suppress your natural energies, allowing the flow of unhappy, dispiriting events. While there are ways to psychically protect yourself from negative energy vortexes, most persons are not even aware that such vortexes exist, much less how to defend against them.

You get the "feel" for a group by observing them. Are they energetic, smiling, laughing, joking, expressing genuine caring for each other? Or are they slumped in low energy, moaning and groaning about their ailments, plotting and scheming behind the boss's back, scratching and clawing in office rivalry? Since the body is a reflection of the higher vibrational bodies, an office full of low-energy, apathetic individuals clues you that the energy vortex, the atmosphere, is heavily oppressive.

The determining vibration of a hierarchical organization like a business is frequently set at the top. How does management view its workers? With respect, good pay, generous benefits, a healthy and safe work environment? Or as shiftless, lazy, dishonest serfs, to be hounded and spied upon and tested for drugs? Such expectations are unconsciously transmitted to the workers. Any worker stepping into such an environment is unconsciously apprised of the expectations of management, without a word being spoken. The worker's coordinate blends with the overall energy vortex, and the "events" of high or low energy, contentment or dissatisfaction, honesty or thievery, find easiest expression along the lines of the expectations. The coordinate, acting as a magnet, pulls into expression those events in line with management's expectations.

This principle carries over into every field of human endeavor. You know that children live up to expectations. If told they are lazy, dishonest, and stupid, they will act lazy, dishonest, and stupid. The expectations need never be openly announced; they can remain unspoken. The child, who suffers far less blockage between conscious and unconscious data than an adult, will understand precisely what the expectations are. Because the parent is viewed as big, strong, and omnipotent, the child seeks to please the parent in line with the expectations. Even at the expense of one's own growth and fulfillment, the child will perform according to negative expectations, so strong is the desire to please the parent.

Examples are legion of troubled, delinquent, or scholastically failing children who spring to life and heights of achievement when one person, one lone adult, breaks through the cloud of negative expectations to say, "I care about you. I know you can do better." How the child clings to such precious words! For no one aspires to a reputation of delinquency or failure; all seek their very highest potential level of accomplishment. One adult breaking through the negative vortex of hundreds can inspire a child to feats surpassing even the child's belief in his inner capabilities. One voice declaring, "I care about you," one glimmering strand of love and compassion dangled before the child's eyes like a million Christmas mornings, is latched onto—literally, magnetically linking with the child's coordinate—and the days of delinquency and failure are forever abandoned.

It is possible for a group of relatively stable and content individuals to be disrupted by the arrival of a leech. A leech is one whose vibrational matrix is so weak and low that survival depends on attaching oneself to those of high vibration and sucking their energy dry. A chorus of groans erupts whenever the leech approaches, with the usual litany of accidents, relationship traumas, health catastrophes, financial troubles, and so on, ad infinitum. A formerly cohesive and content group can find itself falling apart, its high communal vibration sucked into the leech's maw.

A dispirited and broken group of inveterate achers and complainers may similarly be disrupted by the arrival of an individual bristling with high and unwelcome vibration. Who needs this happiness, this radiant health, this string of hilarious adventures? Over time, the previously unwelcome member may inspire the broken souls to rearrange their lives along more healthful, productive lines. In this case, the high energy individual acts as a beacon, an ideal to which the others aspire. The group vibration, the energy vortex, accelerates from the love of aches and pains to the love of life.

Every group of individuals, from a couple, to a neighborhood, to a nation, to a world, manifests a group vibration, an energy vortex. Those coming in contact with a vortex will be instantly—albeit unconsciously—apprised of its nature. This operates, on an individual level, to steer you toward those groups among whom you can find growth and fulfillment, and away from those too disparate for there to be any commonality. A group too far "lower" or "higher" than yours offers no comfortable home base. You seek those of relatively sympathetic vibration as a bed of security from which you sally forth to pursue your private purpose.

You create your own reality. But as your body is essentially electromagnetic vibration, you are unavoidably affected by all other vibration with which you come in contact. "Creating your reality" does not mean that you stand invincible, an unmovable pillar against the crashing tides, but is instead a recognition of your place within the overall scheme. The reason your vibrational bodies perceive the levels of information they do is to feed such awareness to you, the better for you to consciously fashion your experience.

On an individual level, you become aware of the core vibration, karmic material, and beliefs of those you meet, the better to understand if a potential relationship holds promise of growth. Further, any group will carry a communal vibration, an energy vortex, which will affect the nature of your experiences within the group, for better or worse.

A consciously lived life is one in which you are aware of the nature of vibration and its effects on the events of your life, upon which you deliberately fashion a vibrational environment in harmony with your private goals, growth, and fulfillment. You do not stand aloof and immune in the world of your fellows, but accept your place among them, seeking and avoiding them as befits your purpose. The more sensitive you are to the messages of your higher bodies, funneling their perceptions into unbidden "feelings," the clearer the course you steer through the world of human events.

Thirty-One

∽

Bedrock Vibrations

It may seem obvious and apparent that the energy fields carried by others of your species carry potential effects upon you. Yet you are also affected by any energy field with which you come in contact, whatever its degree of consciousness. Even bedrock objects carry consciousness, of a quiescent dreaminess, and offer an attenuated exchange of information when against your skin.

The purpose of human life is to manipulate the physical world, the world of bedrock, fashioning the raw materials of the earth into signposts of progress in art, religion, and technology. This is where human consciousness meets bedrock, where bedrock is manipulated, molded, and reshaped into the tools and symbols of meaning to your species.

At base, all is vibration. Your body is vibration; your thoughts are vibration; bedrock objects are vibration. Because vibration travels in distinct and consistent patterns, and because exchanges always occur when vibrational fields intersect, every bedrock object created or molded by your species will carry within its structure an imprint of intent from its creator. The thoughts and designs of the artist, the inventor, the craftsman, are transmitted to the objects flowing from their hands; these vibrational intents remain with the fashioned objects long after release from their creators' possession.

Just as a consciously lived life is one in which you recognize and respect the effect others can have upon you, so also do you become aware of the objects in your life, their origin, their creators, and their creators' intent while fashioning them.

First, let us explore the process by which a creator imprints intent upon bedrock objects.

Any material that you can see, touch, and manipulate is essentially bedrock. Bedrock objects carry high charge, of similar pattern, sparking low resistance. They are the densest form of event, slowed to the earth pulse and allowing charge to fill their primal cells with each earth pulsation. The higher the charge, and the lower the resistance, the denser and more impervious to change the object will be.

Your physical body manifests as bedrock, as it is the slowest of your four vibrational bodies, the only one vibrating slowly enough to permit charge to fill its cells. This enables you to manipulate the world of objects, as you and the physical world share a commonality, a mutual construction.

Remember that an event's intensity is determined by the matrix of event units that must be dissipated through the media of space and time. Yours is the power to juggle space and time, minimizing spatial expression and lengthening temporal duration, or spilling an event rapidly in time and reducing its spatial expression.

In the world of objects, your power to juggle space and time is relative to the density of the object at hand. Consider that your intent to manipulate an object is, in itself, a swirl of energy that must be dissipated through space and time. This is literally the case. You must impress your intent upon the object spatially and temporally. Your ability to do so is determined by the density of the object, for your intent can squeeze into an object's primal cells only to the extent that they are not filled with charge.

In other words, a given beat of the pulse will spark a certain charge within each primal cell forming an object. Any leftover space within each cell can be filled with your intent—for your intent exists on the level of thought, carries no bedrock charge, and therefore will not compete with charge for space within the cell. Still, there are limits as to your power to impress your intent upon an object. The first priority is to maintain the object's stance in the physical world. The primal cells must fill with sufficient bulk to sustain the object's endurance in space and time. Beyond that, you—or any other conscious species—can impress your intent upon the primal cells, filling the gaps with your nonphysical thought vibration.

Consider two examples, a rock and a marshmallow. Which is easier to manipulate, more malleable in your hands? The rock, because it carries such high charge, has little space left within each primal cell to allow your intent to squeeze into the molecular structure. You cannot bend a rock, nor squeeze it, nor twist it around your finger. There is no room within the primal cells for your intent to seep in and allow such manipulations. The marshmallow, on the other hand, carrying little charge within the cells, can play host to a far greater bulk of intent, for your intent can wash through the cells almost without hindrance, impressing upon them your desire to manipulate the marshmallow into a variety of shapes.

Taking the rock and the marshmallow, you decide you will work with your hands to make each assume the shape of a pancake. Your intent in both cases is the same. The size of the two objects may be the same. Are you able to render both rock and marshmallow into pancakes within the same amount of time, using the same amount of energy?

The difference lies in how much space each cell of an object carries in addition to its charge. There is much more space within the marshmallow's cells. Therefore, you can feed more spatial intent—more event units expressed in space—into the cells with each passing moment. You therefore accomplish the marshmallow pancake in little time. The "event" of your marshmallow pancake has been expressed principally in space, and little in time.

By contrast, the rock, carrying high charge and virtually no leftover space for your intent to seep in, forces you to play out your intent over a far greater span of time—for there is little free space with which you can work.

Space and time are the parameters through which you express intent. The higher an object's charge, the less leftover space into which your intent can insinuate itself, stretching the event's expression over a greater spread of moments.

While you are working on an object, manipulating it to your design, you are unconsciously impressing upon it the nature of your thoughts and beliefs. All of the material carried in your vibrational matrix, blended into your coordinate, will be imparted to the object you manipulate. Because your nervous system's impulses are transmitted through the spine, they necessarily are imbued with the flavor of your coordinate, and this impression is transmitted to all that you touch.

This level of thought, because it exists above the level of bedrock, is imprinted not within the primal cells, but upon their walls, where only pattern finds expression. The walls of a cell also carry pattern, in addition to that sculpted into the charge. It is this envelope of pattern around a cell that is most susceptible to the vibrational energies carrying the mark and meaning of your coordinate.

The intensity of your thoughts will determine the intensity of your vibrational impression upon an object. If you manipulate an object with little emotion or interest—tying your shoelaces, for example—you leave little imprint. If, on the other hand, you are suffused with emotion as you manipulate an object—preparing a meal for a loved one—your imprint upon an object will be that much stronger. The stronger your emotional and intentional imprint, the greater the rearrangement of the pattern carried in the primal cells' walls—the more it reflects "you."

This explains the sentimental value people place on objects given them as tokens of love, or objects belonging to a family member now dead. The person's intent lives on—quite literally—encoded in the object. Over time, this energy will dissipate, as it is not strengthened by intent on a daily basis, or is altered by the handling of others.

The implications should be obvious. Begin to consciously consider where the objects about you originate, who made them, for what purpose, under what conditions. For all such information is encoded in the objects, and carries potential effects upon you. Further, consider that every object you touch will be imprinted, to however small a degree, with your thoughts at the moment of contact.

Let us observe some ramifications of this process in the everyday world. Which means more to you on your birthday: a store-bought card smudged with a quick signature, or a laboriously constructed, personalized card? Is the intent not the same, to wish you a happy birthday? Yes, but you see how the intensity of the varying intents manifests. Assuming that the cards are the same size, their spatial expression is identical. So any variance in intent must be expressed through time.

Buying a card carrying a rhyme dreamt up by a stranger, with a quick signature on the bottom, takes little time and thought. Sitting at a table with construction paper, scissors, glue, sequins, yarn, and magic markers might require half an hour to render a beautiful card.

Observing the two cards, you unconsciously recognize the intents lying behind their creation. One was created by a stranger for profit, sold by a stranger for profit, to a friend who cared only enough to scrawl a hasty signature and drop it in the mail. The other stands unique in all the universe, an irreplaceable creation designed to celebrate one person's birthday, marking one year's progress, lovingly designed to reflect your personality and interests, tickling your sense of humor.

The key element is love. The greater the love, the more intensely it burns, the more time and effort you are willing to expend—the more time and space you need to fully express your feelings. This is why the home-made card is so precious while the store-bought card leaps straight into the wastebasket. You recognize the intent behind their construction, clinging to the love of one while discarding the thoughtless irrelevance of the other.

If one object were to be selected as the most evocative symbol of your culture, what would it be? The automobile. Yours is a mobile society, always rushing from place to place, to work, to school, to the store. Much of your waking time is spent behind the wheel. Many take more pride in, and lavish more attention upon, their cars than they do upon their families and friends. A car is a symbol of one's inner life, as it represents one's status, one's self-image, and one's place in the culture. Little old ladies drive different models than macho young hot rodders. The poor parade their poverty in beat-up jalopies while the rich trumpet their opulence behind tinted glass and polished chrome. While all objects are symbols, few are so blatantly symbolic as the automobile, for the car you drive marks your place within the culture.

Because you spend so much time behind the wheel, in direct physical contact with the seat, steering wheel, and controls, over time a car will absorb the patterns of your thoughts and beliefs. Because the materials used in a car's construction are so dense and sturdy—therefore, filled with charge—they are impervious to any slight, temporary variations in the occupants' energy fields. For instance, carrying a passenger for a while will have no strong effect upon the human vibration implanted in the car. But, over time, with you consistently at the wheel, the car will quite literally be magnetized in line with your thoughts and beliefs. Your car is not simply your possession. Your car is you.

A brand new car would seem to be free from such influences, for it has known no long-term owner. Yet the process of imprinting intent begins at every level of an object's creation. Cars do not drop from the sky or spring from the earth; they are fashioned from raw materials. Each stage of creation, each hand upon the materials shaping the car, will affect—however slightly—its energy matrix before delivery to the showroom.

There has been some comparison between the quality and repair records of American automobiles versus their Japanese counterparts. Which fall apart more readily; which can drive to the moon and back without a hitch? Searching for the causes of the disparity, you uncover a marked difference in the atmosphere of the two countries' automobile plants. American plants are riven by strife between management and labor, management standing aloof while sewing their golden parachutes, labor viewed as mere cogs in the wheels of progress. Japanese factories are run on a more democratic system, where each worker feels like a member of a family, input is encouraged and appreciated, and a communal sense of solidarity imbues the enterprise from top management to lowest rung.

Who do you think would produce better cars? What is the intent behind all those hands fashioning the raw materials into the car's finished form? Would you rather have your car put together by angry, surly, disgruntled, disparaged, mistrusted workers; or by troops singing their company song at the start of the day, filing in to work together as a family?

Any automobile rolling off the assembly line will already carry a human imprint, for better or worse. Building upon this, over time you imprint your car with your unique thought patterns, literally magnetizing the car.

Because you spend so much time in your car, and because it becomes an extension of you, your car may offer clues reflecting conditions of your inner life that may well be unconscious. A frequently recurring trouble spot may be a clue that a corresponding aspect of your life is in need of attention. Is it the engine—the power, the get-up-and-go, the drive? Is it the brakes—meaning safety, security, rest? Is it the radiator—keeping cool, holding pressure under control? Is it the exhaust system—the elimination of waste and poison? Is it the oil—the lubricant that keeps all parts running smoothly?

We do not mean to suggest that any time a part breaks down in your car, you must immediately run to a psychiatrist and uncover your latent, repressed psychological blocks. Frequently, however, there is a correlation. Many mitigating factors come into play. How long you have owned your car, imprinting your unique vibration over that imparted by its makers, enhances such a relationship. The intensity of your thoughts and feelings while driving will influence the degree to which you affect its functioning. Steaming and fuming in rush hour traffic day after day will carry greater effect than tooling down country lanes without a care. Finally, the extent to which you identify with your car, viewing it as an extension of yourself, will affect the power of your imprint upon it.

The next time you have car trouble, ask yourself if there is not a correlation, a symbolic relationship, between the faulty part and the condition of your life. Feeling frustrated and without direction (engine)? Recklessly charging ahead without thinking through your goals (brakes)? Hot temper, inability to deal with pressure (radiator)? Poisoned by relationships and thoughts you had best leave behind (exhaust)? Unable to integrate the components of your life into smooth harmony (oil)?

Over time, as you magnetize your car in line with your thoughts, in a sense it will come to "depend" on you. We recognize the danger in anthropomorphically projecting human qualities onto bedrock objects. A car is not a pet or an infant. Still, because you magnetize your car with your thought patterns, and because like attracts like, when you slip into the driver's seat, your presence is "welcomed" because it bolsters the extant energy patterns imprinted by you in the past. It confirms and energizes what you imparted before. Each trip you take further energizes your car, making it more "you," and deepening your imprint.

While you may sense a reluctance to lend your car to others, out of fear of what might happen while another is at the wheel, your apprehension more deeply reflects your unconscious knowledge that another cannot be "recognized" by your car. In a sense, although the tank is full of gas, a car driven by another lacks full energy and cohesion because the human intent, upon which the car "depends," is lacking. Have you heard of those whose cars function perfectly for years, only to break down ten minutes after being lent to others? This "coincidence" is largely due to a car's "dependence" on its owner. With the owner's energy lacking, the energy field surrounding the car cannot be recharged or sustained in full strength, and any latent mechanical problem may suddenly find nothing blocking its physical expression.

Your car carries an energy field about it which you recharge and sustain every time you drive. Because bedrock metal's toughness is impervious to temporary alterations in energy, your car cannot suddenly alter its energy field to match that of a new driver. The energy field about the car is weakened. While this should find no immediate deleterious effect, it can carry potential for trouble that the owner would not experience while driving the same course.

Another implication is the importance of evaluating the owner of a used car before you buy it. You are better off probing the psyche of the owner than poking around under the car's hood. Recognize that thoughts are electromagnetic vibration, and that they magnetize objects over a period of time. A car will carry the imprint of its owner. Just as you evaluate a prospective employer on conscious and unconscious levels, so do you benefit from a similar evaluation before buying any second-hand "charged" object like a car or house. The psychically aware can pick up many clues from handling objects, clues about the owners and their inner lives. Magic? Miracle? No, electromagnetism. You charge any object you habitually use or contact. The stronger your thoughts and emotions, the greater the imprint.

We use the example of an automobile because it is so central to your culture. You project your self-image into the car you buy, and over time you magnetize it, imprint it with your personality. The same holds true for all other objects you own. The greater your attachment to them, the longer the time you possess them, the stronger your emotions and thoughts while in contact, the greater will be your imprint.

The implications are twofold: First, recognize that any object strongly imprinted by your thoughts will offer clues as to the nature of your inner life, whether consciously available to you or not. Second, respect that others imprint themselves onto their possessions, and that any transfer to you will carry the force of the prior owner's inner life, carrying potential effects and ramifications on yours.

Every used car salesman knows this. It explains why all their cars were driven by little old ladies only on their way to church each Sunday.

Food is love. The first nourishment you take flows effortlessly into your embryonic potential, floating in its infinite sea of possibility. Sprung from the womb, you suckle at the breast, gazing into the eternal eyes of maternal love. Food flows naturally, gracefully, endlessly, affirming the return to physical life and its boundless horizons of growth, learning, and love. From the first embryonic nourishment, from the first moment at the breast, food is love.

This unconscious understanding, this unspoken symbolism, is never lost. A family gathers for the evening meal, holds hands, and offers a prayer of gratitude for the bounty before them, and for each other. Holidays fraught with divine significance feature lavish feasts replicating the flow of divine love sustaining your world. An angry and misguided parent deprives a child of food, not out of desire to harm the child's growth but as symbolic withdrawal of the breast, severing the bond of love. A lone diner in a restaurant evokes compassion, even pity—for food is meant to be shared with loved ones.

The intent behind food is love. The Source did not cast you upon a hard and barren planet, or a penurious desert island, to watch you squirm and writhe with hunger. Yours is a planet blessed with a munificent cornucopia of foods, miraculously restoring themselves season after season. The perpetual cycles of nature and her limitless bounty reflect the desire of the Source that you shall know Its loving intent to sustain you as you pursue your purpose: to be and to grow.

Where have you gone wrong? Why is the world of food so strewn with dire warnings and threats about the dangers carried in the foods you eat? Why do you attribute so many of your society's most intractable and widespread health problems to your diet?

Food is love. That is the intent behind food. Any alternative intent, any less worthy purpose between a food's creation and its delivery, will diminish its nutritional value.

Any object will be affected by the intent of those handling it. This intent is literally encoded in the walls of the primal cells sustaining the object. The pattern carried in the cell walls will be reconfigured, magnetized in line with the intent and thoughts of those handling the object.

All food is bedrock. All food is susceptible to the imprint of others as they handle it. This imprint cannot help but affect a food's nutritional content—for better or worse—before it reaches your plate.

When you enter a supermarket, do you feel loved? Have the rows and rows of standard, uniform, quality-controlled boxes and jars been created out of loving intent to sustain you, out of appreciation for your divine, unique spark? Are you greeted with hugs and kisses at the checkout line? Do you feel exhilarated, recharged, energized by your visit to that purveyor of love and nutrition, driving from the parking lot singing a hymn of gratitude?

You are a stranger in a supermarket. The rows and rows of boxes and jars that greet your eyes are the same rows and rows greeting every other customer from coast to coast. You do not exist in the eyes of those who manufacture your food; you are unknown, anonymous, a consumer, a statistic, but nothing more. A checkout clerk greeting you may smile in recognition and offer "hello," but if your wallet is stretched a bit thin, would the clerk treat you as family and bag your groceries anyway?

Food is no longer love. Food is profit. Food is created by strangers in distant places, stripped of variety and uniqueness, ground into uniformity, poured into colorful boxes and jars, dangled before you like a worm on a hook.

Your body, even if overweight, is undernourished. The nexus between food and body, love, has been cut out of the picture. Your cells cannot maintain full vitality. The earth, seen as boundless love at the breast, now seems cold and indifferent. The body's desire to race free and vital from first breath to last weakens, retreating from its tight embrace of life's potential. Why expend full, vibrant energy in a world that knows no love?

You attribute many of your health problems to additives, preservatives, artificial coloring and flavoring, and the like. In deepest terms, no such links exist. Restricting yourselves to the physical world, you force a causal relationship where none exists. The truth lies deeper. What is the purpose of a preservative? Is it to buoy your body's health and explorations? Or is it to enhance shelf life of the product, ensuring greater profits for the manufacturer?

The intent behind lacing food with preservatives is to increase profit. Love and profit do not mix; they are like oil and water. When food is manipulated with profit as the overriding motive, the "love" intent is sullied. When food is colored with dye to entice your eye, laced with flavorings to fool your tongue, the intent is not to love but to deceive. When the uniqueness of each ear of corn, stalk of wheat, golden apple, grain of rice, is not cherished and appreciated, but ground into quality-controlled uniformity, a loving appreciation for the earth's bounty is lost, replaced with avarice.

How is "love" encoded in the cells of a foodstuff? "Love" respects diversity, upholds freedom, and fosters growth. All of these attributes are encoded in the pattern of a primal cell's wall, configured to link most efficiently with the cells of the person or animal ingesting the food. A healthy individual, and a natural, unsullied food, carry virtually identical pattern in the walls of their primal cells. This allows the food to link with the body in the most efficient way possible, sparking the maximum energy, raising the vitality of the body, spurring it on to new growth.

To the extent that food has been sullied with motives other than love, the pattern carried in the food's cells will be altered. There is less commonality between the food and a body, less mutual configuration which can link and spark efficient utilization of the food and new growth. The more the food has been sullied by motives like avarice and prolonged shelf life, the greater the alteration to the cells' pattern: the less "love" is offered to the body.

Unconsciously, you recognize this. But as your culture grants validity only to the physically perceivable, restricting itself to the lowest level of event, it wrenches causal relationships where none exist. You find your bodies falling apart, prey to cancer, heart disease, obesity, hypoglycemia, high blood pressure, AIDS. You search for causes among the symbolic shards of truth carried by your senses, and point the accusing finger at bleached flour, white sugar, preservatives, additives, processed and packaged products, and fast food.

No such causal relationships exist, in deepest terms. For it cannot be honestly stated that eating a given food will, without exception, lead to a given breakdown in the body. Since the essence of scientific law is a given cause leading to a given effect, without variance or exception, it defies even the limited understanding of science to claim a causal relationship between food and your health problems.

Unconsciously recognizing that there is some link, but thrashing about on the level of symbol, the best you can do is to proclaim red meat the cause of heart disease, and preservatives the couriers of cancer.

The underlying connection between processed foods and disease is this: there is no love in such foods. The Source's intent, that food revitalize and nourish your bodies, is absent, ground out by automation and packaging in search of profit. The cells of your body are not nourished as they should be. Over time, their cohesion, their strength, and their vitality weaken. This can provide an opening, a foothold, to a condition seeking expression as illness.

Remember the fundamental importance of belief in creating the events of your life. If you believe that certain foods are harmful, what belief underlies this view? That your body is not under your control, a projection of your mind, but is instead a helpless pawn in the random chess game of existential meaninglessness. You do not trust your body's resilience, you do not hear its harmony, you do not absorb its wisdom. You do not know your body. It is a stranger to you, a sack of flesh and bone carrying your brain from place to place.

Because you do not know your body, and cannot hear its wisdom, you assume it to be mute and helpless. In the cold, dark, cruel Darwinian world of natural selection, it exists solely to toss your genes into the generational lottery, then collapse and decay.

With such beliefs lying behind your view of the body, you are highly susceptible to any suggestions of the body's weakness and helplessness. Cirrhosis from alcohol! Cancer from sodium nitrate! High blood pressure from salt! Hypoglycemia from sugar!

You are at the mercy of nothing, nothing except that which you choose to believe and find faithfully manifested in your body. Your body is a symbol, a symbol of your inner life. It is the "slowest" of your four vibrational bodies, a symbol of your private truth. When you believe it susceptible to breakdown and decay, helpless against the attack of virus and carcinogen, you roll out the red carpet for those conditions to appear.

This may appear to contradict our recent material, in which we outlined the extent to which you are influenced by the energies of others, and the energies imprinted on objects by others. Indeed, our point is that food is literally sullied and deprived of nourishment to the extent it is processed for profit. But there is a vast difference between acknowledging the influence of outside energies and the expression of your beliefs in the symbol of your body. The buck stops at the skin. Your body is your private creation. It is the reflection of your soul. It is your spirit in flesh. It is a mirror of your inner life.

Simply eating foods sullied with avarice, weakening love's intent, is insufficient to cause any breakdown in the body. Your body is far too resilient for that. There are many who eat what modern thought would consider to be atrocious diets, and they sail through life without a hint of ailment. In such cases, while a more "natural" diet might spark even greater vitality, the individual's body still retains enough cohesion and exuberance to sustain all adventures.

Remember that the body is the slowest of your four vibrational bodies, the one most cloaked in symbol. Bedrock foods, which you consume to sustain the body, are also largely symbol. It is the imprint of your thoughts and beliefs, sizzling at far higher frequencies, that carries much greater impact on your body's condition. An exuberant embrace of life, an appreciation for the body and its delicious sensations, is far more important to sustaining health than counting out roughage by the gram. Your body simply reflects the higher levels of vibration from which it flows. Starting at the top, your thoughts and beliefs "trickle down" to find corporal expression. One who loves and cherishes life's precious moments, while eating a diet of earthworms and slugs, will enjoy far better health than the morose guardian of existential angst, munching on tofu and sprouts.

When you divide the world into "good" and "bad" foods, you assert the fallibility of your body, its natural inclination to disease and decay. When you fear a world of carcinogens rampaging through your body, threatening tumors from head to toe, you grant permission for such tumors to sprout.

Although food's loving intent can be sullied and bruised by others, by far the most significant imprint is that imparted by you while you eat. Your beliefs have an electromagnetic reality. When you eat a food while believing it to carry harm, you literally "coat" the food with your belief as it enters the body. If you bring an ice cream cone to your lips while thinking, "Ice cream is so fattening," then you imprint that belief onto the ice cream's cells. You literally alter the electromagnetic pattern such that the cells find it easier to be converted to fat cells, rather than digested and passed on without effect.

Even when you allow yourself to eat only "good" foods, you still assert the body's weakness and susceptibility to disease and decay. For you choose "good" foods not so much out of appreciation for their qualities, but out of fear that "bad" foods will hurt you. The fear, itself a powerful burst of intent, imprints even "good" foods with the belief that the body is frail and weak. As ye believe, so shall ye find.

The growing emphasis on natural, whole foods reflects your unconscious recognition that food is love, that it should be unsullied and unadulterated, springing directly from the earth to your stomach. The more "natural" a food is, the less it has been handled and altered for profit, the more it will retain its natural loving imprint, its ability to link with your body's cells in the most efficient way possible. Raw fruits and vegetables, whole grains, unprocessed rice and beans, carry little damage to their intent to sustain you. They are most easily absorbed by the body, sparking its energy and vitality.

You call this revolution in eating habits a return to "natural foods." The original, primal, fundamental food of the universe is love. Gathering fruits, vegetables, and grains from the earth, fashioning them out of love for self and family into tasteful and aesthetically pleasing meals, restores you to the "natural" meaning of food. What intent lies behind those who create your food—love for you or love of profit? Which do you find easier to swallow?

A more comprehensive overview of the body and the battleground of food in your society will be offered later in this book. Our intent now is to trigger your thinking and awareness, nudging you toward a deeper under-standing of the world about you and how it operates. Any object—a birth-day card, an automobile, a breakfast cereal—will be imprinted by the intent of those handling it. The degree of imprint depends upon the con-struction of the material (the denser an object, the more impervious to imprint), the length of time it is handled, and the intensity of the thoughts and beliefs of those involved. This discussion should not evoke fear, fear of your susceptibility to others, but should simply spark an awareness, a recognition of how the world is constructed and influenced by your species.

You need not fear that every fast-food cheeseburger you swallow plants banners in your cells proclaiming, "Tumors Wanted—Apply Here." But knowing that the natural intent behind food is love, and that your body is more vital and exuberant when suffused with loving intent, would you choose over time to eat your meals on the run, purchased from strangers seeking profit, or take the time to fashion your own meals from natural, whole ingredients? Which would you rather feed to your chil-dren?

This is the consciously lived life, the recognition of the principles lying beneath the physical world, a respect for the power of beliefs and thoughts, and the conscious choice to live life at its highest, healthiest pitch.

Thirty-Two

℘

Memory

What is memory?

All animals, whatever their degree of consciousness, possess memory. For memory is the basis of rational thought, and any organism must "reason" to survive. It must distinguish between harm and succor, food and poison, life and death. At the most rudimentary level, memory is the recognition of conditions experienced previously, coupled with a judgment as to the effect of experiencing those conditions. A "negative" experience will be actively avoided. A "positive" experience will be pursued.

Remember that any experienced event is split in the brain into two components of sense data and interpretation. As incoming vibration is transmitted from the sense organs to the brain, the brain immediately interprets the vibration, based upon experience. A given sight, sound, tactile sensation, taste, or smell will be reduced to an electrical matrix of impulse, an electromagnetic configuration unique to the specific triggering stimulus. This energy matrix is then linked with the universal "library" of all such matrices to determine "what is it?" Once the vibration is recognized, it travels along neuronal pathways, constructed by belief, to link with a corresponding interpretation.

Incoming vibration is compared with similar previous experience, as a way of determining the potential effect the environmental conditions hold. Memory serves as the storehouse of experience, from which are drawn interpretive analyses bearing on one's present condition.

The "higher" an organism is in the hierarchy of reason, the more sophisticated its memory. Insects live largely on instinct, and while they can learn to avoid certain conditions and seek others, their capacity for conscious recall is virtually nil. The neuronal structures simply do not exist to allow for a greater depth of recall and evaluation.

As the human species' unique filter is a rational mind, it stands to reason that human memory is more sophisticated than in any other terrestrial organism. For you need not have a given set of conditions before you in order to trigger similar remembered experiences. Merely daydreaming can trigger a free association of memory. Another asking you about an experience can trigger it to consciousness, though it carries no bearing on your immediate situation.

The greater the brain's capacity, and the more complex the neuronal pathways within it, the more sophisticated the power of memory will be. The human memory stands supreme above all other terrestrial animals, for as yours is the specialized power of reason, yours must also be the ability to recall, sift, and evaluate your store of memories with precision and sophistication unknown to the earth's other creatures.

Memories—the actual records of events—are not stored within the brain. Instead, the parts of the brain responsible for processing memory consist of the neuronal networks between sense data and interpretation. Each such pathway has a terminus in the interpretive side of the brain, and each terminus acts like a magnet when stimulated, pulling a given memory down from superconscious thought to conscious awareness.

Every experience of your life is recorded electromagnetically as sense data and interpretation. While you enjoy physical life, each experienced event is recorded and stored in your coordinate. When a new situation demands that all associative memories be brought to conscious awareness, the energy matrix representing the incoming vibration is linked with memories holding similar configuration. These associations are then pulled from memory storage into consciousness. With the background material in mind, you can evaluate and interpret the present experience in line with your past.

Memories are not stored in the brain. They stand apart from the electrical whir and buzz of the brain's activity. Only when triggered by external stimuli, or your thoughts, are they pulled from storage and presented to conscious awareness.

At the point of death, the brain and its neuronal networks cease functioning. Your store of memory is released from the coordinate, vibrant and vital as your first breath, and free to imprint the universal ledger with your life's story.

Memory is the reverse of the process by which incoming sense data is perceived. Your present condition is fed to you as sense data, which travels neuronal pathways to find interpretation in line with your beliefs. Memory begins as electromagnetic storage, attracted toward consciousness by the pull of the interpretive side of the brain, and is then reduced, in the mind, to the experience of sense data. When a memory is triggered, you recall the place, the environmental conditions, your mood and actions.

The superconscious memory is drawn down to the level of object and experience, painted in the brain as sense data.

Whether incoming sense data is triggering interpretation, or memory is being drawn down to reexperienced sense data, the process is filtered through belief. Your belief screen stands as the middleman between sense data and interpretation, throwing switches and triggering associations colored by your beliefs. As each fresh experience is channeled to the interpretative lobe along the pathways etched by belief, so are memories triggered most easily along the existing pathways.

More, those memories brought to recall will be reinterpreted by the condition of your present belief screen. An event evoking sheer terror at age five may now provoke guffaws of laughter as you recall your fright at the shadows on the wall in a dark and monster-filled bedroom. The original interpretation of the event is lost; the sense data is reinterpreted in line with your current worldview.

Just as perception is selectively colored by belief, so is memory similarly brought to awareness. Your belief screen filters out memories incompatible with its worldview, allowing passage only to those memories confirming and enhancing that worldview.

You may believe that you had a miserable, lonely childhood, neglected by your parents, taunted by your classmates, ridiculed and ignored by your teachers. Built upon these memories will be a belief screen viewing the world as a dreary, threatening, hostile place, a preview of hell while on earth, holding the miserable human race and its terrors of rejection and scorn. You justify such a worldview by pointing to your miserable childhood, holding this as irrefutable proof of the correctness of your outlook, confirmation of the human race's intrinsic depravity.

Now, wasn't there even one occasion—one occasion?—when you experienced kindness from others as a child? When your views were listened to and thoughtfully considered by others? When you were shown love and affection? Not even once?

If such memories are allowed any conscious recall at all, they are dismissed as irrelevant, isolated incidents, in no way refuting your worldview. The neuronal pathways do not exist to allow such memories to play out in full strength, forcing air and light into your worldview's shuttered gloom. For if such memories were allowed full expression, they would threaten the validity of the worldview, forcing a reconsideration, a more balanced evaluation of the peaks and valleys of childhood. Because the status quo is the most comfortable—and the most efficient—place to be, a belief screen will resist any meddlesome tampering by memories contradicting its stance. Such memories, if recalled at all, are summarily dismissed.

Each new experience will be split into sense data and interpretation through the extant belief screen—life is miserable, people are awful—thus seeming to confirm the selectively recalled events of your childhood, bolstering your worldview. Perception and memory travel along a two-way street, passing through the belief screen controlling the flow of traffic. When neither perception nor memory challenges the belief screen, each passing day further cements it into place, confirms and justifies the correctness of its vision, ignoring and dismissing any distracting, contradictory data.

Another individual experiencing an identical childhood could hold a worldview that people are basically good, though prone to impatience and sharp words. Another could selectively recall the events of warmth, tenderness, and affection, dismissing the trauma with a quick, "Yes, there were some bad moments," before returning to a worldview holding life and the human race as proof of God's love and mercy.

You can never recall every moment, every incident, of your life's experience. Your conscious mind can hold in awareness only a tiny fraction of the past when evaluating your present and future. The memories triggered to awareness will be those compatible with your worldview, filtered through your belief screen.

Not only do you create your present and future through your beliefs, you also create your past. You cannot recall every moment. You carry shards and fragments, and proclaim them your life history. Which fragments you carry about will be determined by your beliefs. They will seem to confirm your beliefs, your overall worldview, when in fact it is the worldview that determines which events are available for recall.

Further, recalled events are reinterpreted through your present belief screen. If forced to recall an event incompatible with your worldview by the queries of another, the recalled event may be squeezed through the belief screen and emerge as not contradicting your worldview, but confirming it. Your worldview of life as hostile and threatening will flavor your recall of moments of tenderness and warmth, casting in doubt the motives of those offering kindness, suspecting them of cynically jockeying for advantage or other base designs.

If unquestioned and unexamined, your belief screen will interpret fresh experience along the same lines, seeming to confirm your interpretation of the past. This cycle can be vicious or sublime, either confirming a negative worldview and drawing in future negativity, or confirming that the world is a luminous crucible of divine harmony, attracting future events of refulgent joy.

The purpose of memory is to enable you to chart a clear course through life, instantly able to analyze a situation in line with your previous experience. Memory is the foundation of reason.

Memories are triggered most easily along the neuronal pathways etched by belief, linking sense data with interpretation. Your beliefs flavor and color your memories, determining which will reach conscious recall. As perception is selective, so is memory. You remember what you want to remember, those events confirming your worldview.

You create your reality through your beliefs. You create your past through your beliefs, building up an association of events confirming your worldview. Change your beliefs—alter your belief screen—and you alter your past, drawing into awareness events long forgotten. More, each recalled event will be reinterpreted in line with your new beliefs, the sense data sent charging down new neuronal pathways to find fresh interpretation, further altering your belief screen.

You create your life's history through your beliefs.

Thirty-Three

౨

Fear

From the smorgasbord of emotions pumping through body and soul, few carry the intensity, the power, and the physiological impact of fear. Like any emotional state, fear is the surface expression of a deep and tangled web of beliefs, whose many strands stand snarled, blocking sight of their ultimate source.

What are the physiological responses to fear? The heart quickens; adrenaline cascades through the blood; the body's "fight or flight" potentials are activated. Perception is heightened, each strand of incoming vibration seized upon and milked dry of every drop of information it carries.

Clearly, the core belief standing behind the physiological reactions is this: "My body is in danger." Its security, its integrity, its desire to live free and whole, are threatened. The body prepares for fight or flight: either a superhuman resistance to the perceived danger or an accelerated retreat.

In the specific instance of actual physical threat to the body, "fear" is the set of physiological responses to perceived danger. In such a situation, the responses are justified and necessary. They aid you, in heightened awareness, strength, and mobility, in keeping your body safe and unmolested. This is *genuine fear*. Genuine fear is your body's reaction to a clear and present danger to its integrity, stimulating enhancement of its normal strength and capabilities.

One of the most damaging, and most prevalent, abuses of your body's miraculous response-ability is *anticipatory fear*. This occurs when you trigger the body's "fight or flight" reactions when no clear and present danger threatens its integrity. Your society is drowning under a sea of anticipatory fears, worrying about nuclear war, environmental catastrophe, global instability, the collapse of the economy, the corruption of politicians—all the growing fissures threatening to sunder the foundations of Western civilization. Fear—for your health, your safety, your job, your children, your nation, your world—grips you from opening your eyes to the morning headlines until you again seek the sweet release of sleep.

Fear's damage is twofold. It springs from an unconscious, unexamined, skewed matrix of belief about the nature of reality, and it eats like a corrosive at the symbiotic partnership of body and mind. Let us examine this in detail.

Genuine fear springs from the belief that "My body is in danger." Incoming visual, aural, and tactile information feeds to the brain a message of impending threat to the body's security. The brain responds by triggering an avalanche of hormones into the blood, infusing muscle with sudden strength, boosting oxygen efficiency, accelerating the heart rate. Fight or flight—you stand ready.

Consider what happens when you read a newspaper article or book about the dangers of nuclear war and its aftermath. Your eyes are drinking in vibration—the symbols of written speech—which carries a message of potential bodily harm. You react with fear. What is fear, again? The belief that your body is in immediate danger. So your brain responds with its instinctive reaction to perceived threat—triggering physiological responses designed to enhance your ability to fight or flee.

Yet you sit on a sofa in the comfort of your home. Where is the clear and present danger? Who threatens you? No one. So the body and mind are left confused. On the one hand, you are drinking in vibration informing you of great potential bodily danger; yet when the body reacts appropriately, it finds its reaction to be groundless. The hormones, the strength, the efficiency, are never pressed into service. Rather than finding quick release, healthy release, they dissipate slowly, lingering in the vague atmosphere of fear your reading evokes.

Over time, the normally clear channel between body and mind is clouded. The mind begins to doubt the verity of the body's sensations. Then, when the mind reacts to an imagined threat by triggering a physical response, the body cannot dissipate the hormonal alarm in quick bursts of action, but dribbles it gradually, pointlessly, from the blood. The body, possessed of its own consciousness, sends the message that the mind is in err to have triggered such a response. Where body and mind are meant to work in matrimonial harmony, now they stand apart, regarding each other warily, lacking full trust in each other. The mind questions the validity of the vibrational sensations fed to it by the body's organs. The body resents the mind's irrelevant screams of alarm when no danger threatens. The smooth symbiosis becomes a cold and suspicious standoff.

The implications of this are enormous. For fear's corrosive shredding of the mind-body channel washes over into all emotional states. Any time your body drinks in vibration, your mind must pause to question and verify its validity. Any time the mind seeks to trigger a physiological response in line with its beliefs, the body resists the urgent entreaties, having suffered too many false alarms. Where body and mind were originally designed to carry you through life on two sturdy legs, now you hobble on crutches.

The atmosphere of fear, which hangs over your society like a noxious miasma, poisons your mind and body, sowing seeds of discontent between them, blunting and crippling your full experience of life's emotional richness.

Since all emotions are physiological responses triggered in line with your beliefs, let us follow the strands of belief leading down to the core belief giving rise to fear.

Genuine fear is a response to an immediate, present danger. Anticipatory fear triggers the same physiological reactions in response to an imagined danger occurring sometime in the future. So the first element of anticipatory fear is: "I believe this event may take place in the future." You do not fear what can never happen, only those events which you believe to be within the realm of possibility.

The next step in the belief matrix is this: "I believe the event carries potential danger to my life." Fear is always a response to threat, so anticipatory fear carries the belief that one stands to be harmed by the event's expression—physically or otherwise.

The next step in the belief matrix is this: "I am powerless to escape the event's expression." You believe you can do nothing but passively await the event's inevitable crash through the roof. What can one measly human being do to prevent nuclear war? Nothing, you believe. You feel powerless, helpless to prevent the expression of what you fear.

And whence arises this belief in one's powerlessness? Now we toss aside the last few spadefuls of belief, exhuming the ghastly specter, the sorrow and terror of the ages, the worm-eaten curse of the millennia: "*I do not create my own reality.*" Embedded deep and hidden within the layers of belief upon which your culture is built, seeding and fueling its religious, scientific, and political schools of thought, lies the final, irreducible core belief: "I do not create my own reality."

This is fear's genesis. This is the foundation of the Era of Unconscious Life. This belief colors every aspect of your culture. From it spring pantheons of gods and demons—Zeus, Jehovah, God—all reigning over the earth with firm, unsparing, and capricious hands. Modern science builds its "factual" hierarchies of knowledge on this belief, postulating haphazard evolution, vicious natural selection, and the universe's birth in a random and accidental explosion of hydrogen. Politics feeds upon and reinforces this fear, as the populace begs the government to take control over its lives, and those in power happily oblige.

You live in fear. Fear of God, before Whom you throw yourselves, begging for mercy—or fear of living in the atheist's meaningless wasteland. Fear of science's marvels and wonders—nuclear weapons, toxic wastes, genetic engineering, a vanishing ozone layer. Fear of poverty, illness, and aging in a hostile and cruel world, forcing you to sacrifice liberty for the paternal protection of government.

You see, fear is not the measured, appropriate response to a world in crisis. Fear is the cause of the crisis. Fear feeds the crisis. For any fear is based upon the core belief that one does not create one's own reality. This violates the fundamental nature of reality, upon which all else is based. You do create your own reality. There is no other rule.

Beyond the damage to the mind-body channel, beyond the fearful worldview so at odds with the truth, fear carries a further harm: *You create what you fear.* Remember that all potential events of your life, and of your society and world, already exist. They hang suspended in the realms beyond space and time, awaiting the proper moment of physical expression. As they near expression in time, those probable versions most in line with the condition of your thoughts and beliefs—private or communal—will be pulled into expression.

When you fear a potential event, you automatically carry the belief that the event is likely to occur. This, in itself, pulls the feared version of the event closer to expression. Further, by concentrating on the event, triggering physiological reactions in expectation of its manifestation and repeatedly playing it out in your mind, you energize that probable version most in line with your fears. Mind and body work in tandem, building a powerful grid of energy around the expectation of what you fear.

You create your reality through your beliefs. When you so energize a probable event through worry, fear, and bodily distress, you act as a lighthouse boring its welcoming shaft through the fog, guiding the feared event home to safe harbor in your life's experience.

Once the feared event finds manifestation, you take this as confirmation of the appropriateness of your fear—it happened, just as I expected—and the mechanism is strengthened; the matrix of thought and belief with which you pull feared events into your experience is rewarded and empowered. Afraid of illness? Afraid of abandonment? Afraid of rejection? Afraid of poverty? Afraid of attack? Afraid of cancer? Afraid of nuclear war? Afraid of failure?

You create what you fear. In perverse self-immolation, the mind-body symbiosis—created for the purpose of charting a safe and healthy course through life—is turned against your happiness and fulfillment, employed to energize those events you most fear, pulling them to physical fruition.

There are no judgments, no sense of "good" and "bad," beyond your private interpretation of events. When you find fears physically materializing, you are viewing yourself in a mirror, observing the physical reflection of your inner life. This is your power, your freedom, your gift. It can also be your curse, your bane—but all such judgments remain on your level of experience.

The universe works for you, not against you. Its fundamental energy is joy, not sorrow. It is far easier to experience the positive versions of events than the negative. Yet you carry always the freedom to override the universe's basic warm support, experiencing instead the cold, dark press of fearful events against you in the night.

Because anticipatory fears all spring from the core belief that one does not create one's own reality, all such fears are, by definition, irrational. Reason is the human species' unique and precious filter through which earthly life is experienced. To believe that one's fate is in the hands of others, or—even worse—in the hands of no one, is to shatter the sturdy foundation of reason, toppling it into the quicksand of random meaninglessness. You cannot chart a clear and healthy course through life when you do not believe yours is the power to create your life. The more plentiful and vibrant are your fears, the greater the blow to reason, and the more you stagger about in blind panic, drawing painful events to yourself and perpetuating the vicious cycle of fear begetting trauma begetting fear.

Fear corrodes the bond between mind and body. Fear flows from a fundamental contradiction of truth, the belief that one does not create one's own reality. Fear is, by definition, irrational, robbing you of reason.

Private fears lead to private miseries. Communal fears lead to a world in crisis.

Part Five

CONSCIOUS LIFE

Thirty-Four

୬

A New Creation Myth

In this final section of our book, we turn from the theoretical to the practical. It is all well and good to explain physical universe construction, how human consciousness is seeded into the earthly medium, the nature of events, and the power of mind in creating one's life experiences. But how do these principles translate into everyday life? How can one utilize them to create health, wealth, and wisdom, or any other worthy goal?

The fundamental message of this book, upon which all conscious life rests, is that you create your reality through your thoughts and beliefs. Herein lies the key to unlocking your power to consciously fashion your life's events. Conscious life begins not with a voyage to the stars but with an inner journey, traveling the corridors of belief upon which your worldview is built, determining which paths lead through the swamps and quicksand of outdated dogma, and which glow with the radiant luminescence of truth.

Earlier, in our belief screen quiz, we began the process of challenging you to examine your beliefs, with an eye toward determining which remain valid in light of your new understanding and which are rooted in old-order belief systems no longer valid. For to effect lasting and salubrious change, you must examine your belief system down to its very core, its most basic fundamentals. Merely changing surface beliefs by suddenly affirming their opposites—"Okay, there is no God separate and apart from me"—is insufficient to realize enduring change. You must dig deeper, past the many layers of belief built up over the centuries and inculcated from your first breath, down to the axioms upon which all religious, scientific, and social schools of thought are based.

Such work can be painful. Remember that the brain resists attempts to forge new networks of belief, for it is more efficient, and more comfortable, to process incoming data along existing neuronal corridors. A deliberate overriding of your extant belief structures will therefore meet with some initial resistance, as the brain fights altering its comfortable neuronal networks. Over time, however, as your conscious and deliberate work overrides the brain's resistance and installs a higher level of truth as your operating core vibration, you will feel an eagerness to absorb and process information along the new belief networks—for the "higher" your core vibration, the more efficiently your brain operates. And since the brain is wired to process information as efficiently as possible, it will come to welcome your explorations into higher levels of truth and understanding.

Again, merely changing surface beliefs while leaving underlying core beliefs untouched cannot bring about the revolution leading to a fully conscious life. So let us first examine the core beliefs upon which Western culture is based.

The fundamental theme threading its way through all areas of Western culture is *separation*, isolation. Humanity is separate from God. Humanity is separate from nature. The mind is separate from the body. The natural world is a seething battlefield of competition and survival of the fittest.

This theme is so deeply rooted in Western culture as to be virtually invisible. Yet it fuels both religious and scientific fields, even while those in both camps staunchly defend the veracity of their beliefs and condemn the godless rationalism, or gauzy-eyed mysticism, of the other.

For example, observe the creation myths promulgated by the religious and scientific communities. Every human culture devises a creation myth in line with its beliefs, a symbolic, mythological explanation of how the world and its creatures came to be. Such a creation myth will always interweave its culture's fundamental beliefs about the spiritual forces beyond the earthly plane, the human race's position and importance in the grand scheme, and the purpose and meaning of life on earth.

Because Western culture is riven into opposing camps of science and religion, it has sprouted two starkly discordant creation myths. The Judeo-Christian creation myth outlined in the Bible's first book posits a God, a Being separate from humanity, existing before the universe's first atom danced to life. God created the universe, created humanity, and gave it dominion over the natural world.

Immediately, then, the theme of separation is woven into the myth: humanity apart from nature. Further, when Adam and Eve eat the fruit of the forbidden tree of knowledge, a cat-and-mouse game ensues, in which they try to hide from God's sight while God searches for His fallen creatures so as to expel them from the Garden and condemn all succeeding generations to carry Adam and Eve's sin as their own. Immediately, from the first, humanity is separated from God, from the spiritual force presiding over the world's creation. This creation myth neatly contains both humanity's separation from God and its separation from nature.

Science posits a Big Bang, in which all the matter of the universe lay latent in a tiny ball, which upon exploding flung the primal material to the far reaches of the cosmos—creating the cosmos in the process—and set into motion the expanding universe, at some point to reach the apex of its expansion and contract toward apocalyptic collapse. Just by chance, the third planet from the nearest star happened to contain conditions conducive to life, to animate beings inexplicably endowed with consciousness, who over the millennia evolved from single-celled sea organisms to larger aquatic animals, until one or several species hopped onto land and began the long march toward the emergence of humanity, the very pinnacle of earthly life.

This evolutionary process was governed by random genetic mutation and survival of the fittest, the earth's seas and forests host to furious competition between and within all species, with reproduction the sole motive for existence. In this scenario, humanity evolved from the apes and is, therefore, the "highest" form of life, separated from nature by its magnificent brain, standing above and apart from all other earthly creatures and their inferior intellects.

It is a fine irony that science—the guardian of "reason"—should hatch a creation myth as patently irrational and ludicrous as one requiring all the matter of the universe to squeeze into a tiny ball. Science is forced to such absurd lengths in order to squeeze any possibility of spiritual influence or design out of its creation myth. Yet notice that the Big Bang myth carries the same result as the Genesis myth: Humanity is separate from nature—it has evolved from the primordial slime to stand as the highest creation of "evolution"—and separate from God—for, in science's scenario, there is no God.

Science and religion, for all their surface differences, weave creation myths reflecting the deeper theme of Western culture from which they both spring. This is one small example of the process we urge on you now, to dig deeper than the mere surface and begin to appreciate that the most fundamental beliefs fueling your religious, scientific, and social realms are just that—*beliefs*. As such, to the extent they block your apprehension of higher truth, they prevent you from stepping fully into a consciously lived life.

As the first step on your journey toward such a conscious life, let us summarize and reaffirm our perspective on the meaning of your existence—our creation myth, if you will.

You are a part of the Source, never apart from the Source. You float securely in the eternal seas of intent fueling your world's journey through time and space. No good works are required to win the Source's favor; no banishment to the depths of hell awaits those who transgress universal law: for you are of the Source, in the Source, by the fact of your existence. No wall, no boundary, no pearly gate stands between you and the Source of your being. You are the Source.

Strung between sun and moon, water planet Earth plays host to a glorious profusion of life. Each species represents a unique slant or focus, a flavor or twist, through which the Source spills Its intent to explore Itself and Its world in as broad a variety as the earth can sustain. Each species carries its unique focus while contributing to the health, vitality, and growth of the larger world. Each is an integral strand in the finely knit web of life sewn into the larger fabric of mountain, forest, plain, and sea. For the earth carries its own consciousness; the earth is itself a living organism, both dependent upon and contributing to the multitudinous species swarming upon its rocky flesh. The earth is alive.

You spring from a family of consciousness taking a particular slant on human life. Your greater entity oversees all your reincarnational experiences, searching the grand historical sweep for those times and places most conducive to its fulfillment. You are who and where you are because your greater entity chose to enjoy life through the miracle of your flesh, poised in your time and place, standing utterly unique and irreplaceable as one final, irreducible expression of intent and desire. On levels unseen, your every thought and action reverberate throughout the cosmos, echoing your uniqueness and etching your life's story in the ledger of the universe.

Unknown to your species before the present age (save among the most enlightened), the human race has always carried the ultimate power and responsibility: to create its own reality, to find its beliefs and thoughts miraculously reflected in the experiences of the flesh. Through the millennia this power has remained hidden; personal power was projected onto hierarchies of gods, the forces of nature, the vicissitudes of fate, accident, and serendipity.

Now you stand at the dawn of a new age, as the veil masking your true source and power evaporates like morning mist under the sun's amber heat, and you behold what you have always known but pretended to forget. The physical world is symbol, a reflection of deeper unseen truths, the intersection of flesh and spirit. You experience a linear flow of moments on a seemingly bedrock earth, yet both space and time are illusions.

Here lies your power, for all "events" of ancient "past" and distant "future" lie latent, now, awaiting activation and physical expression through the force of thought and belief. Your desires, your fantasies, your hopes are not simply the stuff of idle daydreams; they are realities, existing now, there for the plucking. To you falls the power and responsibility of ripening those events most conducive to your fulfillment, then harvesting the fruits of your effort.

There is no divorce between you and the Source; you are the Source. There is no divorce between you and nature; you are nature. You are never alone, but stand forever as a unique and irreplaceable strand in the web of life upon your planet. You are divine. You are unique. You are eternal.

It is no accident that you live in this time and place, playing your part in the transition between the Era of Unconscious Life and the Era of Conscious Life. Before you now lies the choice to slough off the demeaning, belittling, life-scorning dogmas of yesteryear, and embrace instead your birthright, the power to create your own reality.

This, we offer, is the true source and meaning of your life. In which do you choose to believe: the Garden of Eden, the Big Bang, or Conscious Life?

Thirty-Five

֍

Affirmation

We will return later to the process of digging through layers of belief to determine which hinder your growth and fulfillment, but now we turn to an examination of the tools and processes used in conscious life creation.

The centerpiece of conscious life creation is a daily time set aside for the express purpose of using the tools we will soon outline. Just as you plan times to eat meals, go to work, pick up the kids from school, or exercise, it is important that a specific block of time be set aside each day to consciously create your life's tone and future events. This block of time need not be lengthy; as little as five minutes will suffice.

The importance of a consistent daily session is that it sends the message to all levels of mind and spirit that this routine—conscious life creation—carries as much weight as every other aspect of your life, if not more. Treating it cavalierly, once in a while when you can grab ten minutes, doesn't carry nearly as much significance as a regular, consistent routine of effort.

Each session must be conducted in a time and place when you are assured of being undisturbed for the duration. For you must create a state of deep relaxation and be able to maintain this state for the whole of the session. If you are familiar with meditation or self-hypnosis, you already have a comfortable method of inducing deep relaxation. If you have no favorite technique, we offer the following:

Sit in a comfortable chair or lie on the floor. Your clothes should be loose, nowhere binding or pinching the skin. Close your eyes. Begin drawing deep breaths, breaths that fill your lungs to their fullest. Release each breath slowly, calmly, allowing it to gently flow through your nostrils or mouth. After ten such deep breaths, start the process of relaxation. Beginning with your feet, focus on each part of the body and mentally tell yourself that this part is now relaxing, relaxing, relaxing. Feel the tension draining from your body into the floor, leaving the body warm and tingling. Move up through your legs, your hips, your abdomen, your chest, your arms, your face, your scalp, and your brain. Take as much time as you feel necessary to ensure that each body portion is thoroughly relaxed; *feel* the waves of relaxation as they soothingly envelop you.

At the procedure's end you should feel a tingling, vibrant alertness. You are not falling asleep, you see; you are actually heightening your mind's alertness by releasing its concern for the body. Your mind should be alert and vital, while your body rests in blissful relaxation.

Let us consider for a moment the purpose of this relaxation. Recall that you have four vibrational bodies: psyche, aura, etheric, and physical. During your waking hours, the higher bodies focus their energy exclusively toward the physical body, for the sole purpose of maintaining your safety and security in the physical world. Each vibrational body receives and transmits a certain level of information, all fed down to the physical body in a never-ending stream. While you are awake, the energy flow is strictly one-way from the higher vibrational bodies down to the physical.

By inducing deep bodily relaxation, you are deliberately reversing this energy flow. You see now the importance of choosing a quiet and secure spot in which to conduct your relaxation. Any extraneous noise or stimuli rippling to your senses automatically triggers your higher vibrational bodies to alertness. In a quiet, secure environment, you are able to deliberately release the body's tight, sharp focus on the physical world. As you do so, the energy flow begins to course in both directions: always from higher bodies to the physical, but also from physical up to the higher bodies.

This is necessary because the work you do during each session is to inform the psyche of your intent and desire to experience certain events in your future. Since the psyche stands at the portal of the primal pulse, where all events are simultaneous, you are literally signaling that you desire certain events to be brought down to physical expression. You are talking to your psyche, in other words, instructing it which events you wish to manifest. Only in a relaxed state, when the energy flow runs in both directions, can you contact and communicate with the psyche clearly and without distortion. Only in a relaxed, undisturbed, and comfortable state of relaxation can you employ the tools outlined below with greatest efficacy.

The first tool of conscious life creation is affirmation. An affirmation is a statement of intent. It signals to your higher bodies that you are focusing on a specific theme or event that you wish to manifest physically. It is an order, a command to the psyche that an old, limiting belief or value is being discarded in favor of a higher, life-affirming one.

The two key elements of an affirmation are *formulation* and *repetition*. First, you must formulate an appropriate affirmation. To aid in our understanding, let us review what language, particularly spoken language, is and how it ties in with our earlier material.

You know that words are symbols, thought-forms stepped down into the field of speech and written language. A word is not the thought behind it, but merely the transmitter of the thought. Each word you speak or write must be translated in the mind of the beholder, stripped of its symbolic wrapping and returned to its original nonverbal thought-form.

Consider for a moment the process occurring when you speak to someone. Your thoughts are stepped down into symbolic words, which you speak aloud. The spoken words are interpreted by the listener's ears, understood as symbols, then stripped of their symbolic clothing and restored to pure thought-form.

In other words, because the human race was set up to experience a camouflage physical system, your thoughts whir on frequencies undetectable to others. You are not all telepathic. So you override your inability to transmit pure thought-forms by reducing thought to speech, which is restored to thought-form in the listener's mind. You still communicate your thoughts, but must do so through the symbolic middleman of speech.

Each word of any language is the symbolic expression of a pure thought-form existing before and above written or spoken words. The human race is connected to a universal dictionary, in a sense, in which each language's symbolic words spring from an underlying, universal bank of concepts. If, for instance, you say "cat" to a Spaniard, the word means nothing because he cannot translate the symbol to the thought-form behind it. If you say "gato," however, instantly the word is recognized, stripped of its symbolic shroud, and both you and the Spaniard hold the universal concept "cat" in your minds, entirely apart from any specific symbolic expression. You are both tapping into the universal dictionary, where "cat" exists as pure thought-form.

Each concept in the universal dictionary carries a certain weight or importance, a certain effect upon the body. For each such concept sparks a unique configuration of electrical impulse in the brain, reducing the concept to the brain's operating frequency. Because the brain operates on electrical impulse, and because your body is essentially electromagnetic energy, each word you hear or speak carries a literal effect upon the body.

Most often this process passes unnoticed; for particularly in Western culture, you have been taught to disregard the messages and signals from the body. Still, you have all experienced the effect of hearing "fighting words," the rush of adrenaline and the heart's acceleration, in response to the speech of others. While this is an extreme and obvious case, understand that every word you speak or hear carries a physical impact on the body.

Now, this seemingly esoteric digression bears heavily on the formulation of an affirmation. Above all else, it underscores the necessity of formulating a *positive* affirmation. It is futile and potentially damaging to replace an old belief with its negation.

For instance, if your belief work has uncovered a belief that you are unworthy of love, which you now realize lies behind your string of unsuccessful romantic adventures, you would not phrase your affirmation as, "I am not unworthy of love." Recognizing that each word you speak is stripped of its symbolic wrapping and that the thought-form behind it carries a literal impact on the body, by stringing together such a phrase you are still transmitting the key phrase "unworthy of love" to the body, and thus to the psyche.

That you are negating the phrase is insufficient to override this process, for on the levels of which we speak, sentences do not exist; each word or concept is individually expressed as impulse and felt in the body. It is in the mind that words are glued together to form sentences and complex thoughts. At the level of the psyche, words are felt in pure intensity, split out of context into a series of discrete impulses.

Thus, you must phrase your affirmation positively. To follow our example, you would say instead, "I am worthy of love." Or, better, "I am loved."

A crucial element of phrasing an affirmation is clarity and brevity. An affirmation must be short, sweet, clear as glass. For the clearer a word's meaning, the less open to distortion and confusion, the greater the impact it carries on the body and psyche. A clear, concise statement hits home in a way that a heap of oratory bombast never can.

Another crucial element of phrasing an affirmation is that you must state what you want as if you already have it. For, you now understand, *you do already have it.* In the realms beyond the psyche, where no time exists, all probable variations of your life float in equal potential. They exist now. So when you state that you already have something you desire, you are not idly daydreaming, but making a statement of fact.

Whatever you want, you already have it. Whatever you desire to achieve, you have already achieved. Whatever you want to feel, you have already felt. From your perspective, in a space-time world of linear moments, you have not yet found your desires manifesting physically. No matter. You know they exist; they exist now; and you are merely alerting the higher levels of your mind to activate them and drop them into physical expression.

You see, for instance, that the phrase "I want money" carries a verb implying that what you want you do not have, and there is a chance you may not get it. This is the hidden, underlying meaning behind the verb "want." So it is this meaning that is transmitted to your psyche—and it naturally will heed your bidding and activate those probable futures in which you may or may not find money accruing to you.

Understand, again, that there are no judgments on the higher planes, no determination as to "good" and "bad" experience. There is only growth and learning from that perspective. The entire universe is set up to manifest your thoughts and beliefs precisely and without interference. So don't perceive a malevolent universe at work when you choose an inappropriate phrase and find your desires not manifesting. It is your responsibility to choose your words with care and precision, to ensure they carry clear and unambiguous instructions to the psyche as to which probable futures it is to activate and manifest.

After formulating a concise, clear, positive affirmation, the next step is *repetition*. During the daily session set aside for such work, you will repeat the phrase aloud. Let us examine the underlying reasons for this.

Understand the distinction between your mind and your brain. Your mind is "you," the nonphysical though physically focused expression of intent to experience earthly life through a human body. The mind holds your hopes, your dreams, your aspirations, your loves. The brain, in contrast, is the organ responsible for processing your mind's decisions, translating them into physical action. It is a transmitter and conveyer of energy and intent, stepping the mind's thoughts down into neuronal impulse and feeding them to the body. The brain is where incoming sensory experience is split into the two components of sense data and interpretation; the mind then ponders these on its higher, nonphysical level, floating above the furious electrical activity of the brain.

Your beliefs are literally, neuronally, etched into the brain, into comfortable grooves along which sense data travels to interpretation. The process of affirmation is one in which the mind deliberately rewires the brain. There is no battle here, no Freudian division into battling components of the psyche. The brain is merely the processor of information, doing its synaptic duty faithfully and accurately.

Since much unhappiness springs from the brain's being wired into certain neuronal networks from earliest childhood, affirmation overrides the brain's existing networks to replace them with more life-affirming belief patterns. From this flows a healthier level of impulse fed down the spine into physical action, automatically reconfiguring the coordinate and altering its magnetic pull toward future events.

This process begins with affirmation. The affirmation must be spoken aloud. Through this process, thought is stepped down into the brain's electrical networks, channeled through the spine to the act of speech, thus imprinting both brain and coordinate with the affirmation's power. Simply thinking the affirmation is insufficient, you see; the brain must be literally rewired, and can do so only when converting impulse to action: thought stepped down to speech.

How do you judge your progress; how do you determine if the affirmation is "working?" Nothing could be easier: you note the body's reaction every time you speak the affirmation.

In Western culture, where mind is divorced from body, where the body is seen as a machine prone to disease and decay, or host to swarms of malevolent impulse, the easy symbiotic flow between mind and body is largely lost. You are not accustomed to noting the physical effects of speech, either yours or that of others. Among other things, the process of using affirmations will help restore that camaraderie you enjoyed at birth, mind and body joined in easy harmony.

After each spoken affirmation, pause to notice the body's response. Feel the effect the phrase has upon the body. Determine what area of the body, if any, seems to resonate after you speak the affirmation.

The extent of your body's resonance with the affirmation reveals the extent to which new neuronal networks are being forged in the brain. At first, when you begin affirmation work, you may feel nothing, no bodily response. This indicates that the affirmation contradicts your brain's present wiring, and the brain is unable to split the sense data—your spoken words—and interpretation, as efficiently as it wants to. You may even detect a confusion in the body, a slight resistance, as the brain struggles to process the unfamiliar thought phrased in the affirmation.

The same occurs during a "lie detector" test. A person speaking what he knows to be untrue may blush, sweat, or find his heart rate accelerating. All these responses are detected by monitors and clue the operator that the person under interrogation may be lying. On a more common level, speaking a lie frequently causes the face to blush; this is especially true among children, not yet masters at the art of routine mendacity.

Why? The brain is unable to process the words spoken under the mind's direction. If a child knows she stole a cookie, the sensory experience has been duly filed away that at a certain time, and against Mother's wishes, the cookie was stolen. Now, when the mind, under fear of punishment, forces the lips to speak, "I didn't steal a cookie," the brain is forced to do the impossible: to process information contrary to its previous storage of the event in question. "But I did steal the cookie!" cries the brain. Because the incoming sensory data—the spoken lie—can find no easy home along existing neuronal networks, the impulses "back up," in a way, and spurt down into the body, provoking the skin to flush and the heart to race. The brain's confusion translates into a physical confusion.

This same process occurs when a spoken affirmation contradicts the brain's comfortable wiring. The brain is constructed to process vibration as efficiently as possible, which means shipping incoming data along existing corridors of belief. When a contrary affirmation is first heard, the brain struggles to process it. "I am loved?" asks the brain. "But I've been unlovable since childhood!" And so the brain will initially resist the affirmation, which may be felt as a confusion or resistance in the body.

This underscores the importance of repetition. Merely speaking the affirmation once is insufficient to rewire decades of negative programming. In a given daily session, an affirmation should be spoken aloud between five and twenty times, until you "feel" that all has been accomplished that can be for one day. The process of rewiring the brain's neuronal networks is not one accomplished overnight, but must proceed strand by strand.

Eventually, with a consistent, daily program, you should feel the body beginning to respond to your affirmation. You may feel a little crack, a little opening, in the brain, the throat, or the heart. This little opening, a burst of air and light squeezing into the tomb of moldy belief, is the signal that the process is working, and the brain is hesitantly rewiring its networks to allow flow in line with your affirmation. When the resonating ceases, repeat the affirmation once again.

Within a week, if your affirmation is appropriate and you have no deeper beliefs blocking its implementation, you should begin to notice that the theme of the affirmation ascends in your daily experience. That is, you notice people talking about the theme more often; you find more mentions of it in your reading material or on television; and your daily experiences seem to be imbued with the theme to a greater degree than before. You may also notice that "negative" events related to the affirmation's theme arise. For instance, if your affirmation relates to financial security, you may find elements of your financial life going haywire: banks and credit card companies making unusual mistakes; unexpected expenses showering upon you; a pay cut or outright loss of a job.

Some beneficent universe! you cry. What good is making positive affirmations when they bring such a flood of "negative" events!

Here is what underlies such ascending events of both positive and negative flavor during your affirmation work. The brain, under the onslaught of your repetition, is forging new networks of belief, new channels to split sense data into interpretation. As it does so, in the interim period before fully installing the new neuronal network, it literally carries two corridors through which to process incoming sense data.

In addition, the confusion caused by your deliberate overriding of old programming carries a certain intensity, and this intensity will be bound to the affirmation's theme, making it more likely that "events" related to that theme are pulled to physical expression. The "negative" events are drawn down by the old neuronal network, while the "positive" events spring from the new network. While the brain juggles both networks, and suffers a certain confusion as well, the affirmation's theme will be highly charged, making passage to physical expression more likely for events of all stripes and colors.

As you progress with your work, and assuming all other belief-coasts are clear, you should find that the body resonates more strongly with each passing session. Each spoken affirmation will bring a stronger, clearer, more vibrant bodily response. This clues you that the new neuronal networks are being built in the brain, and that your coordinate is being reconfigured as well—for it is this energy swirl carried in the spine that is responsible for your body's reaction to the phrase, whether confusion or warm tingling. As you move toward a higher level of living, a happier plane of life, your body responds by embracing your affirmation, tingling and glowing upon hearing you speak the words.

One day, you will find that speaking your affirmation produces sweeping, tingling waves of warm acclamation from head to toe. This is your signal that your work is finished: The brain has forged a new neuronal network of belief; your coordinate is reconfigured to allow free passage to experience in tune with your affirmation, and is sending beams of intent to the highest levels of mind, up to the psyche, informing it that henceforth you will experience only those events in line with your affirmation.

It is important not to worry during the process, not to psychologically peek into the oven and see if the affirmation is fully baked and ready for frosting. For what does worry signify? Underlying any worry is the belief that what you desire may not come to pass. It may or it may not; you lack full confidence. And by worrying, you throw your psychological weight to the possibility that the affirmation will *not* succeed, do you not? You therefore grant it validity. And the brain, the ever-compliant and obedient brain, forges a network of belief that your affirmation probably will not succeed. The coordinate responds likewise, sending up to the psyche the instruction that the affirmation will not succeed and that the old program-ming should remain intact. Thus you continue to experience events in line with the theme of your old belief programming.

So leave it alone. Do your daily affirmation work and then forget about it. Don't stop and ask yourself during the day if it's working. Trust. Trust in the inherent beneficence of the universe, and of your soul. Know that what you affirm, you already have. And if the path bumps and grinds as both negative and positive events drop into your lap, understand that they signal the efficacy of your affirmation, harbingers of its eventual success.

The universe is at your command. The brain, the coordinate, the psyche, the auric and etheric bodies, they exist for one purpose: to grant physical expression to your thoughts and beliefs. They weigh neither good nor bad, performing flawlessly and silently as they are instructed to do. To you—spirit made flesh—falls the power and responsibility to instruct and inform all levels of body and mind that you choose a life at the highest, happiest possible pitch: a conscious life.

Thirty-Six

Visualization

The second primary tool of conscious life creation is *visualization*. Visualization is the conscious fashioning of an event in the mind's eye. It is a consciously constructed dream in which your waking mind directs the action. It stamps the imprint of a desired future event onto your psyche.

Visualization is best conducted during the daily session of conscious life creation, when you are deeply relaxed and undisturbed by external stimuli. As was mentioned in the last chapter, the process is most effective during deep relaxation because the energy flow runs in both directions, from psyche to physical body and back up again. Your desires, sculpted into physical images, float unhindered to the highest reaches of mind and spirit.

Let us examine the procedure for effective visualization.

First, understand that visualization's purpose and impact are on an entirely different level than affirmation. The purpose of affirmation is to rewire the brain's neuronal circuitry, thereby reconfiguring the coordinate and the nature of events it pulls into your life. The principal tool of affirmation is speech, precisely formulated and repeated. Visualization, in contrast, is where you deliberately fashion a specific, concrete event that you wish to have manifest. The principal level of vibration employed is that of sight, although a richer picture can be created by enhancing sight with other sensory material.

Affirmation's effect is essentially upon the body—the brain and the coordinate. Visualization's effect is directly on the psyche, floating up through the levels of mind to link with the highest vibrational body, stimulating it to pull a specific event into physical expression.

Just as you must choose an affirmation of clear and unambiguous meaning, recognizing that each word carries an impact on the body, so must you also fashion a visual scene with utmost care and attention to detail, suffusing it with intensity. For as a word is a symbol, carrying a thought-form but not being the thought-form, you now understand that everything you perceive through your physical senses is also symbolic, your private interpretation of swirling grids of electromagnetic energy. So when you visualize a scene, recognize that it is not the image itself being transmitted to the psyche, but the elements of the scene stripped of their visual artifice, carried in unmasked intensity to the upper reaches of mind.

It might be helpful, therefore, to consider the scene to be visualized before you are in a state of deep relaxation. Consider all the elements carrying crucial meaning; ponder the flow of action precisely as you want it to unfold. For it is best not to create a static picture—that is not real life—but a flow of action, a scene unfolding in real time.

Next, your visualized scene must be realistic. It must be an experience you could reasonably expect to find occurring sometime in the near future. Remember what you are doing: instructing the psyche to probe among your probable futures and manifest the event most closely aligned with your visualized scene. If your concern is to increase financial security, you would be unwise to visualize a scene in which a hole opened in the ceiling and a river of cash poured into the living room. How likely is such an event? What are the chances the psyche would find such a latent possibility among your future selves? Better, then, to focus on the realistic: a new car, new clothes, a bigger house, a comfortable checkbook balance, and so on.

Visualization should be an ongoing process, in which each step of the desired path is visualized, pulled into physical expression, and followed by the next incremental step. Visualizing the ultimate goal of your life, years and years ahead, is largely futile, for probable events that far in the future lie dormant, unreceptive to activation from your present. The closer in time your visualized scene is, the greater the psyche's ease in linking it with a fully vital probable event, swelling with readiness.

Now that we have established the importance of choosing a realistic scene, and one relatively close in time to your experienced present, let us turn to the process of crafting the scene in all its particulars.

First, understand that the scene you create need not be fashioned precisely as you will ultimately experience the event. For example, in any physically experienced event, you can perceive the action only through your own eyes; you do not step aside and watch yourself perform. Yet this can be a powerful tool in visualizing a scene: placing yourself in the action, seeing yourself as part of the unfolding drama.

Remember that all perceived objects are symbols—your body included—and that the underlying meaning behind a visual symbol will be transmitted to the psyche. To place yourself within the scene, therefore, ensures that your presence is indelibly inscribed in the psyche's instructions; that you wish not to be a tangential player, but the lead (if that is your desire). So rather than always visualizing a scene as if it were playing out before your eyes, feel free to place yourself within the scene and consider your "eyes" as belonging to a disinterested observer.

It is important that the visualized scene entirely fill your field of vision. Although you are creating a miniature movie, you do not want to project it as one, with the borders of the screen clearly visible and the audience tossing popcorn. As with any experienced event, it must fill your eyes to the periphery.

As with a short, cogent affirmation, visualized scenes are most effective when relatively short, concise scenes of unambiguous intent. A long, drawn-out montage building slowly to its climax may stand one in good stead among academic film criticism circles, but it defeats the purpose of visualization. Remember, above all, you are striving for intensity; and intensity carries more punch when delivered in quick, rich, powerful bursts. So a visualized scene should last no more than a minute in most cases, including all the necessary action but driving immediately to the point, the desired goal.

This leads to the next consideration: your scene must carry emotional intensity. For despite your every effort to reduce life to manageable, "rational" chunks, such is meaningless on the higher levels of mind. There, your life is recorded and guided by means of energy and intensity. The more intense an experience, the greater weight it carries in your life's ledger.

For instance, if we ask you to recite exactly how you celebrated your last five birthdays, could you instantly rattle off where you were and with whom? In contrast, if we ask you to describe five recent occasions of intense anger or intense love or intense joy, your responses would flow much more smoothly. For this is how events are primarily recorded: as emotional intensities, with the surface perceptual data attached as tangential record-keeping material.

So an effective visualization will build in emotional intensity, producing a palpable emotional response. If you visualize a new car, don't simply see the car, but *feel* your response on acquiring it, driving it for the first time, showing it to friends. Let the joy flow through you, consume you. Let this emotional intensity be the "background music" of the visualization; for in deepest terms, it is the emotional intensity of the event you wish to transmit to the psyche, not the surface visual data.

As with affirmation, repetition carries great benefit during visualization. Within your daily session, if time allows for five repeated viewings of the same visualization, such a routine is far more effective than only once daily. The psyche operates on intensity; the more times you send it a scene, the greater the intensity imparted to the scene. And the higher the intensity, the stronger the pull toward physical expression of the desired event.

We confess some reservations about using the word "visualization" for this process, as it implies that only one band of sensory vibration is employed. True, sight is your species' most powerful sense. But any visualized scene is immeasurably enhanced by buttressing the visuals with other sensory data. For this is how you experience real life, is it not: as a fabric of various bands of vibration, seamlessly sewn together into your experience of a rich, whole world alive with sight, sound, texture, smell, and taste.

To the extent that other senses can be assimilated into the scene, try to include them. In almost all cases, of course, sound will naturally occur, as people speak within the scene. Without losing your sharp, intense focus on the main purpose of the scene, if you can include a modicum of background sounds - traffic, music, the television—you therefore bring the scene closer to "real life" and strengthen its intensity.

The senses of taste and smell may be more difficult to routinely introduce into a scene, as they carry less everyday significance. But recall that smell and taste are the "highest" of your senses, perceiving the highest level of vibration, the life force emanating from all living organisms. As such, including them in a scene will bring the picture to "life," particularly on the level of the psyche. For at the psyche, you see, your species' hierarchy of sense interpretation is loosened; there, the "higher" senses carry much more weight and intensity than they do in your everyday experience.

You know, for instance, that each person has a different smell, though this rarely rises to awareness unless you are pressed skin to skin. As your visualized scene unfolds, and again while not losing your focus on the imagery, try imbuing each person in the scene with a unique smell which you easily perceive. If the others are well known to you, suffuse them with the smell you normally associate with them. In this regard the psyche operates like a dog's nose; it "recognizes" people more by smell than by sight, for smell arises organically from an organism, while sight is merely your perception of it, divorced from its intrinsic properties.

To the extent that taste can be introduced into the scene, whether through food or drink, this too rounds out the sensory vibration of the scene. We will not go so far as to suggest tasting the other individuals in the scene, for this would almost certainly distract you from the desired event of your visualization, unless you are under twenty years of age.

To summarize the elements of a carefully crafted visualization: Choose an event both realistic and fairly close in time. Build the scene around a significant moment of high intensity, a climax, eliciting powerful emotion. Flesh out the scene with other levels of sense perception, including sound, touch, taste, and smell to the extent possible without distracting from the scene's focus. Keep the scene brief, no more than a minute long. Repeat it up to five times within a given daily session.

Now that you have crafted an appropriate scene, you must provide the raising and lowering of the curtain on either end. Before each visualization, with your mind blank, say aloud something to the effect of, "Trusting in the goodness of the universe and myself, I now instruct my psyche that the following event will manifest in my life." You should find specific wording comfortable for you.

Upon ending the visualization, preferably on a high, intense pitch, allow your mind to go blank again and say aloud, "This event now manifests in my life exactly as I envision it." Now, release the emotional intensity built up by the visualization; feel it rippling from your brain and body in concentric circles, pulsing through your etheric and auric bodies out to the psyche, about six feet beyond the skin. Understand that this is not mere fantasy but a deliberate manipulation of energy, for your thoughts are carried on bursts of electromagnetism to the boundary of the psyche. In your relaxed condition, you can literally feel the process as waves of energy and intent radiate from your body outward to the higher levels of mind.

When the waves of intent have fully dissipated, and you lie in quiescent peace, you can begin the process again with your spoken introduction to the visualized scene. Because the intensity of a proper visualization cannot be sustained for long, you should offer no more than five repetitions during one session.

Again, a crucial understanding is that it is not pictures or sounds you are sending to the psyche, but waves of energy and intent. The brain automatically strips perceptual data of their surface patina and translates them into the underlying thought-forms. You intensify this material by visualizing a scene carrying emotional weight, building up to a climax. This intensity is married to the thought-forms behind your visualized images, propelling them with great force to the psyche, carrying clear and undistorted messages of your intent. The psyche responds by activating those probable future events most closely aligned with the thought-forms and intent broadcast to it by your visualization. If no belief-impediments block the event's expression, it will slide into your life's flow seamlessly and effortlessly.

As a general rule, it is best not to include both affirmation and visualization in a single daily session. For the two tools are born of starkly different purpose and carry vastly different effects. Affirmation is used to rewire the brain's neuronal networks so that incoming sense data is shipped along new corridors of belief, thus altering the coordinate's pull toward events of a more beneficial nature. The focus is exclusively on the body—the brain and coordinate—and rewiring its circuitry, its inner magnet.

Visualization, by contrast, is a message sent to the psyche. Visualization does not address the brain or coordinate—it assumes they are in sympathy with the desired event—but ripples its intent out through the higher vibrational bodies to the psyche. It is here that specific events are activated and pulled toward physical expression.

Because the energies involved in affirmation and visualization are starkly different, it is best not to combine them in one session. Best to allow your energy to focus fully and sharply in one area at each session.

As you can see, for visualization to be effective, there must be no belief-impediments blocking an event's expression. For that reason, a carefully crafted Conscious Life Plan will generally begin with affirmations, repeated daily until the body tingles its message that the new neuronal network is fully installed. Then, with the brain and coordinate reconfigured to allow "positive" events to flow, you turn to visualization, instructing the psyche specifically how you wish your life's events to unfold.

With this material as background, we can now turn to specific areas of concern in contemporary life, and see how our tools of affirmation and visualization can be used to consciously create the life of your choice.

Thirty-Seven

Health

Of all Western culture's beliefs, few reveal themselves as intellectually and spiritually bankrupt as those pertaining to health. For while medical technology has brought unprecedented sophistication to the practice of medicine, and scientific explorations daily uncover new secrets of the body's inner life, Western culture remains among the unhealthiest ever to people the globe. Billions upon billions are spent every year on health care; the rise of degenerative diseases mocks the technological advances which can never keep pace; and the cost of maintaining the health care system affects everyone, in sickness and in health.

You create your reality through your beliefs. Knowing this, and observing the epidemic of illness permeating Western culture, what can you conclude about the belief systems underlying the culture's approach to the body and to health?

Since the Reformation, Western culture has been riven into two increasingly polarized camps, religion and science. In a healthy individual and culture, intuition and reason are united in happy symbiosis. Western culture wrenched apart this easy alliance, throwing intuition and emotion to the keepers of religion, while reason was stripped of its intuitive balance and held supreme by the world of science.

As we have seen, both religion and science cling to creation myths hatched to explain the creation of the universe and humanity's appearance on earth. Such creation myths are bound into far broader cosmologies and dogmas, frameworks of belief through which experience is filtered. Science's framework is no more "rational" than religion's, for it excludes any hint of divinity, of a spiritual life beyond the realm of the senses, and thus forever sloshes about a symbolic quagmire, the fiction of a physical world, and upholds it as the sum total of reality.

Science's need to squeeze any hint of the vast unseen realms from its cosmology reduces all of life to chance, to accident, to mechanical processes observable to the eye and ear. Science reduces the universe to its physically perceptible symbolic coating. Science further reduces every organism to a machine, to be understood by picking it apart and examining its constituent building blocks—thus the term "reductionist" describing science's approach. Fueled by Descartes's rigid separation of mind and body, science imposes its reductionist perspective on the human body, considering it a machine—an exquisitely crafted specimen, perhaps, but still a machine—and herein lies the core belief underlying Western culture's sad state of health affairs. The body is a machine.

While science arrogates to itself the "rational" approach to the body and to health matters, religion offers another perspective grounded in its mythology. The Genesis creation myth, as we have seen, plants Adam and Eve in the Garden of Eden, naked and unashamed. Upon eating the fruit of the forbidden tree of good and evil, their nakedness is revealed to their eyes and, in shame, they hide the offending body parts behind cleverly arranged fig leaves. Before the first human child is conceived, then, the race has already learned to feel ashamed of its bodies, to cloak its sinful flesh from sight. Humanity, already separated from God and nature in this creation myth, now further divorces spirit from flesh, considering the body debased and immoral, tainted flesh raging with evil impulse.

A fine mess you are in, strung between the two pillars of Western culture and their cosmological perspectives on the human body. On one hand, an accidental machine prone to disease and decay. On the other, sordid flesh driving the soul to damnation. And, further, as the individual is considered powerless and incompetent, you are taught to believe that you can play no role in maintaining your health, that such must be left to professionals bestowing the benefits of technology to patch up the decaying heap you cart about beneath your neck.

Is it any wonder Western culture should be so riddled with illness?

The body is a physical reflection, the physical version, of a grid of electromagnetic energy standing behind it. Every feature of the body, every miraculous birth of a cell, every beat of the heart, reflects unseen rhythms and processes occurring on the higher realms, as energy is stepped down through the psyche, the aura, and the etheric body, finally to manifest as the symbolic expression of intent standing before you in the mirror. The body, therefore, is essentially vibration manifesting in various frequencies and patterns, weaving bones and blood and muscle into the smooth harmony of the healthy body.

Each such vibration is tuned to an identical frequency of earth-stuff. Each element of earth carries a unique vibration formed by its atomic structure and chemical bonds. In a sense, every earth element "sings" in a unique voice. The body is formed when the various frequencies and patterns pulsating from the higher bodies link with earth elements carrying identical vibrational patterns. Like a pointillist painting, each point of intention behind the body bonds with an identically contoured earth element. Each earth element is instructed precisely where it is to stand in the overall matrix. As you know, the body's cells are constantly dying and being swept away, replaced with fresh earth material. How do the earth elements "know" to form a liver, a toenail, a brain cell? They "know" because they magnetically bond with the higher, unseen points of intention pulsing their unique vibrations, weaving the body's invisible pattern.

The cosmos sings. It sings out a vibrational pattern of unfathomable complexity and harmony. The earth sings in reply, meeting the cosmos note for note, element for element. Between cosmos and earth you stand, a divine song, a miraculous harmony, woven into the thundering symphony of creation.

It is important to recognize that many of the so-called "progressive" or "New Age" approaches to health are merely new voices trilling the same old song, the antiquated cosmologies of religion and science bound up in pretty new wrapping and sprinkled with megavitamins and crystals. For everywhere you hear of alarming threats to health, of carcinogens oozing from the woodwork, of the dangers of cigarette smoking, the certain doom awaiting those enjoying alcohol or other drugs, and so on. Indeed, it seems as if the very world has launched a full-scale attack against the human race, and that you must shield yourselves behind strict and unyielding regimens of diet and exercise to protect yourselves.

Most pernicious are those "scientific" findings "proving" causal links between certain substances and specific disease states. Cigarettes cause lung cancer, refined flour causes hypoglycemia, cholesterol causes heart disease: You know the litany. Know now that it is false.

Take the broader perspective. You live in a safe universe, in which your existence is forever buoyed by unseen realms of energy and intent. The universe works always toward your happiness and fulfillment, and toward radiant health. A breakdown in health symbolizes a breakdown in your higher life, your thoughts and beliefs, and a lack of faith in a beneficent universe.

Yes, Western culture is plagued by diseases and illnesses of every stripe and degree. All such disease states are symbols, symbols of a culture collapsing as its twin cosmologies, religion and science, rot and crumble beneath it.

Remember also that you are connected to the universal mind, the collective unconscious, at the level of the psyche. However private your experience, however isolated you may feel from your brethren, recognize that at the level of the psyche you are inextricably linked with the ebb and flow of human culture. A sickness in the culture's worldview will find manifestation in the bodies of its members, *but only those members who also carry private reasons for manifesting disease.*

This cannot be emphasized too strongly. You are at the mercy of nothing. No carcinogen can spark a tumor within you if you do not carry a private reason for allowing its manifestation. First, always, forever, there must be a private reason for expressing disease. Following that, connected as you are with the collective unconscious of your species, you may well agree to manifest that disease as a symbolic expression of the culture's pathology. You serve both yourself—disease manifesting for private reasons—and the larger culture—your disease state expressing a hidden truth about society. You never sacrifice yourself for the culture, wasting away in symbolic martyrdom, but use the personally chosen disease state to also express your cohesion with your race.

Your views of health are largely based on fear. Fear of disease and decay, fear of the body's unworthiness, fear of your helplessness to maintain vital health in the face of a carcinogenic onslaught. Remember—you create what you fear. You can, quite literally, worry yourself to death.

If the body is a reflection of the higher vibrational bodies, and any disease state merely the symbolic expression of a higher disharmony, are all attempts to treat disease through physical means—drugs, surgery, herbs—futile and misguided? Should the body be cured solely through mental work, from the higher realms?

While all disease states originate in the higher realms, they are hardly impervious to treatment on the physical level. Your body, as a physical organism, operates within a certain range of frequencies. Obviously, any physical substance, from a drug to an herb to a crystal, must also operate within the same approximate band of frequencies.

Because sympathetic vibrations carry strong effects upon each other, the body indeed welcomes appropriate treatments, lovingly applied. The most effective plan of healing incorporates both physical and mental work, alleviating the body's immediate suffering while altering the mental programming that brought the disease to expression.

In considering physical treatments, recall the power of intent, how one's motives and purpose are indelibly stamped onto the physical materials one handles. Using this understanding, consider the various schools of treatment available in your culture. One of modern medicine's primary tools is the use of drugs. Viewing the body as a machine, a perceived lack or imbalance is corrected through chemical means and, thus, the machine is restored.

Consider how your culture's drugs are manufactured. Are they crafted by Mom and Pop outfits, operating at a low profit margin out of love and concern for the health of the citizenry? Far from it: pharmaceutical companies are often huge, politically powerful bureaucracies bent on maintaining their market share and high profits.

What are profits? Surplus. As nature knows no surplus, no deliberate hoarding of resources beyond need or reason, surplus is a violation of the natural order. The desire for surplus springs from Western culture's intrinsic distrust of the natural world, does it not, its divorce from the natural order. And what is the hidden value fueling the thirst for profit, motivating the capitalist machinery? *Money over life.*

You see now the framework of belief upon which traditional Western medicine is based. Beginning with a divorce from the natural order, medicine views the body as a machine, requiring periodic tune-ups and pharmaceutical oil changes to retain health. In capitalist culture, the requisite drugs are manufactured by profit-seeking firms; thus, each drug allegedly designed to enhance health carries the imprint of its manufacturer's valuing money over life. Quite literally, *contempt for life* is carried in every drug manufactured by profit-seeking firms. Swallowing such a drug, that message is carried to every fiber and cell.

Observe, for example, the frenzy among drug companies to discover and market a drug effective in the "war against AIDS," when the disease was new. Did the successful companies then offer their creations on a nonprofit basis out of loving sympathy for the afflicted?

Begin to peel away the surface of life, to perceive the intent lying behind the deeds and creations of others. For it is intent—the thought-forms behind an object's creation—that carries a literal impact upon the body. That aspirin in the jar, manufactured by a stranger for profit—is it the best way to cure a headache? Or would the intent behind a soothing scalp massage by a friend, motivated by love, perhaps not offer greater healing?

An aspirin cures a headache while ulcerating the stomach lining. This is one example of how many drugs carry unhappy side effects, damaging other organs and processes while "curing" the focus problem. Nowhere is the reductionist perspective more apparent: to cure one part may require sacrificing others. Can you see the contempt behind such an approach, the ignorance? The body is a unified, harmonious gestalt. To deliberately violate any part of the body is to violate all of it, and to wound the spirit behind it as well. How can such an approach make you well?

Obviously, in one brief chapter, we can just barely scratch the surface of issues relating to health and healing. Recognize that your society's unhealthy state reflects the sickness of its religious and scientific cosmologies, which in turn are based upon Western culture's divorce from the natural order. Recognize that the "toxins" and "carcinogens" seemingly threatening you are almost always creations of your species in its divorce from the natural order, and the host of disease states they cause meant to force examination of the culture's crumbling spiritual foundation, not to aggravate it through fear. Begin to appreciate the power of intent, how it coils itself within every thought and gesture, and how a medical system built upon profit, not love, carries capitalism's value of "money over life" to every cell of those treated with manufactured drugs.

Any Conscious Life Plan concerned with health and healing must, obviously, begin with affirmations designed to clear away the wreckage of old worldviews, the cosmologies of religion and science, and replace them with life-affirming beliefs built upon appreciation for the body's innate health in a safe and supportive universe.

If health is an issue of concern for you, the first step is to examine your beliefs about the body, about health, about your degree of power in maintaining health, about the nature of aging and death, and so on. For from these beliefs will your health or illness flow; merely altering surface beliefs while leaving core beliefs unexamined cannot bring lasting change.

Beginning with an affirmation program, then, it may be necessary to first install new beliefs of far deeper, broader impact than those specifically focusing on health. For a belief hierarchy must be consistent and in harmony from top to bottom in order to change one's reality in the deepest and most enduring permanence. The first step, therefore, is to replace Western culture's core beliefs with those more in line with universal reality.

If you lean toward the scientific side, having abandoned the fairy tales of religion in childhood and hewing now to the "rational," your Conscious Life Plan should begin with affirmations designed to restore you to the cosmos. For you have drifted apart from your true source, your true reality, and must reclaim your place in the divine cosmic sweep.

If you retain a firm grounding in traditional religious dogma, believing yourself born in sin and groveling at the feet of God for forgiveness, you must replace such beliefs with those affirming your innate divinity. You are moving beyond Judeo-Christian divorce from God and nature, restoring yourself to the divine order, tossing aside guilt and fear of punishment as the tools of ineffective parenting, bearing no relevance on the conduct of a self-realized adult.

The precise wording of an affirmation must, of course, arise from within. Only you know how words resonate inside, and you therefore search for those words and phrases carrying the greatest impact, the strongest resonance, when you speak them. For the purpose of restoring yourself to the cosmos, whether to counteract scientific training or to dismiss guilt-ridden religious dogma, you might fashion an affirmation from these suggestions: "I am divine." "I am God." "The cosmos pulses within." "I am part of all that is." "I am light." "I am music." "I live in a safe universe." "Love surrounds me." "I am eternal." "I shine like the sun."

Again, these are only suggestions, and you must find your private wording. But the point of such phrases—seemingly nonsensical in some cases—is to awaken your long-dormant bond with the universe, to affirm your oneness with creation, to claim your rightful role in the cosmic plan. Thus, these affirmations are not meant to bring specific events into your life, but are merely the foundation, the core belief, upon which more specific affirmations can be built. The foundation must be sturdy before the house can stand tall.

Having found a comfortable phrase, and speaking it aloud in your regular daily session until your body tingles its acclamation, you can move on to more specific affirmation work regarding health issues. Here you focus more specifically on your body as the spirit made flesh, embracing it with words affirming its divine origin and temporal beauty. Again, building our belief hierarchy from broadest to most specific, at this stage you would fashion an affirmation of fairly amorphous structure, restoring your body to its status as spirit-made-flesh while not yet focusing on any particular organ or area of concern.

Affirmations at this level might be phrased as follows: "My body is spirit in flesh." "My body radiates divine light." "My body is perfection." "My body sings divine music." "My body radiates beauty." "My body glows with stardust." "My body graces the earth." "My body is a symphony." "My body is the Temple of God." "My body flies on divine wind." "My body dances through the stars."

You can see that the "rational" mind may sputter and protest at affirmations such as these. My body glows with stardust? What nonsense is this? it asks. At this point, remember, you are laying the groundwork, the fundamentals; to do so, you must override the detritus of the decades, including the "rational" perspective of the body as a machine. To affirm something as outrageous as your body glows with stardust, or dances through the stars, is to forge a neuronal network of belief allowing for miracles—for miracles spring from a faith in the divine, limitless potential bursting into the universe at every moment, an eternal spring of promise from which you can drink if you believe you can. So the purpose at this level of affirmation work is to install neuronal networks painted in such broad, cosmic strokes that "miracles" become your everyday experience.

Obviously, at this stage, there may well be resistance from old beliefs as they are pried loose in your mind, clinging tenaciously like barnacles to their familiar mooring in the psyche. The "Voice of Reason" may scoff at your spoken affirmations, scorning your attempts to live at a higher pitch, whispering doubt and confusion.

When such voices and doubts arise, rather than trying to squeeze them from consciousness, instead bring them fully into focus, say, "I release you, now go in peace," and feel the old belief drifting from you, out into the cosmos, out toward the Light. In doing so, you inform all levels of mind that you are perfectly aware of what you used to believe, that you lovingly release those anachronistic values, and replace them with those allowing a higher vibration to guide your life.

When this level of affirmation work is completed, and you will know when your body tingles in response to your spoken affirmation, the time has come to move to affirmations more precisely relating to health. You may have a specific area of concern requiring attention, or you may simply wish to install "preventive" beliefs as a way of releasing any potential illness.

Assuming you suffer from a specific malady, before you begin affirmation work you need to take several intermediate steps. First, you must accept the responsibility for having brought the illness to corporal expression. Any gnashing of teeth and rending of hospital gowns over your cruel and tragic fate is a mechanism of abdication, whereby you project your personal power and responsibility onto the world at large, releasing you from blame.

There is no blame, no divine finger of retribution pointing at you from the heavens and mocking your illness. Instead, recognize the immense power you hold, the power to literally manifest your thoughts in the body. Imagine the power! And now, reclaiming that power as your own, accept responsibility for what you have created, and resolve to turn that power to creating healing instead of illness.

Second, mentally probe the malady for clues as to its symbolic meaning. What area of the body is affected? Does it affect your mobility? your looks? your relationships? your job? your sex life? your energy level? Working backward from the effect of the illness, try to determine the hidden cause. Ruthlessly examine your life for pockets of unhappiness, repressed and masked behind elaborate sang-froid or forced cheer. Leave no mental stone unturned. Does the affected area have any special significance, any private meanings carried from childhood? Examine your life in toto: are you happy and fulfilled, or do you carry regrets and frustrations?

Your investigation must be as thorough as a bone-rattling physical examination. Knowing that the nature and location of your malady is a symbol, you must uncover the private meanings and energy blockages springing to symbolic life.

Knee trouble may symbolize issues of dominance and submission—getting down on your knees before others, or requiring others to do so before you—or perhaps a retreat from full, active participation in earthly life, for your mobility, your power to scoot about the earth, is crippled.

The heart is the organ pumping in harmony with the primal pulse, unconsciously recognized as the organ of love, so heart disease or a heart attack may carry overtones of life bereft of true connection with others. Heart attack victims are most often men, those trained from childhood to avoid genuine intimacy, driven to chase hollow trinkets like wealth and power as balms on the throbbing emptiness in their hearts.

Cancer is an exquisitely crafted symbol, carrying both Western culture's most threatening consequence of divorce from earth—unbridled growth—and frequently arises in response to the body's exposure to man-made toxins and carcinogens, again expressions of the human species' divorce from the natural order.

Unsightly skin disease may reflect difficulties in "facing" the world, a symbolic barricade fencing the threatening world out, repulsing others before they can gain intimacy and confirm fears of rejection.

Obesity frequently springs from the equation "food is love," whereby an unhappy, unloved person compensates by symbolically returning to the unlimited, loving flow at the breast. Obesity may also carry sexual fears, deliberately making one unattractive to the opposite sex and removing one from the threatening messiness of romance, intimacy, and physical closeness.

These brief sketches are by no means laid down as immutable laws, but are simply suggestions to spark your thinking. It is you who must uncover the private symbolism behind any unhappy health issue. Having done so, you craft an affirmation designed to counteract, contradict, and cancel the old, limiting beliefs.

To our knee sufferer: "I am complete and secure." "I embrace all others as my equals." "I embrace life in a safe universe."

To the man with heart disease: "I am loved." "I offer love freely." "I trust others with my inner feelings." "I cherish my family." "I am whole and complete." "Love flows through me always." "My heart beats with love."

To those with cancer (who must also determine the symbol behind the specific site affected): "The universe is safe." "I embrace the natural order." "I am of the natural order." "I cherish the earth." "I embrace life." "I live in a safe universe."

To our friend with unsightly skin: "I embrace life." "I affirm the goodness of every person." "I trust the world with my feelings." "I cherish all I meet."

To the overweight sufferer: "I am loved." "I am an essential part of the universe." "My value is beyond counting." "I am divine." "I am eternal." "I cherish my sexuality." "I embrace romance." "I face intimacy with confidence." "I am beautiful."

Again, these are simply suggestions, and you must fashion your private affirmation with words carrying deep power and rich resonance, for it is emotional intensity for which we strive.

You will notice a creeping case of broken record-itis in the list above, particularly regarding the safe and secure universe. Science's cosmology— of your random body floating in a meaningless universe—lies behind many of today's health problems, and must be counteracted before genuine healing can occur.

Affirmation is also effective in a program of "preventive" medicine, releasing any probable future selves carrying disease and discomfort. But note the intent behind such affirmations: Do you *fear* ill health, or do you *affirm* good health? Your intent is the rocket on which the affirmation rides to the brain and coordinate. The identical phrase, spoken out of fear or out of trust, will carry entirely different effects. Affirmations designed to maintain radiant health might be phrased like these: "I am a living body of light." "My body is divine music." "I maintain perfect health." "I live in a safe universe." "Health flows through my every pore." "Divine light suffuses me." "I glow with health." And so on; once again, the precise wording must be of your own choice.

Now let us turn to our second primary tool of conscious life creation, visualization. In matters of health, visualization is most often used, and most effectively so, when an illness has manifested in the body. You see, if you are of sound and radiant health there is little for you to visualize, for visualization is meant to pull you in a new direction, to attract future events of a different order toward expression. If you already maintain good health, you certainly don't want to veer off that track! So visualization is a tool employed to counteract the effects of illness already finding corporal expression.

If the afflicted body part is external, then you have little difficulty in visualizing it as healthy, for you know exactly how it would appear. Visualizing internal organs is a different matter, however, for even though you may have a good idea how the organ looks, you still lack a solid understanding of how it appears during the body's never-ceasing activity. A photograph may reveal the organ's contours and color, but not how the organ affects and is affected by its neighbors, nor how it moves or changes shape during a day's course. Remember that visualization is most effective when the created scene is a dynamic flow, a slice of life, rather than a static picture.

Our point is that it is better to dispense with renderings of an afflicted organ instilled by photographs and the like, and instead create a more personal conception. Treat the organ as would a cartoonist, perhaps exaggerating certain qualities, painting it with vibrant color, even giving it a face and personality. Now, what is the purpose of transforming an organ into a cartoon character?

Remember that when you visualize, what you see in your mind's eye is not what is transmitted to the psyche. Long before the message ripples to that level, the visual imagery has been discarded, the symbolic clothing tossed aside, revealing the naked truth beneath. Further, that truth is transmitted based on the emotional intensity propelling it to the psyche, and that intensity is imparted by the extent of the image's resonance with you.

For you to fancifully create a cartoon image of an organ, to endow it with a personality and free will, is to make that organ "yours" in a way that dutifully re-creating a photographic image of the same organ never could. You want to make the organ "you." You want to imbue it with the stamp of your personality, for just as you love your own children more than those of others, you "care" more about an organ whose imagery you have created than you do for a generic version. Remember, always, it is emotional intensity for which we strive; the more personal and private your imagery is, the stronger your connection with it.

Few are the tools of healing more powerful than humor and the laughter it provokes. A good, rippling laugh massages both body and spirit, as every cell is invigorated with the pleasant sensations of laughter, while that joy ripples to the highest level of mind, confirming one's delight in earthly life. We are not tossing mindless metaphysical crumbs your way, nor speaking metaphorically. Laughter literally heals the body.

Humor is thus a powerful tool in visualizing the body back to health. When you visualize an organ, endowing it with a personality and facial features, go all the way and create a humorous cartoon character. Give it a name: Stan Stomach, Harry Heart, Carol Colon. Give it a distinctive accent, a few personality quirks, a colorful banter with neighboring organs. Or, if you prefer, graft the personality of a well-known cartoon figure onto the organ, visualizing it with that character's face transplanted onto the organ, carrying the familiar personality and mannerisms with it.

Now, what is all this nonsense about, Alexander? Sickness is serious business! Pain is no laughing matter! How dare you reduce suffering to the level of a cartoon!

Yes, restoring health is serious business, and pain is not to be cavalierly dismissed. But beyond humor's automatic beneficial effects on body and soul, there is a further subversive purpose to employing humor in healing; it is a way of declaring: *I will not be defeated!* Cancer? I laugh at cancer! Heart disease? I guffaw in your face! AIDS? My sides split at your impotence!

You see, underlying the humor is the recognition that you create your own reality and that what you have brought into physical expression, you can just as easily dismiss; and your power to do so is so immense that disease is literally a laughing matter, to be regarded as a trifle, sent packing back whence it came with a chortle and a friendly kick in the pants.

Remember—and again we wear deep the grooves on our broken record—you create your reality through thought, energy, and intensity. The more intensity you impart to a thought-form, the stronger its physical manifestation will be, meaning it must fill a greater space and time to find full expression.

When disease strikes, if you recoil in horror and despair, moaning and groaning endlessly about your cruel fate, what are you doing? You are *strengthening* the disease, granting it permission (if not outright welcome) to take up permanent host in your body, to ravage and break it. When you rush to doctors and gobble pills at their bidding, you confirm your belief in your powerlessness and impotence to heal yourself, to create health as you have created illness.

Despair, fear, anger, denial, resignation: these are all powerful energizers, confirming your impotence in the face of illness. And what you energize, you experience. Humor stands this process on its head, for it shows how little effect the illness has on your mental well-being, on your outlook, on your love of life. It cuts the rug out from under the disease state, blocking replenishment from other highly charged emotional reactions. Not only does humor carry literal healing to the body, it also undercuts the emotional intensity sustaining the disease.

So, returning to our visualization, you craft a highly personal character for the affected organ, granting it a personality and facial features, if that be your wish. Make it a strong character, full of sass and vinegar or glowing with radiant love and kindness, depending on your choice. The personality should be one you admire as one of strength, courage, and fortitude.

During the daily visualization session, craft a scene in which the affected organ is engaged in strenuous activity along the general lines of its function in the body. Stan Stomach might be seen sorting through the contents of a meal, muttering about the dietary wisdom of his master, but vigorously breaking the food down into components and sending them on their way to sustain the body's health. Harry Heart ripples with muscle and power as he squeezes hot red blood through his chambers, patting happy red blood cells on the head as they pass, never tiring, never straining. Carol Colon might join Stan Stomach in groaning about the content of her raw material, but nonetheless performs her job efficiently and tirelessly—we leave the details to the scatologically minded.

Most important: *There must be no evidence of disease or impairment in your visualization.* You are not visualizing what is, but what will be. You are alerting the psyche as to which probable future it should activate and manifest, and your purpose is to restore radiant health to the organ in question. No mention should be made of the illness responsible for the visualization.

It is the practice among some proponents of visualization in health matters that the afflicted visualize an internal battle, in which the "good" white blood cells attack and devour the "bad" invading cells. Cancer patients are often guided to use this imagery. Perhaps you see the potential danger in such a scenario. You set the body up as a battlefield, an "us" versus "them," thus crippling the image of a harmonious, indivisible gestalt. You necessarily impart great power to the "bad" invaders, for they are worthy of being fought in a visualization; thus the intensity you grant them ensures their perpetuation. You transplant the fundamental malady of Western culture—divorce from nature, divorce from spirit, leading to isolation and separation—into the body. You confirm your belief in your helplessness under the world's malevolent onslaught, for you have been "attacked" by the "bad" invader cells.

This is not to say that such visualizations should never be used, but to caution you to consider what the unintended effects might be. Always consider the underlying symbolism of a scene, the worldview fueling it, and to what you grant intensity, for therein lies the effectiveness or ineffectiveness of a visualization.

If a battle scenario seems appropriate—if you do feel you have been violated by external forces—then try to weave humor into the visualized battle. Portray it more as a cartoon shoot-out, or children playing cops and robbers, than a real life, battle-to-the-death struggle. Treat it lightly; see the invading cells as actors, playing a part, spewing fake blood and dying exaggerated deaths as in a Hollywood movie. By doing so, you still conduct a battle of "us" versus "them," but by treating it lightly and humorously, you don't impart intensity to the sense of being invaded, of being powerless, of viewing the body as a battlefield.

What if your illness isn't focused in a particular organ, but is instead a general, evenly distributed malady like carrying the AIDS virus or a blood disorder? How should one craft a visualization to counteract such an illness?

Most important, again, is to avoid any hint or mention of the disease itself within the scene. The point is to magnetically attract a future self glowing with health. So that is precisely what you depict. You might project your body as a glowing body of light, each organ and tissue radiating a different color, sewn together into a pulsing fabric of luminescent beauty. Or you might depict the body as a symphony, with each organ and tissue issuing a different note; you might assign traditional symphonic instruments to the various body parts.

This is not as fanciful as it sounds, for as we have endeavored to explain throughout, your body is light and your body is music. For, at base, your body is vibration and so are light and music. Visualizing your body as a glowing rainbow of infinite color, or hearing it thundering the divine song of the cosmos, is actually closer to reality than the image staring back at you in the mirror.

As you visualize your body in this way, mentally squeeze as much intensity as you can into the sense of harmony suffusing the body; feel, see, and hear the different vibrations complementing each other, contributing to the majesty of the body's harmony. Intensity should be focused more on the sensation and appreciation of harmony than on the images or sounds themselves. For it is this intensity—of a body suffused with radiant harmony—that you wish to project to the psyche, stimulating it to manifest such health in the future, restoring you to full vibrancy.

As with affirmation, it is essential that you not worry about your progress, that you not examine yourself minutely and constantly for evidence of healing, that you not set deadlines for when healing must occur. All such mental fiddling harms the process because it springs from a lack of faith, a lack of trust, in the beneficent universe and in your power to heal yourself. No healing regimen can succeed when the sufferer surrenders to illness, builds his self-image around his condition, and abandons a regular routine of work and leisure in frenetic pursuit of a cure. The cure lies within. You need only clear away the beliefs that brought the illness to expression, then trust in your power to restore full health.

We would be remiss not to again mention briefly that there are illnesses chosen for reasons beyond the easy reach of affirmation and visualization. Deeply imbedded karmic triggers, designed to create the experience of illness as a reincarnational balance, or the unconscious choice to leave life at an early age, may be immune to reversal through the affirmation and visualization process.

Nothing is ever set in stone; nothing is fated or predetermined beyond your power to change. If a steady program of affirmation and visualization does not yield measurable results within two months, it may be that the choice to experience illness carries deeper significance than the learning that healing would bring about. Also, if one has not thoroughly cleared away old beliefs, then affirmation and visualization cannot be as effective as they are when built upon a clear and unambiguous foundation of belief in a loving universe and one's irreplaceable part in the cosmic dance.

If the expected healing does not occur, and you are certain you carry no limiting beliefs blocking a cure, you might benefit from a counseling or hypnosis session, guiding you to an understanding of your purpose in manifesting disease or the hidden karmic reasons for it.

Our focus on affirmation and visualization—all mental work—is not meant to slight therapies aimed at the body, working directly with the afflicted area. Again, the most effective regimen will be one incorporating both mental and physical elements, working in tandem to alleviate the symptoms while also releasing the need for disease on a higher level.

When choosing a physically oriented therapy, most important is to consider the intent behind the treatment, and the intent on the part of those administering it. For intent, once again, makes the universe go round. And the intent behind a treatment can carry a greater impact upon its efficacy than the elements of the treatment itself.

Many medicines are made from plants; in this case, Western medicine acknowledges the wisdom of native peoples in their use of herbs and flowers to effect healing. Now, what is the difference in intent between a plant fresh from the earth, applied or ingested, versus a drug containing the same plant, manufactured for profit? A plant fresh from the earth carries only universal harmony and respect for all life; a drug manufactured for profit carries "contempt for life" within its molecules.

Which offers the greater healing: a massage offered by a friend or family member, or a massage performed by a stranger for a fee? The strokes may be identical, the massage may last the same stretch of time, so only the intent behind the act differs. Which would your body more likely respond to in joy and radiance?

We offer two small examples simply to trigger your thinking, to emphasize the importance of determining the intent behind whatever physical treatments you choose. Your body is your divine vessel, your spirit made flesh. Treat it as you would a child, placing it only in the hands of those whose motives are pure.

What of crystals? Another New Age fad, or facilitators of health and healing? Having passed Professor Alexander's introductory course on physical universe construction, you can now analyze any substance for its potential effect on the body. A crystal, obviously, falls in the category of bedrock. Bedrock's qualities are high charge, uniform pattern, little resistance. Further, you know that pockets of high vibration urge neighboring areas of lower charge to raise their vibrational level. What conclusions can we draw about the efficacy of crystal in matters of health and healing?

The human body, primarily composed of water, is built upon a bedrock frame of bone; and the body carries enough bedrock cohesion that it retains its shape and size. A crystal is much sturdier, more impervious material; therefore, its charge must be higher and more uniform than the human body's. Placing a crystal upon the body will therefore amplify the body's energy in that area, urging it to stronger, richer pulsations. Within limits, this property of crystal can carry physiological benefit. As the sculpted spires and precisely angled planes of natural crystal reveal, crystal's molecular structure differs from that of most rocks. Without going into detail, this unique structure more closely resembles the body's patterns than other bedrock substances, granting crystal higher power to work with the body's rhythms.

Remember also that bedrock objects absorb the vibrations of their owners over a period of time. Crystals routinely worn or handled become "yours," and, in a sense, come to recognize the unique vibrational patterns of their owner. Crystals charged up in times of health would then be more effective in curing illness than a cold stone carrying only the imprint of its miner.

Because crystal is bedrock, and carries greatest effect on bedrock, it is not as effective in enhancing mental work, healthy thought processes, as some aficionados claim. For thought pulses at a far higher vibration than crystal; the sympathy is lost. Crystal carries little impact on affirmation and visualization work, for example. It is upon the body, upon the symptomatic symbols of illness, that crystal carries greatest effect.

This discussion is intended only to offer our perspective on the use of crystal in healing, not necessarily to endorse such use. The danger lies in ascribing magical properties to bedrock, once again surrendering personal power to forces and elements outside the body. Crystal is not essential to health and healing; it can aid, perhaps, but is no substitute for life-affirming, health-embracing thoughts, which are the only foundation of true health.

Space limitations prohibit a more detailed discussion of the manner in which environmental conditions and the habitual use of certain substances may make a disease state more likely, but never certain. In rejecting the notion of absolute causal links between environmental conditions and disease—like cigarettes and lung cancer, or alcohol and cirrhosis—we do not mean to suggest that there is no relationship nor that one can pummel the body with toxins and poisons, then disclaim any responsibility for the diseases which result.

Once again, the fundamental issue is intent. What is the intent behind the use of a substance? And, equally important, what is the intent in avoiding that substance—refusing to touch cigarettes or alcohol or preservative-laden food? Is it an affirmative lust for life and respect for the body that fuels your activities, or fear for its security in a hostile universe, a certainty of its impotence to maintain health in the face of environmental assault?

Affirmation or fear? Which motivates your choices?

We are not suggesting that you are free to smoke a carton of cigarettes a day, wash down your tarred throat with a case of beer, chase the beer with a meal of bologna and processed cheese, and expect to maintain fine and vibrant health to your dying day. Possibly you could. But we hope to steer you in a new direction, to a higher level of life.

We hope to restore the symbiosis between mind and body you enjoyed at birth, but which was beaten out of consciousness as science and religion stuffed you into their straitjackets, slapped blinders on your eyes and plugs in your ears. Thus crippled, the thought of the body possessing its own consciousness, sending signals and messages to your mind, was beaten out of possibility.

A program of affirmation work affirming the body's innate health, its place in the cosmos, its precious expression as the spirit in flesh, should gradually awaken the long-dormant body consciousness. In its own way, after its own fashion, the body will communicate. And what is your response to those signals—scorn or respect?

Rare is the body that shouts for joy upon swallowing an alcoholic beverage. For alcohol is a poison, as you understand from its effects on the brain and, over time, the liver. So an awakening body consciousness may well steer one away from imbibing alcohol, communicating its desire to remain vital and alert at all times, the better to carry out your desires in unhindered efficiency.

Conversely, the body may welcome a glass of wine over dinner with a loved one or family. The warmth the wine brings to the skin, the convivial atmosphere such a gathering evokes, may offer refreshing variety to a body which craves diverse experience.

Cherishing your body as the divine vessel it is, as the miraculous expression of spirit made flesh, and respecting its clear messages, you restore yourself to the easy symbiosis of childhood, of mind and body working in tandem, partners in the joyful miracle of earthly life.

So let the proscriptions, harangues, and histrionics of others fall lightly upon you. Surrendering to fear of disease, building a fortress of organic foods and rigid temperance, is a violation as surely as shooting your veins full of heroin. For both rise from disrespect—lack of faith in the body's innate health and healing capacity, or a deliberate overriding of the body's frantic cries. Neither cavalierly disregard the body nor treat it as a brittle china doll, to be fretted over and zealously guarded. Respect its messages, respect its innate health, respect its wisdom. You and your body are at the mercy of nothing.

Health is a given, your natural condition. Illness is a symbol of higher disharmony, stepping down into physical expression. With your views of the body now firmly based on an appreciation of its intrinsic divinity, its power, its being an integral strand in the web of life, vibrant and radiant health are yours until your last breath.

Thirty-Eight

の

Abundance

We use the term "abundance" rather than "wealth" because our perspective on the issue differs considerably from most of Western culture. Before discussing specifically how you can increase the flow of abundance into your life, we must take a broader look at the planetary fabric in which you live.

The natural world knows neither wealth nor poverty, neither surplus nor lack. Animals carry an instinctive trust in the universe, an unconscious faith in its miraculous design, providing food and shelter for all. Western culture, divorced from the natural order, stands apart, unconsciously threatened by the divine harmony about it, for such contradicts its fears and beliefs. Evolution, the Big Bang, Jehovah setting humanity above nature, are all projections of Western culture's innate distrust of the earth—separation and competition spewed outward onto the natural world, masking its divine harmony under the opaque canvas of mechanistic randomness and aloof divinity.

Divorced from nature, divorced from God, divorced from one another, each person stands alone, driven to erect a fortress of security, a cocoon of wealth, protecting one from the vagaries of a hostile universe, an angry God, or one's indifferent fellows. The quest for wealth springs from fear, fear for one's security in a penurious world, born of humanity's divorce from earth.

It is not our intention to merely instruct you in the mechanics of increasing your personal wealth, while leaving intact the fears and falsehoods fueling that drive. Our hope, instead, is to instill an appreciation for the universe's natural abundance.

Step back now from Earth, as if floating in space and regarding the blue-green globe you call home. Recalling that the universe is constructed as a three-dimensional matrix of primal cells, such that every point of space pulsates with life, view earth now as a focused crucible of intent, a concentrated cluster of vibration, standing unique in the universe, playing host to life forms known nowhere else. This rich bed of promise floats between moon and sun, infusing earth life with duality while creating the aqueous dance granting life to infinite swarms of consciousness.

Earth, possessing her own consciousness, plays host to the species swarming upon her, while finding her fulfillment in providing their home. The exquisitely balanced forces of nature are born not of accident but of design, earth's design that all shall live in abundance and freedom from scarcity. So it has been, so it ever will be.

Enter humanity. This species, carrying a unique consciousness allowing rational thought and manipulation of earth-stuff, represents a noble experiment, Earth sharing her powers of design and manipulation with one species treading upon her flesh. The danger in such an experiment—as has been borne out in your time—is that humanity's rational mind would rob it of the animals' intuitive bond with earth, convincing humanity that it stood apart from the forces and protection of nature. Century upon century of Western culture's divorce from Nature now bring humanity teetering at the abyss of destruction, as global temperatures ominously rise while nuclear weapons proliferate among rogue states.

A fundamental feature of earth's design is that energy must flow freely on all levels to sustain the health of the planet and all its species. Blocking energy's natural flow, whether in the outer world or in one's inner life, damming it up through hoarding or repression, results only in detriment. A squirrel gathering five years' worth of nuts will watch his stash rot while his neighbors starve. Blocking the natural flow of emotion, repressing and denying one's inner life, results in psychopathology and psychosomatic illness.

An appreciation of Earth's natural state, her miraculous flow of water, sunlight, and air bestowing plenty to all species upon her, leads one to recognize that abundance is the natural order of things, the inevitable result of a planet suffused with divine harmony. Where wealth and poverty stand in stark contrast, where scarcity prevails, where some feast while others starve, one knows that the natural order has been violated, the faith in nature's abundance abandoned, insecurity and lack of faith rushing into the sterile vacuum of apostasy.

Abundance is the natural order of things. This understanding must precede any effective work in increasing your share of the world's bounty. Further, increasing your abundance must be built upon a recognition of energy and how it naturally flows. Energy may be transformed or exchanged as it passes through your hands, but to block or impede the flow, arrogating it to your private gain, reflects lack of faith in the natural order—once again returning you to your accidental universe, your angry and vengeful God, your contrasts of wealth and poverty, your separation from others.

So to request an increase in abundance is to accept the responsibility that when energy flows toward you in greater generosity, *so must you increase your generosity toward others*. A truly conscious life is one where you appreciate the natural, limitless generosity of the earth—food, drink, and air all provided in unlimited, self-perpetuating abundance—and appreciate yourself as a pulsing strand in the earth's fabric, freely taking and freely giving as energy flows through your hands.

In truth, you can own nothing. True, you can establish a social system built upon the concepts of private property and money as a medium of exchange, erect laws and statutes outlining the flow of money and goods, and lay lawful claim to a plot of land, a shelter, a pile of goods. But "you" are not your body, for your body will die and decay, while "you" are eternal. So the possessions legally linked to your physical body are not "yours," any more than your children, legally linked to your name, are "yours" to buy and sell as you wish. No, the most you can claim of the earth's bounty is temporary stewardship, an ephemeral title to land and goods made necessary and sanctified by your social system.

Stewardship of the earth's abundance, rather than wealth in a hostile universe, must underlie a conscious approach to increasing the flow— both to you and away from you—of the earth's bounty.

As always, a belief hierarchy must be built from bottom to top, from the broadest core belief to those most precisely tuned to your unique situation. So an affirmation routine related to issues of abundance must begin by replacing whatever limiting beliefs you hold with those allowing the easy inflow of the earth's abundance.

Whether you are of a scientific or a traditionally religious bent—or carry a confused jumble of both—recognize how both cosmologies spring from Western culture's divorce from the natural order. So whether you believe you float in a random, meaningless universe governed by natural selection and survival of the fittest; or as the damned and sinful creature of a stern, patriarchal God, the underlying core belief is similar: Humanity is separate from God, separate from nature, separate from each other. So here is where we must begin our Conscious Life Plan to increase abundance.

Affirmations at this stage are painted in broad, sweeping strokes of intent, designed to contradict the mind's comfortable neuronal networks. Appropriate affirmations at this stage might include the following: "The universe is a cosmic web." "The earth is alive." "I am divine and eternal."

"The universe pulses with life." "The universe is divine harmony." "The universe is perfection."

At this stage, you are sweeping away the fundamentals of Western culture's worldview and installing a new framework based upon an appreciation for the universe's divine origin, its pulsation with life and breath, and your place in the cosmic plan. The above are just suggestions; you must find a phrase that resonates with you, hits home with power and poetry, burrowing its meaning in the deepest reaches of your psyche.

You may experience resistance and confusion when you initially begin with such affirmations, as the brain can find no comfortable neuronal niche in which to store them. Recognizing the process, continue to speak your affirmations in daily sessions until the body's tingling its acclamation apprises you that a new neuronal network has been forged, one broadening your worldview, suffusing it with divinity and recognition of your integral role, thus allowing the next step of affirmation work to proceed.

The next stage of affirmation brings you a step closer to the subject of concern, abundance. Between broadening your worldview and formulating affirmations precisely bearing on your situation, you build an intermediate layer of belief, affirming your place in a world of limitless generosity and protection. Affirmations at this stage might be phrased as follows: "The earth cares for all her creatures." "Divine energy flows through me always." "Nature is loving." "Abundance sweeps across the globe." "I am safe and protected." "God loves all His children." "I am part of the cosmic web."

These suggestions, and the particular phrase you fashion for yourself, are designed to forge an appreciation for the earth as a pulsing body of life, providing for all her creatures without limit or restraint. You must believe in such a framework before abundance can freely flow to you.

After this intermediate layer of belief is installed and resonating in every pore, the next step is to formulate an affirmation specifically tailored to your situation. Is it "abundance in general" you seek? The wherewithal to attend college, or to buy a house? A healthier, happier shelter? A finer wardrobe? A new car?

The key is to formulate an affirmation hinting at the desired goal without explicitly mentioning it. That precise focus is the domain of visualization, you will recall. At this point, the affirmation work is meant to clear the way for visualization work to proceed, to forge neuronal networks in sympathy with your vision. So while this level of affirmation is more finely focused, it still must be broad enough to serve as the foundation for a variety of potentials.

As example, if you are unhappy with your current living arrangement and wish to find other shelter for the benefit of physical and mental health, you would not at this point formulate an affirmation describing in detail your new living space. Instead, you would craft a broadly worded statement affirming your right to safe and healthy shelter, and confirming your confidence in the abundant universe's granting it to you. Affirmations of this type might include the following: "The universe protects me." "I live in healthy, happy surroundings." "The earth shelters me." "My physical needs are abundantly met." "Shelter flows to me." "The earth takes care of me." "I have a strong and sturdy shelter."

Notice that the all-encompassing word "shelter" is used, rather than specifically designating "house" or "apartment" or "cave." Allowing the universe to work its magic, you might well end up with more than you requested. Why limit yourself from the first? Using amorphous terms—and this applies to all affirmation plans—allows the universe to guide you toward what best suits your needs—and it may be more than you allowed yourself to dream of.

If your concern is simply for more money, to free you from drudgery and allow you to enjoy life more fully, your affirmation plan should begin with the same two levels of initial work, restoring you to an appreciation for the universe's natural munificence and your security within its loving framework. It is at the last level, the most precise focus, that you would formulate affirmations specifically crafted to drawing in abundance in the form of money.

Other factors may well be involved, apart from holding Western culture's worldview as the basis of your belief structure. If you believe you are unworthy of enjoying a comfortable life, if you believe money is the root of all evil, if you believe the poor are spiritually superior, then you carry belief-blocks hindering the free flow of money to you.

Examine your beliefs about money, about poverty and wealth, about your own self-worth. Money, simply a medium of value, can be neither evil nor good. It simply is. And holding the poor to be spiritually superior to the rich enhances the likelihood of joining the poor in their spiritual paradise—for the psyche always manifests what you believe to carry the greatest potential for spiritual growth. If you uncover such belief-impediments, formulate an appropriate counteracting affirmation and repeat it during daily sessions until your body affirms its complete acceptance.

Once such personally limiting beliefs are cleared away, you can formulate phrases specifically designed to ease the flow of money into your life. Such affirmations might be phrased like these: "Abundance flows to me naturally and effortlessly." "The universe is generous." "My needs are always met." "I have more money than I can use." "I can buy everything I want." "Money gushes toward me." And so on; the point is to create confidence that the universe's abundance flows to you without hindrance, easily meeting or exceeding all your needs.

Once these layers of belief are installed, if you desire a specific item—a car, clothes, a house—visualization is the tool employed to bring the desired object to manifestation. Only you know what you want, so we cannot craft the visualization for you! But remember that the most important element of a visualization is not the imagery but the emotional intensity behind it, for this is the fuel propelling the imagery to the psyche. See yourself with the new car, the new house, the new clothes; but, more importantly, feel your joy at possessing them, your gratitude for the universe's abundance, your appreciation for the privilege of stewardship. Upon these emotional intensities will ride the effectiveness of the visualization.

Just as a consciously lived life means restoring communication between mind and body, and respecting the body's messages, so does it also instill an appreciation for the divine fabric in which you live and your inextricable part in the drama. As such, the need for possessions and wealth as measures of self-worth drops away. The need for the approbation of others as evidence of your importance drops away. The need for hoarding surplus, born of fear and separation, drops away. In their place, you stand confident and complete, suffused with divine importance for the simple fact of existing, cherishing the earth that sustains you and responding in kind with respectful stewardship.

This is true wealth—the precious opportunity to participate in earthly life, treading lightly upon the earth while serving as a wise and foresightful steward, confirming your trust in the world's abundance by matching its generosity toward you with equal generosity toward others, recognizing your common bond with others and cherishing the divine spark in every creature you meet.

This wealth—this you can take with you.

Thirty-Nine

∽

Love And Relationships

Drawing an abundance of material comforts may ease one's life circumstances, but few are those who consider their lives complete and fulfilled solely by possessions and shelter. True happiness, true down-to-the-marrow contentment, depends on the quality of relationships one maintains, the depth of love, trust, and intimacy one shares with one's circle of friends and family. It is within the emotional peaks and valleys of human society that one finds life's richest meaning.

We have earlier explored the source of the human race, the families of consciousness from which it shoots in unique sparks of intent, covering the globe with the rich tapestry of human diversity. Let us briefly review the various levels of consciousness spilling down to flesh.

First, all species populating earth are bound in one common intent: to enjoy earth as the stage on which to play out their lives. From the perspective of the Source, and those levels near It, this agglomeration of consciousness is one indivisible, homogenous cluster of intent, binding with earth's consciousness to create a unique crucible of life. The plant kingdom is included, of course, as it too carries a unique slant of consciousness. Together, plants and the animate species weave the web of self-perpetuating life on earth.

Viewed from a closer perspective, this body of earth consciousness divides into increasingly specialized clusters, plants and animals marking the most fundamental division. Within animate life, countless streams of diversity flow toward earthly expression—forming the insect, bird, fish, reptile, and mammal families. At this stage, far above the primal pulse and beyond the reach of space-time, each species that ever "was" or ever "will be" stands in eternal validity.

Stepping closer to earth, and nearing the beat of the primal pulse, clusters of consciousness increasingly specialize depending upon their purpose in enjoying earthly life. Some choose instinctual behavior as their focus, selecting life forms bound by inner programming, carrying little potential for independent thought and reason. The insect kingdom plays host to such fields of consciousness. Some choose to experience life through the primacy of the society—a bee hive, an ant colony—while others select an independent focus—spiders and flies.

The mammal kingdom plays host to a wide variety of rational creatures, each species precisely balancing instinct and reason in a unique blend through which it filters experience. There is no evolution, no march over time from lower to higher forms of life; instead, mammals spread themselves out along a continuum from instinct to reason, selecting a precise mix through which to filter earthly life. What appear to you as the "higher" forms of life are those choosing to emphasize reason over instinct.

Turning to the human species, we can follow its increasingly specialized strands to the level with which you are most familiar. Originally arising in the undifferentiated cluster of earth consciousness, the human species selected the farthest position on the instinct-reason spectrum, holding reason supreme far above instinctual behavior, allowing for the enormous diversity of human cultures and environmental conditions to which it can adapt. The magic opposable thumb is the mark and meaning of the human species' purpose and design: rational manipulation of earth.

Flowing from the amorphous body of intent desiring expression as the human species are a number of families of consciousness, the first division of labor and approach, where the various tasks and focuses necessary to sustain human society are expressed. From each family of consciousness spills a multitude of what we term greater entities, more finely focused slants of intent, splintering human potential into finer strands of increasing diversity. Each greater entity hovers above the primal pulse, observing the historic sweep of earth as one simultaneous swirl of space-time, searching for places and times most conducive to fulfillment and growth.

Having selected such times and places, the greater entity shoots finely focused beams of intent into the earthly medium, down into the realm of space and time, where each such beam sparks to life a unique human individual, unduplicated in all of time, an irreplaceable strand in the cosmic web: you.

We offer this introductory material as a reminder of the true source of your life and the purpose of your existence, for so often relationship problems and difficulties in relating to others stem from the species' having lost touch with the higher realms from which it springs.

You may have heard the phrase, "We are all one." A head scratcher if ever there was one: Am I one with the neighbors I dislike, politicians I loathe, drug pushers and pimps? At the highest level, indeed you are all one, in the undifferentiated bank of intent giving rise to all species. And you are all one in the body of consciousness choosing to experience earth life through the strongest emphasis on reason above instinct. Below that level, as this body of consciousness splinters again and again, the "one-ness" dissipates as unique strands are forged, bearing more diverse focuses of intent.

At the level on which you live your daily life, with your reality cloaked behind the illusion of a physical world, you naturally emphasize the differences rather than the commonality. Your body ends neatly at the skin, making it "you," while everyone else is definitely "not you." You can see the risk in such a setup—will the species retain enough understanding of its higher commonality, or become ensnared in the illusion of separation? If the latter had not come to pass, we would not be writing this book, offering a hand from the higher realms to pull you from the quicksand of ego and separation.

The happiest balance is to carry an appreciation of the greater commonality from which you and all others spring, while also cherishing your stance as a unique strand of consciousness never to be duplicated. Revel in your "you-ness," while never losing sight of the realms of consciousness from which you spring, binding you to all others of your species and to all other species.

This material bears on our discussion of love and relationships because so often relationships are sought as a balm on the wounds of separation and isolation. Unconsciously understanding the greater source of life, but consciously allowing no such awareness, the schism between the unconscious commonality and the daily experience of separation gives rise to a profound unease, a vague, gnawing discomfort, as one struggles to find one's niche in the human family. Bolstered by Western culture's divorce from the natural order—stripping away appreciation of the common bond and one's irreplaceable role in the cosmic plan—each is left starkly alone, drifting through meaningless space or squirming under the heavy hand of God.

The irony and tragedy is that this sense of isolation and alienation is precisely what drives people to seek the salve of love from others; and yet others, similarly haunted, can offer no genuine loving bond in return. Two isolated, unhappy souls do not together make a happy couple, for each drains the other's energy while offering little in return.

If love and relationships are a problem area for you, the time has come to stop blaming the world for producing such a reprehensible flock of cretins, unable to offer you the love and devotion you deserve, and to recognize that only from a core of true peace, contentment, and a happy outlook can you expect to draw those of similar qualities to you.

As always, we must begin with a program of affirmation designed to counteract whatever beliefs stand in the way of a healthy self-image. Beginning with the broadest canvas, first craft an affirmation designed to restore you to a sense of the overall cosmic design in which you play a part. Again, we are sweeping away the detritus of Western culture's world-view and replacing it with a higher level of truth. Affirmations at this broad level might be phrased like these: "All life is one." "The universe is a divine web." "All life flows from the Source." "God creates heaven and earth." "We are all one."

By now you may notice a rather monotonous similarity between the broadest levels of belief, whether for health, abundance, or love. In all cases, we must first sweep aside Western culture's worldview and install a healthier vision. So, yes, the fundamental work is much the same whatever the ultimately desired goal.

When this deepest level of belief resonates throughout the body, we move to the next level, more finely focused but still fairly general. The purpose at this stage is to narrow the field of view to the human species and one's place within it, while still not focusing too sharply on oneself. Affirmations at this level could include these: "I am part of the Divine Mind." "All persons are my brothers and sisters." "The earth is a family." "I am one with all others." "I cherish the divinity in all others." "We are all spirit made flesh."

The purpose of this stage, again, is to move toward a focus on the human species, affirming its innate divinity and the deep bonds tying all persons together as family.

When the intermediate level has been fully installed, the last stage of affirmation narrows the focus more precisely on the individual, on you, affirming your unique role in the divine drama. For here is where most persons hurt most acutely—they don't know who they are, where they come from, or the purpose of their lives. They feel frightened, isolated, meaningless, alone. To some extent, almost everyone feels this way from time to time. To step into a conscious life, lived at the highest possible pitch, this inner vacuum must be filled with the warm rush of divine understanding. You must feel you are worthy of love before you can attract others who will honor and love you.

This level of affirmation, because it is so precisely focused on you, calls for the most carefully crafted affirmation, precisely phrased to fit your private situation. We can offer some examples, but you must use them only as raw material from which to fashion your own: "I am divine." "I am loved." "I am God." "I am the universe." "I fulfill the universe." "I glow with love." "I am irreplaceable." "I am eternal." "I meet always with acceptance and respect." "The world embraces me."

Now you can see the importance of conducting your daily session in a remote corner, far from eavesdropping ears. Chanting "I am God" is likely to elicit an accusation of hubris, not to mention a request for parlor tricks like parting the bathtub water. As before, the neuronal networks you are installing should be on a higher level of awareness than where you spend your waking hours. You are deliberately forging this higher awareness, sculpting it into your brain and coordinate, as a way of allowing the flow of a higher level of events to manifest in your life.

Restricting yourself to the mundane, the prosaic, the everyday, ensures that that is precisely where you will stay. Opening yourself up to miracles, to the higher realms of love and truth, allows them to flow easily into your experience. Dismiss all thoughts of hubris, of eye-rolling sarcasm, when considering such phrases. In the highest sense, you are God, and you are the universe. You do not daily live on that level of awareness, but that is no barrier to taking a step closer. Reach for the stars.

Probing for beliefs impeding the flow of fulfilling relationships is generally more intensely personal than working on health or abundance issues. For health and abundance are largely the province of universally held values and beliefs, to which almost all subscribe, whereas one's self-esteem and feelings of self-worth are largely shaped by experiences in childhood. The parent's power to shape and mold the child is almost without limit—almost—as the child depends on the parent to teach him the parameters of earthly life. A parent spewing scorn and ridicule at the child's every innocent inquiry and effort warps the child's inchoate sense of selfhood, perverting and stunting his natural growth.

In truth, such a process is based, like all other problem areas, upon Western culture's divorce from the natural order; for only a parent wallowing helplessly in an accidental universe or as a blight on God's good earth could mistreat a child so. Only from a core of self-hatred or, at best, existential despair, could a parent deliberately strangle a child's emotional health. Observe native cultures about the globe: are they plagued with juvenile delinquency, vandalism, drug abuse, and teenage pregnancy?

Having grown up in Western culture, and to some extent suffering the effects of its worldview on your socialization, you may find that beliefs and values implanted decades ago continue to haunt you, poisoning your relationships, making true love seem unattainable, a cruel joke, to be found only on movie screens. In addition to the affirmation work outlined above, there may well be specific messages implanted in childhood that hamper self-worth, polluting your coordinate, preventing it from drawing truly loving persons to you. A single "You stupid jerk!" from an exasperated parent can echo for decades.

We mention this because the wounds suffered in childhood can cut so deep, and though scar tissue covers them in amnesiac relief, the underlying trauma remains. Unless all such scars are washed away, the neuronal networks and coordinate attracting your life's events cannot hum at their highest, clearest pitch.

If your examination unearths feelings of unworthiness inculcated in childhood, and the affirmation work outlined above is ineffective in entirely healing the wound, we have several suggestions.

First is a tool which may appear nonsensical: retroactive visualization. Rather than crafting a desired future event, you return to a key moment in childhood where you suffered wounds to your self-image and replay the scene with a happier outcome.

Remember that memories are stored principally as emotional intensities—so as you review your childhood, searching for such instances, you may well find one particular moment leaping at you in full, bloody intensity, as if the event occurred this morning. Before beginning your daily conscious life session, imagine the happiest possible outcome for the event in question. If you were humiliated, see yourself triumphant instead. If you were struck, see yourself cuddled and stroked. If you were scorned, see yourself celebrated. If you were cheated, see yourself treated fairly. Structure the scene so that it runs as it did in real life until the painful moment arose, then switch to your new, happier ending.

When you have induced full relaxation, say aloud something to the effect of, "Now I relive a scene from my childhood." Then visualize the scene with its new ending. Most important is to exponentially boost your feeling of triumph or ecstasy or love, suffusing the moment with intensity. Feel the emotion race through your every pore and fiber. Closing the scene at this intense pitch, allow your mind to go dark and end by saying, "This is precisely how I lived that moment."

Since we always have subversive reasons for what we do, what might be the purpose of retroactive visualization? What possible use is there in dredging up the hurts of the past and pretending they turned out as triumphs?

The psyche, which feels the impact of your visualization, stands at the portal of the primal pulse, just barely dipping into space-time, communicating constantly with the higher realms where space-time has no grasp. At that level, where time does not exist, your past is laid out in as infinite a range of probabilities as your future. No event is ever finished, complete, locked up in history books as the definitive version. True, you may draw only one version to physical expression. But all other probable versions forever retain their vitality beyond the primal pulse. It is this level of timeless, vibrant potential that you tap into with retroactive visualization.

By telling yourself aloud that this is the version you lived in childhood, and infusing the visualized scene with intensity, you rewrite the history of that event. This is not idle daydreaming; you are literally changing history, your history. For as each moment of life is sizzled into your private store of experience, yours is the power to relive any experience to your script, altering the experience's record and therefore its effect upon you. The single most crucial element is the emotional intensity you impart to the scene; you must hurl burning beams of intent to the psyche, storming across the primal pulse, replacing psychic scar tissue with healthy, glowing memories.

At first you can expect the usual resistance from the brain as it struggles to balance the two competing versions of the past event. "Well, did they slap me or didn't they?" it may well ask. With consistent, concerted effort, you should find that visualizing the newly crafted scene resonates with the body, tingles all over, your signal that the new memory has replaced the old. And as important as the visualization work is, it must be buttressed with a waking acknowledgement that the new version of the event is in fact the genuine one. Throughout the day you might allow yourself to daydream, drawing up the scene, relishing its feeling of happiness, or triumph, or love. Yes, that's the way it happened; it seems like only yesterday.

With the crucial event of your childhood rewritten, you might well find yourself responding differently to people. Those whom you once held dear may drift away, as you find them living on an incompatible level of silent hurt and bottled anger. New friends and lovers may replace them, persons bursting with life, vitality, and high humor. You see, as your coordinate is relieved of its scar tissue, it can hum on a higher level, naturally attracting persons of sympathetic vibration. Your thoughts and memories act as a magnet to others of similar emotional health.

And when your new friends chat about their happy childhood experiences, you can pipe in with, "Yes, but let me tell you about the happiest moment of my life..." and then spill the scene that was once a visualization and is now a fact, your history, indelibly carved into your psyche and the universe as the definitive version of that sublime moment.

If childhood pain springs not from specific instances of abuse and neglect, but rather from deliberate or unconscious mistreatment through the years, a gray pallor woven through the fabric of memory, another tool may be more effective in removing the curse of a bleak and cheerless childhood: forgiveness.

Forgiveness is a process whereby you release from blame those who may have wronged you in childhood. The purpose is not only to remove the energy blockages that anger and resentment create, but to lift from your spirit the stranglehold such memories carry.

Now, it seems to ask much that you forgive those who may have engaged in years of psychological warfare against your well-being. Why forgive them? Why should they be let off the hook? Let us explore what hidden benefits lie beneath forgiving your oppressors.

First, your greatest happiness can be attained only when your neuronal networks and coordinate hum at their highest possible pitch. To do so, they must be clear of energy blockages—for blocked energy always carries detrimental effect. The clearest coordinate is one building confidently upon the past, embracing the present moment, and marching confidently toward the future. Any lingering resentment from the past creates a vortex there, sucking up energy meant for use in today and tomorrow, crippling a richly lived present and future.

To carry angers and resentments for pain suffered long ago is to imbue the perpetrator with present-day power in your life. If the resentment remains, so does that person's power over you, his sway over your mental health. By resenting or hating another, you grant him power, power to manipulate your emotions—even if the person in question is long since dead. Where resentment lingers, the person lives on, a psychic vampire, bleeding dry your health and vitality. To forgive your oppressors is to release them from their privileged roles in determining your self-worth, dismissing them from carrying any effect upon you today. To forgive others is to reclaim personal power.

Another reason for forgiveness is the recognition that you create your own reality. You chose your parents and life circumstances. You magnetically attracted every event of your childhood. *To some degree*, then, you must accept responsibility for the events—both happy and horrifying—of childhood. The process of conscious life creation does not begin with adulthood and reading a book such as this. It begins before birth and is the fundamental law of human life. Children, in fact, carry far greater awareness of their power to influence events than adults do; growing up in Western culture effectively beats such awareness out of consciousness.

To accept your share of responsibility for the events of your childhood is not to absolve from responsibility those who may have wronged you. They must carry that burden, and carry the psychic damage that anyone committing cruelty suffers. You see, there is no escape from one's actions, ever, run as far and fast as one might. The universe is set up to balance every physically expressed act with its opposite—if not in this lifetime, then in another. So thoughts of revenge are futile and damaging, as well as superfluous: Balance will be achieved. Wrongs will be righted.

Another reason to forgive your oppressors is the recognition that whatever they did, their actions were rarely fueled by a deliberate determination to harm you. Especially among parents, even the most barbaric of crimes are fueled by love, however twisted and perverted its expression.

How could such psychic and physical violence be motivated by love? Perhaps the strongest reason for forgiveness is to recognize the milieu in which your parents and their generation lived—back in the Era of Unconscious Life. In those prehistoric times—when people actually believed that the universe was born of a Big Bang and swelled into a random universe supporting meaningless creatures on an accidental planet; or that a patriarchal sky god created the universe in six days, then sat back and watched in haughty satisfaction as his creatures scraped their bellies on the tortuous road to salvation—how could anyone maintain a positive self-image? How could anyone appreciate the divinity pulsing within, when such had been projected outward or abandoned entirely? How could anyone feel significant when floating in a random universe?

This existential insecurity, the core malaise of Western culture, meant that your parents and their cohorts could never truly feel deep self-worth, the highest vibrant self-love one can know. When one cannot love oneself, one cannot truly love others, even one's children. Whether viewing children as random ciphers in cosmic swampland, or as damned creatures born in sin, the result is the same: to rob children of their innate divinity, their intrinsic self-worth and dignity, their carrying a unique strand of consciousness contributing to the growth of all. Even the most loving parent fails at true connection when carrying so many layers of scales upon the eyes, blocking sight of the child's luminescent divinity.

Why resent and begrudge such persons? Why not pity and forgive? Having reviewed all the reasons for forgiveness outlined above, if you find yourself carrying buried resentments against those who raised or influenced you, a forgiveness program is called for. The procedure begins with affirmation, then employs a curious hybrid of affirmation and visualization.

To begin, use the first two levels of belief work outlined earlier in this chapter, those designed to restore you to an appreciation for the divinity of the cosmos and the oneness of all nature. Once those levels of belief are installed, the following step is employed for forgiving and releasing.

After inducing deep relaxation, deliberately create a glowing feeling of love suffusing your body. You might imagine your heart pumping blood-love through your veins, carrying its rich warmth to every pore. Also, imagine a glowing light about your body, emanating from the skin, rising in tendrils and weaving a cocoon of love about you. Love is within you, and all around you. Feel it; boost the intensity as high as you can without straining.

Now, holding that loving feeling—and until now your mind's screen has been blank—speak aloud the name of the person you wish to forgive and release. Speak it as if you were announcing the entrance of a noble personage at a royal banquet, or, if you are uncomfortable with such formality, speak it as if you were seeing a loved one after a long separation, your voice colored with love and affection. In any case, the point is to establish the individual as a valued personage.

After speaking the person's name, bring him into focus. Most effective will be to concentrate on his face, as this carries the strongest impact. If, however, you are most comfortable viewing the person in familiar clothes and surroundings, use that imagery—whatever evokes the strongest resonance with you. The image should remain fairly static, though not frozen, as if the person is listening to you attentively without responding.

You then say aloud, with sincerity, warmth, and confidence in your voice: "I forgive you and release you. Now go in peace." Allow the phrase to resonate through your body; feel the warmth it evokes, as the burden of a lifetime is lifted from your shoulders. Holding the image of the person in mind, see him acknowledge your blessing with a smile and a nod of acknowledgement and gratitude. Then watch as he turns and walks away from you, his back facing you, toward a door or hallway or opening of some sort. Watch as he approaches the opening; see the white light of divinity streaming from it, its tendrils reaching out to envelop him, suffusing him with spirit. Perhaps, just before he disappears, you might see the person turn around, acknowledge you one last time with a smile and wave, then turn and step fully into the light, being absorbed into its refulgent luminosity, disappearing from your sight.

Holding the pulsing warmth of the scene in your body, allow the imagery to go dark. Still glowing, say aloud, "I am free," or "I am released from the past," or "My spirit soars free"—fashion a phrase comfortable to you, to the effect that the act of forgiveness is actually an act of self-love, releasing the hurts of the past to embrace a finer tomorrow.

As with other visualization work, this process should be employed in daily session until it seems somehow stale, as if the body is asking, "What are we going through this again for?" When drawing up the individual's face, a small voice may exclaim, "Are you still here!" These are your signals that the work has been completed, that the hurts inflicted by this individual have been released, and that he no longer carries any power over you. You are unchained from childhood.

We have very briefly outlined some of the causes of unhappiness in relationships, and tools you can use to release the blockages hindering your pleasure in human company. Here we must make clear that of all the topics discussed so far, none is so pregnant with reincarnational influence as the field of relationships. For it is the bump and grind of human relations that carries the greatest potential for growth and learning, and generates the most intense experience. Thus, your bonds with others create the richest medium of exploration and growth, offering potential for soaring triumph and crushing defeat.

The tools and techniques outlined above are primarily designed to resolve relationship problems arising within the boundaries of your present life. They carry less power to penetrate reincarnational thickets. If, after steady and concerted effort, and feeling certain that all belief-impediments have been dissolved, you still find yourself unhappy and unfulfilled in the realm of relationships, there may be reincarnational influences at work.

Further, you can begin to allow awareness of such influences, even if you lack complete understanding of their source. If you find yourself trapped in a relationship with a particular individual, feeling strongly bound in a roller coaster ride of emotional highs and lows, while your mind and friends tell you to wake up and break the tie, such influence may be at work. Upon meeting someone, if you feel a jolt of recognition, or an immediate and unwarranted love or loathing, such influence may be at work. Even while not understanding the precise reincarnational design for joining with others, you can at least recognize that such factors may be at work, explaining the other's inexplicable behavior and your incongruous emotions.

The tools for uncovering such reincarnational material lie beyond the purpose and scope of this book. Self-hypnosis, or a skilled hypnotist, can aid in such work. Any techniques allowing access to higher levels of mind, where you can research past lifetimes, might also bear fruit.

We mention reincarnation only as a reminder that you are not born as a blank slate, but come bouncing from the womb dragging the baggage of centuries. Always, you are at the mercy of nothing, for yours is the power to comprehend and release any influence, whether arising in this lifetime or any other.

As an aside, our discussion should also awaken an appreciation for children and the dangers in squeezing them into narrow paths. Each child is born carrying his own agenda, his own tasks and challenges to keep him busy for the next eighty years. Wise parenting is short on lecture and long on listening, for the child will set about deliberately arranging his life to allow for growth and fulfillment along the lines of his greatest benefit.

A child springing from a different family of consciousness than that of the parent, bearing the stamp of a fundamentally different approach to life, may frighten and upset the parent. Such contrasts are often deliberately chosen to provide growth to both parent and child: The beefy, athletic father watches in dismay as his son trips out the door for ballet and piano lessons. If love prevails, both grow.

Each child is a divine spark of unique potential, the glimmering terminus of a strand of consciousness flowing into earthly life. Each comes fully equipped with a reincarnational history and life plan, tasks and challenges to be met and attacked with relish. The loving parent applies the sunshine and moisture of protection, self-esteem, and love, then stands aside to watch the child sprout and blossom into a garden of soul-flowers.

We have now sketched three areas in which affirmation and visualization work are effective in overcoming hidden psychological obstacles to happiness, growth, and fulfillment. Health, abundance, and relationships, being issues of concern to many, have been briefly explored, along with suggestions for affirmations and visualizations to raise these areas to a higher, healthier pitch. What we offer are simply suggestions; always, you must fashion a Conscious Life Plan which makes sense to you, and whose components resonate strongly. Emotional intensity is the grease lubricating your thoughts' journey to the psyche.

It is not our aim to leave the impression that, with a month or two of affirmation and visualization work, your life will magically change in every way for the better, leaving you without care or problem. That is not the nature of reality. The purpose of earthly life is to effectively meet and handle the challenges that arise, moving past them to unravel the next set of knots.

Conscious life is not the elimination of all problems, but reclaiming the power to master them, to move past them to a higher plane of life, beyond the pull of childhood fears and existential insecurity. It means taking responsibility for the events of your life, the recognition that you pull all experiences toward you for the purpose of growth and learning. It means acknowledging your power to alter the inner magnet pulling your life's events toward expression, changing the nature of those events as they manifest.

An artist is rarely satisfied with his work. Between vision and creation lies an abyss of frustration. Between the ideal and the real stands a mountain of challenge. Yet no real artist ever surrenders, throws up his hands, and abandons the struggle to wrestle vision into symbol. He perseveres, he falls, he rises, he triumphs.

You are an artist, a life artist. Each day is a fresh canvas, built upon the broad strokes and subtle nuances of the past, carrying their meaning as background while offering a fresh start and clean brushes. Never satisfied, no matter how resplendent your work, you face each day as another precious opportunity to reach higher into the stars and wrestle truth into experience. You never surrender, for you arise each day, do you not? As an artist is driven to create even while the process may torment him, so do you embrace the work of life art, struggling to find the most sublime blend of celestial radiance and rich earth tones, marrying them with sure strokes of intent, each day a masterpiece of triumph and growth as life unfolds on your canvas under your sure and steady hand.

Which shall it be—the paint-by-numbers prison of Western culture's worldview or the thundering, divine brush strokes of conscious life?

Forty

ॐ

Ritual

Ritual is the symbolic expression of deeply felt values. Every human culture knows ritual, as the intersection of humanity's spiritual origin and its mastery of physical symbol. Ritual demarcates the flow of time; as the calendar year is built upon the earth's rotation about the sun, so every ritual, whether pegged to date or season, arises from this archetypal pattern. Ritual binds together a tribe, a community, a nation, symbolically affirming the commonality beneath the surface diversity. Ceremonies, celebrations, religious holidays, birthdays, national days of independence and triumph, weekly religious services, the ringing in of the new year: all these are rituals, familiar niches in the sweep of time, binding one year to the next.

Ritual, known only to the human species, arises from its need to impose rational order upon the world, to slice the flow of time into manageable chunks, to create traditions stitching generation to generation in a seamless fabric. Singing Christmas carols at Yuletide binds you to the cathedrals of the Middle Ages; Jewish boys undergoing circumcision binds them to the Old Testament fathers of the race; taking communion binds you to Jesus in the Garden of Gethsemane, even as Jesus's ritual offering of his blood and flesh bound him to the pagan religions predating his time. Ritual is an anchor to the past.

Ritual is symbol, a formal series of structured actions hinting at deeper truth while never fully expressing that truth. For ritual is born of mystery, the urge to wrestle truth into symbol, even while acknowledging that the ritual's actions are but a pale reflection of the truth underlying them. Where ritual retains full meaning and vitality, it is bound to an appreciation for the deeper truth from which it arises.

Over time, as a culture's cosmology and spiritual life evolve, ritual must keep step or lose its vitality. Ritual divorced from underlying truth becomes stale, no longer holding power and mystery, but standing as a desiccated remnant of its culture's past. Each generation must refashion its rituals to match the flow of spiritual evolution lest the ritual lose all meaning.

Such is commonly seen today, where many religions cling to rituals born centuries—even millennia—ago, arising from the Zeitgeist of their culture. As time marches steadily on, a ritual frozen into place loses its bond with the culture, no longer speaking to the deeply felt spiritual tone of the time. How many actually believe they eat the literal flesh and blood of Christ when they swallow wafer and wine? How many believe they witness deepest spiritual truth when the keepers of religious ritual are all male—while women, the spiritual guardians of earth, can only watch from the pew? To be vital and strong, to carry mystery and power, ritual must arise organically from the spiritual life of a time and place.

Briefly turning to a more prosaic exploration of the deeper purpose behind ritual, how does it fit into the conscious life scheme outlined so far? Is it the pathetic grasping of the ignorant, to be dismissed by all self-realized adults, or is it a powerful tool of conscious life creation?

Remember how your beliefs are etched into your coordinate: through action. Any time you act, your brain triggers electrical impulses which travel down the spine to spark the desired action. In the spine, the intent behind these impulses shapes the coordinate, molding it according to the beliefs fueling the action. In this manner, your beliefs are literally written into the coordinate, which in turn magnetically attracts the events of your life.

Remember also the importance of repetition. In affirmation and visualization work, once is never enough. Repetition, the constant expression of desire and intent, ultimately rewires the brain's circuitry, reshapes the coordinate, and signals to the psyche which events it is to manifest. The more often such work is done, the greater the intensity imparted—and intensity equals power.

With this understanding, you can appreciate the importance of ritual. First, any series of actions signals to the brain and coordinate that you believe the actions to be of importance or benefit. Whatever actions you perform, whatever they symbolically represent, the beliefs fueling them are encoded in brain and coordinate. Second, a ritual performed regularly drives home the beliefs behind it with increased intensity. This intensity, of course, serves to carry your beliefs to the psyche, where events in line with the underlying beliefs will be pulled closer to expression.

The daily session during which you conduct affirmation and visualization work is itself a ritual, a regular pattern of behavior arising from deeper beliefs and values. Ritual, when consistently employed, and when expressing deep inner truth, is a powerful tool for those fashioning a conscious life.

Ritual falls into two main categories: those performed alone and those performed with others. Obviously, each type carries a distinctly different purpose. Private rituals turn one's focus inward, emphasizing one's uniqueness, one's inner world of dreams and thoughts, one's private bond with nature. Group rituals shift one's focus outward, into the larger human community to which each is bound, celebrating affectional ties and shared values.

We might begin, then, with private rituals. As you cast about for familiar rituals on which to base your own, you find a dearth of material to work with. What rituals has your society spawned that emphasize the individual's private truth and inner life? None—for even solitary prayer is a projection of power outward, onto a patriarchal sky god, asking him for guidance and assistance, underscoring one's ignorance and impotence.

A conscious life is one lived in full appreciation of one's inner power, one's unlimited energy and knowledge, and one's irreplaceable role in the cosmic scheme. Private rituals serve to declare and celebrate private power—for only from a center of confidence and self-love can one truly connect with others to better the world.

Rituals benefit from implements carrying special meaning, tools and objects suffused with meaning beneath their everyday utility. Candles, bells, incense, special clothing, herbs or other plants, elements from the earth, all serve to create a mood, a sense of specialness, setting the ritual apart from prosaic, everyday activities. Over time, after repeated use, such implements will naturally absorb the energies evoked during ritual, literally imbuing them with spiritual power. Implements of ritual are thus best kept sheltered from casual handling and use, for such can diminish their high vibrations.

Especially in private rituals, the implements chosen must carry deep personal meaning; they must resonate with you as symbols of higher truth. For this is the purpose of ritual: bonding spiritual truth with earth elements and action. If you own no objects carrying special significance, no heirloom items binding you to your forebears or other cherished items, you might purchase a few items expressly for use in private rituals. If you love the dance of flame from a candle or oil lamp, such could only enhance your ritual. If certain toys or dolls evoke happy memories from childhood, try to find a similar item. A stone or cloth or flower bearing your favorite color carries the power of your inner life. These are just suggestions; as always, only you can sort through your store of symbols and memories, gathering those items carrying the strongest pull.

A ritual is like a play: The curtain must rise, and it must fall. Every religious ceremony carries this dramatic structure: The lighting of the candles and the call to worship on one end, and the snuffing of the candles and the benediction on the other, provide the framework for the spiritual celebration strung between the rising and falling curtain. So should all rituals be built upon a consistent pattern of distinct opening and closing.

In a private ceremony, any number of actions can serve to open the ritual. Lighting a candle while saying, "This is the God-light of protection," or "I light the universal lamp of truth," or "My light burns with the stars," is a way of performing a precise and consistent action—lighting the candle—while also affirming the higher purpose of ritual. Action and spirit: these are ritual's ingredients.

Lighting incense serves the same purpose, literally imbuing the room with a distinct, ritual-linked scent. As the sense of smell perceives a higher level of vibration than sight or hearing, using incense or other olfactory stimulants is especially effective for inducing a spiritual mood.

To close a ritual, snuff out the candle or the incense while speaking aloud that your attention now turns away from the celestial realms, back to the earthly medium in which spirit finds its growth. You might fashion a closing phrase upon these suggestions: "The God-light now remains within me as I embrace earth life." "The universal flame glows within me always." "In peace and love I return to my brothers and sisters." The closing phrase may also be influenced by the nature of the ritual, summing up its meaning in one richly evocative phrase.

Because private rituals are just that—private—we prefer to refrain from offering specific routines lest we rob you of finding your private symbols. You know the elements of ritual—music, readings, dance, meditation, prayer, invoking higher spirits, food and drink—and you must fashion rituals springing from your inner life, carrying private truth. A variety of rituals can be devised for diverse purposes, often used in conjunction with affirmation and visualization work to alter the course of life events. Only private symbols, and a personally devised order of ritual, can grant expression to your needs and celebrations.

We can, however, offer one ritual designed to heal one of Western culture's most gaping wounds, the division between mind and body. Having been raised in Western culture, it may well be decades since you enjoyed the young child's easy symbiotic flow between mind and body, and you may claim to feel no ill effects from the rupture. A blind person may similarly swear to get about just fine using sound and his hands to navigate through the world—and would you applaud his wisdom if he declined a sight-restoring operation? Just as the blind man's eyes would suddenly offer a flood of sensation previously unknown to him, so may you find unimagined benefits in restoring the easy flow between mind and body.

The best place for this ritual to be conducted is the bathtub. Indeed, many private rituals are best held while soaking under warm water. Water is the foundation of life, the child of sun and moon, the only one of earth's three main elements to carry appreciable resistance and thus the only element sparking growth. To envelop the body in warm water is to plunge into the primal sea of life and creation. Thoughts of growth and change literally carry greater impact, for the body's stimulation at all points by water's play of attraction and resistance unites it as one with the mind's urge toward growth.

The room holding the bathtub should be dim or dark, reducing visual stimulation to a minimum. A candle or incense may be lighted, along with the phrase you routinely use to begin private rituals. Step into the warm bath and lower yourself into the water. If you can submerge all but your head, do so. Allow a time of deep breathing, eyes closed, concentrating on the warm velvet cocoon in which you float.

Now, open your eyes and say something to the effect of, "I now affirm my love and appreciation for my body." Place your hands on your toes, gently massaging and exploring them, studying their design and perfection. Allow plenty of time for this; think of all the times your feet and toes have served you well, all the adventures they have carried you on without complaint or your acknowledgement. If you wish, you might say aloud, "I cherish my toes," or "My toes are perfection," or "I feel the universe in my toes." The phrase should be deliberately crafted on a suprarealistic level, above the mundane, everyday opinion you hold of your toes. We are reaching for miracles.

Now, lovingly releasing your toes, move up to your feet. Again, gently massage them, exploring their curves and folds, admiring their design, recalling their years of stalwart service. Speak aloud whatever phrase you used for the toes, sending your appreciation now to your feet.

Work your way up along your ankles, your calves, your knees—what wonderful knees! think where they have taken you!—your thighs, your hips, up to the sexual organs. Now you understand why we suggest this be a private ritual. For, yes, you must express the same appreciation and love as you have for every other body part, underscored with a gentle massage. If the thought unnerves or repulses you, consider your reaction and its appropriateness. Do you really wish to carry the legacy of Adam and Eve's original sin, passed like a genetic mutation through umpteen generations and festering in your genitals? Or would you rather release shame and guilt and embrace the site of sensual pleasure and procreation?

Nowhere is Western culture's division of mind and body more apparent. For what sensations do your sexual organs bring you? Pleasure. Pleasure means you feel good. And what does society preach about sexual experience, except inside legally and religiously sanctioned marriage? Pleasure is bad. The body says "good," the mind says "bad." This confusion, implanted at a tender age, splits mind from body, crushing their easy symbiosis under the baggage of centuries.

The body never lies—that is the province of the mind. If it feels good, it is good. Period.

As you massage the genital area and send it your appreciation, check your feelings. Are you feeling guilt, embarrassment, shame? Call such feelings up, acknowledge them and their source, and lovingly release them. You might project them into the glowing candle flame, watching them evaporate in the divine light of higher truth.

Continue to move up the body, appreciating both the skin and the internal organs lying beneath them. You carry enough anatomical knowledge to guess where various organs are located; as your hands pass over their skin-wrapping, pause to send appreciation. The stomach, for instance—flawlessly processing everything from breast milk to adolescent sugar binges to the beaujolais and sushi of polite society. What a miracle!

Moving up the chest to the neck, trickle one hand down the other arm, admiring its design and perfection, the miraculous joint at the elbow, greased for life at birth. Then reverse hands and appreciate the other arm.

Take particular care to examine, massage, and appreciate your hands. For these are your primary tools of manipulation, the intersection point of your soul with earth, with which you embrace and act upon the world. Study their design, flex them, ball them into fists, then wiggle each finger alone. Have you ever known any human invention, however inspired and exquisitely crafted, to exceed or even match your hands' design, subtlety, responsiveness, power, sensitivity, durability, intricacy, adaptability, or flexibility? No such creation has ever sprung from the hands of man, or ever will. The hands of man are themselves your greatest miracle.

Using your miraculous hands, move up to the neck and face. Here you pause to appreciate the sense organs, feeding constant details of your stance in space. Your lips, teeth, tongue—explore them all, offering gratitude for the gift of taste and the power to pucker up for a loved one. Your nose, bringing you the highest level of vibration, the life energies about you. Your eyes, painting a picture of a physical world with a palette of infinite color, shading, and nuance. Your ears, carrying the laughter of children and music's healing thunder. Your scalp and hair, beneath which lies the brain, that inconceivably complex maze of circuitry through which belief and intent are translated into action. Pause to appreciate the brain, its faithful translation of belief into experience, its neuronal circuitry through which you experience the power of your thoughts.

When each body part has been lovingly appreciated and massaged, close by affirming the unity of the body, offering an appreciation for its cooperative harmony. You might run your hands from your toes to your scalp once again, fairly quickly this time, not breaking the body into parts but feeling your fingers' path as a journey along a glowing body of light, indivisible and perfect.

After lying silently in the water for a few minutes, allowing the appreciation for each body part and the harmony of the whole to sink in, you might close the ritual by saying aloud, "I love, cherish, and respect my body," or "My body is perfection," or "My mind and body are one." The point is to affirm the bond between mind and body through the mind's active appreciation for the body and respect for its miraculous design and harmony.

We offer this ritual as a suggestion, and you must adapt it to suit your purpose. With this fleshed-out ritual as an example, you can devise rituals designed to heal other wounds or lacks, or to celebrate success and harmony, as you see fit. Rituals such as this are best not conducted every day. They should be imbued with specialness, the high importance accorded to events riding above the cycle of daily concerns. Allowing spontaneity to determine the use of ritual enhances their power—for you conduct a ritual when "the spirit moves you," offering respect to the hidden cycles pulsing beneath daily life.

Group rituals celebrate family, community, and shared values. They weave persons together in a common web, upholding shared qualities and beliefs as the basis of community. Further, group rituals can affirm shared spiritual understanding, acknowledging the unseen realms from which you spring, or renewing the race's bond to the earth. In group ritual, the focus is on the underlying commonality binding persons together, or on the even larger earth-web of which the human race is but one strand.

As mentioned earlier, rituals evolve as the species' consciousness evolves, if the rituals are to retain power and mystery. Rituals born of ancient dogma, no longer relevant or inspiring, fail their purpose. In your age, the time of transition between old and new orders, it seems apparent that the time is ripe for new rituals to reflect the grinding spiritual gears rolling the race forward.

One such ritual would be a celebration of the family. While there is much talk these days of "family," your society has no rituals designed to celebrate family, has it? As the mother provides the fetal womb, so is the family a social womb, in which young children enjoy comfort and security while gradually kicking and stretching toward the day of independence. A ritual affirming the supreme importance of family, and the inexpressible value placed upon each person within it, serves to celebrate each person's worth as well as the ties binding each to the others.

A deeper purpose lies behind such celebrations, for you choose your parents and family, and you choose your children. More precisely, they agree to join with you for mutual benefit and growth. So to celebrate family is no idle exercise in Norman Rockwell anachronism, but instead acknowledges the choices made before birth, lost to memory, binding parent to child.

Such a family ritual can be as simple as going around the table before a meal and having each person speak appreciation for each of the others, offering a specific moment of warmth and laughter shared that day or a broader appreciation for the love and support the other offers. Children will have little difficulty finding reasons to appreciate their parents, as parents are meant to guide and protect; but parents must also come to appreciate each child as a unique, divine spark, carrying flesh and blood from his parents but brought to life by a soul all his own. No sarcasm, ridicule, scolding, or lecturing should infect the ceremony. Each is to cherish and appreciate, and offer these aloud in tones of respect.

A more elaborate ritual of the same type can be devised to suit each individual family. An annual "Family Day" could be established during which handmade gifts are exchanged, recitations of respect and appreciation offered all around, followed by a special trip to the park or other outing. We do not mean to encouraging limiting expressions of appreciation to only once a year! But setting aside an entire day annually when the only concern is the pleasure in each other's company underscores the more frequent appreciation ritual.

Of special importance is that husband and wife reaffirm their marriage vows in the presence of their children. So often, in life's frantic rush, a couple loses the passion and tender respect they knew in courtship. Of all the elements of a child's security, none is so central as to rest securely in the hermetic bond between his parents, for from their love for each other flows a common love for the child, that love being exponentially stronger than one adult alone can offer.

We recognize that we address a culture in which half of all marriages end in divorce, and the notion of romantic love can seem a cruel farce. In the long run, as the race restores itself to the natural order, and as the number of those consciously creating their lives increases, the overriding factor splintering marriages apart—unreasonable expectations—will diminish. No longer will each depend exclusively upon the other for every need; no more will marriage be seen as an escape from the cold isolation of modern life; and an appreciation for each person's uniqueness will diminish the need to reshape one's partner in one's own image.

Of course, the family ritual outlined above can be performed in a single parent family. In a divorced household, if the tension level permits, the divorced parents could join in the ritual for the purpose of reassuring their children of the marital love they once shared, and from which love the children grew.

The unstable nuclear family leads us to the next level of human affiliation, that of the extended family and community. The extended family brings grandparents, aunts, uncles, and cousins into a circle joined by blood. The community steps outside those blood bonds to embrace friends sharing common values and affectional ties with the family. Building in hierarchies, the great human fabric is slowly stitched together in circles of increasing size.

The ritual outlined above, for use with the nuclear family, can also be used with an extended family gathering. It might be particularly evocative during the holiday season, when the air is redolent of spiritual truth and gratitude spills more easily from the lips. A Thanksgiving dinner in which gratitude is offered not only to the spirit of nature that laid its bounty upon the table, but also bathes each person in the spotlight of love and appreciation, bonds spirit with earth, love and family, in a way that carries power and resonance.

The point is to set aside a time to recognize that the spirit of God, and Christ's message of love, can be more than dry texts dusted off once a year and dutifully repeated by rote. They spring forth anew every time a child offers heartfelt gratitude for the love and guidance of his parents, and the parents respond with words thanking the child for the gift of his presence.

Of particular importance to young people are rituals celebrating their movement toward manhood or womanhood. All of childhood is preparation for full flowering into self-realized adulthood, and a ceremony in which a community's adults acknowledge their acceptance of a boy or girl as taking steps toward adulthood binds generation to generation in a way that few other rituals can. Each child longs for the acceptance and approval of adults; to make the child a center of attention, hearing the words of his or her elders welcoming the child into the adult tribe, spurs the young one on to even more determined efforts at achieving manhood or womanhood. The Jewish culture has such ceremonies, the bar mitzvah and bat mitzvah, but the broader society can devise its own rituals released from a specific religious orientation.

A puberty rite for modern Western culture might be fashioned as follows. On the chosen day (whether a specific birthday or when the time feels right), the boy or girl would leave home in the company of same-sex relatives and adult friends. All men for a boy, or all women for a girl, the celebrants would travel to a location suitable for a private ceremony. Of course such ceremonies are best held outdoors, in a park or forest, where paternal sun meets maternal earth.

With the adults standing around the child in a circle, each could offer personal thoughts about what it means to be a man or a woman. Such reflections could include sharing deeply held values, and how they have been tempered and proven by the passage of time, a discussion of how one's body changes as puberty takes its course, a code of morality for dealing with others, and so on.

Each group must decide for itself how structured a ritual it is to devise. A responsive reading could be used with those groups desiring more structure: A leader offers a series of encouraging and illuminating insights about adulthood, while the others responsively speak their affirmation. Of course, music can play a vital role, offering songs of youth and growth, or as the background for dance.

An informal group might simply take the boy or girl for a walk in the woods, allowing the child to ask questions about adulthood that until now he or she has kept locked in private wonder. Encouraging free and frank discussion, the child hears a variety of perspectives on what it means to be a man or a woman. Sex is generally the number one topic of curiosity in such discussions, and it should be discussed without shame or guilt, as a natural and joyous part of life, binding great pleasure with a moral code.

Following the same-sex ritual, the group returns to the home where friends and relatives of the opposite sex have prepared a party or feast. Here the boy or girl is welcomed into the arms of the opposite sex, celebrating his or her steps toward adulthood. Bread is broken after toasts to the child's long and happy life. Individual recitations may be offered, as with the previous ceremony, in which the opposite sex adults describe how their lives are enriched by the presence of the other gender, encouraging the child to grow toward the day when the other sex will be embraced in love and responsibility.

Hugs all around, of course.

In addition to the large ceremony outlined above, at the day's close the boy or girl might retreat with the same-sex parent to a bedtime chat about issues raised and discussed throughout the day. This tender, private ceremony might be held with just a lone candle bathing parent's and child's faces. After both parents have bestowed a good night kiss, the boy or girl drifts off to sleep, dreaming visions of mastery, freedom, and responsibility.

Larger community rituals may affirm the shared values binding unrelated persons together, or joining together to acknowledge the spiritual world from which the human family springs. All religious services are of this type, drawing together those who share a common cosmological perspective on the origin and meaning of life.

We suggest that in the future such rituals will change to follow the evolution of consciousness as the race returns to the natural order. Such rituals will rely less on offering worship, prayer, and hope of forgiveness to a paternal sky god—out there somewhere, divorced and distant—and will instead affirm the divinity immanent in all things. As in all other areas of life, a conscious life is one reclaiming personal power, no longer dribbling it away to the keepers of religion and government. As such, a ceremony celebrating humanity's spiritual origin will move toward celebrations of the God burning in each heart, the divinity coursing through all veins, the redemption that one owns at birth simply for being alive.

This shift in consciousness will also restore the race to the natural world, to the earth granting life and freedom. If there is a divinity "out there" to worship, it is the earth, that living organism upon whose flesh you live. Recognizing that human consciousness and earth consciousness have deliberately joined to explore the manipulation and mastery of physical life cannot help but restore you to appreciation for the inconceivable complexity, the divine harmony, that suffuses the earth.

Naturally, rituals born in this spirit will be conducted outdoors. No more will you need the rigid floor blocking earth's healing energy, while the walls and roof seal you off from nature's rambunctious sport. No, you embrace the play of sun and wind and rain, gladly accepting your part within the fabric of life, affirming your kinship with the elements and forces of nature.

Rituals might be devised to honor specific elements of the natural world. A tree ritual would celebrate their steady forbearance and fortitude. Every autumn they drop their leaves, from which they drink in the sun's energy, in the faith that the earth will turn to spring and support their tender buds and sprouts. What person alive can match such faith? Appreciate also the theme beneath the falling and sprouting of leaves—from death springs birth—a universally held spiritual truth, another expression of which is Jesus's death and resurrection.

A water ritual would celebrate the elixir of life, the building block of creation, the primal sea from which you and all other creatures spring. Such a ritual could be held at a lake, a stream, the seashore, or even on dry land, with water in a bowl or urn. Knowing water's underlying pattern—a pulsating fabric of attraction and resistance—forges a new appreciation for water's role as the spark of growth. You carry it inside you now, fueling the constant death and rebirth—again—of cells as your body is reborn anew in every moment. To celebrate water is to celebrate life, creation, growth, change, fulfillment.

A sun ritual turns your gaze skyward, toward the shower of resistance sparking light and heat, the perpetual river of cosmic energy warming earth's surface, preparing the bed of life. From the sun, which is the male element, come vigor, action, mastery, construction, destruction, and adventure, all confirming man's role as the material keeper of earth. A sun ritual is particularly effective as a celebration of manhood and masculinity, men and boys joining together to acknowledge their guiding celestial influence.

By the same token, women and girls join hands under the moon's warm glow, celebrating the moon's especial qualities of spirit, nurturance, love, stability, and security. Recognizing the bedrock construction of the moon, her steady pull on the oceans' tides and woman's chemistry, binds woman to her role as spiritual keeper of earth, the bearer and nurturer of life.

All other elements of the natural world are ripe for ritual celebration as well—the wind, the rain, the plants and animals with whom you share the earth. We refrain from offering specific rituals, precise formulations of recitation, music, and dance, for to do so would be to rob you of devising personal rituals resonating with you, arising organically from your life and values. Each person, and each community, must devise rituals speaking to them where they stand. Rituals must evolve as each of you evolves, changing to reflect the deepening spiritual life of their keepers.

It may seem as if we are urging a return to pre-Christian times, to pagan festivals worshiping earth's elements and celestial companions. Indeed we are. For only when you recognize the spiritual wind blowing through all of creation—in every blossom, under every rock, in the veins of a fallen leaf—can you appreciate your own divinity, pulsing within, binding you to all creation. Our aim is to heal the rupture between mind and body, between you and your fellows, between the human race and the natural world. Rather, our aim is to encourage you in such a direction— only you can take the steps returning you to the natural order. Rituals and celebrations suffusing all of creation with divine wind are one step on that path.

Only an appreciation for the divinity immanent in all things can provide the foundation for a fully conscious life. Rituals and celebrations, both private and communal, are powerful tools in affirming one's spiritual source and the divinity suffusing all of creation. Between the lighting and snuffing of the candle lies the magic and mystery of the soul.

Forty-One

ᔥ

Being Peace

If there is one universal cry swelling in the hearts and rising in the throats of all the globe's peoples, it is this: Peace! From Central America to Africa to the Middle East to Asia, the anguished chorus rises in melancholy despair: Peace! Why is it so unattainable? Why must lives and limbs be shattered in the endless squabbles over territory, religion, and politics? Why must children be broken and bloodied over the obtuseness of their elders? Is there no end to it, no prayer of laying down arms and settling differences through reason and respect?

Building on the principles outlined in this book, perhaps we can take a fresh look at the causes of war and the hopes for peace.

All events hover in eternal validity above the primal pulse, beyond space and time. From this infinite bank of potential events, individuals and societies pull events into physical expression, each "event" being one version of a larger master event. Individually, each manifests private events through the magnetic pull of the belief structure sculpted into the brain's neuronal circuitry and the coordinate. On a mass level, the beliefs and thoughts of many are pooled in the collective unconscious at the level of the psyche, there attracting mass events most in harmony with the communal vibration. As each individual creates his own reality, so does the larger human society create its mass experience.

The nature of the collective pool's vibration determines the nature of events pulled to expression. Where a majority enjoys lives of vigor, growth, and fulfillment, couched in a network of loving, supportive family and community, the collective pool hums in high harmony. Where a culture's worldview leaves each standing utterly alone, isolated, separate, forgotten, or trembling before the throne of God, couched in a competitive economic system of victor and vanquished, wealthy and homeless, the nature of the collective pool will suffer accordingly. It is the communal vibration, the sum of all private vibrations contributed by a people, that determines the nature of mass events finding expression.

Native cultures know warfare, as issues of territory, pride, and dominance play themselves out within the context of those enjoying life in the natural order. But to Western culture belongs the prize of fouling its history with the stench of countless corpses, writing its march through time with the blood of slaughtered millions. For Western culture, divorced from the natural order and suffering under scientific and religious cosmologies hatched upon that rupture, collapses into existential insecurity, life without meaning. Unable to turn inward for sources of love, comfort, and divinity, Western culture looks outward for security, hoarding surplus as protection against the imagined cruel vagaries of nature and one's untrustworthy fellows. Territory also builds a buffer zone of protection against enemies and gnawing emptiness.

Such a culture naturally blends its collective thoughts and beliefs into a pool of vibration weighted heavily toward events of isolation, separation, and fear—culminating in war. War brilliantly symbolizes Western culture's core malaise, for in both its origin—the need for dominance and control as a balm on insecurity—and in execution—murdering one's brothers, blind to the underlying commonality—it feeds back the beliefs breathing it to life. This is how the universe works: It lays before your eyes the nature of your thoughts and beliefs. A culture recounting its history through millennia of youth bloodied and broken in battle is one whose collective unconscious is fed a constant stream of negativity born of ignorance.

At the level of the greater entity, not only is war futile, but each act of murder is an act of suicide. Over the sweep of history, every action is balanced with its opposite. The law of karma is simply the law of consequence: Every action carries a consequence, flipping the action over to experience its opposite. What is not balanced within one lifetime will be carried over to the next. Because this reincarnational balance is lost to Western culture, foreign to its religious and scientific cosmologies, the self-restraint evinced by those mindful of reincarnation is absent. Further, a culture secure in the certainty of reincarnation is one automatically imbued with a sense of divinity, a cosmic design, and a deep purpose to each life.

From an even loftier perspective, in the undifferentiated bank of intent from which all human life springs, all acts are experienced as a single organism acting upon itself. The atrocities of war carry no meaning in terms of victors and vanquished, but reverberate as a uniform agony throughout the human host consciousness. On the level where the human species is united as one, there can be only one winner or one loser.

Returning to our understanding of thoughts and their electromagnetic reality, recognize that your inner flow of thoughts, while private on your level, is fed in a constant stream to the collective unconscious, where all persons are bound together. At the level of the psyche, each contributes private experience to the communal store of vibration pulling mass events toward expression.

Energy is simply energy. Thoughts carry power and energy toward the object of their attention, whether borne on the wings of love or hatred, anger or gratitude. To participate on either side of a battle is to strengthen the pool of intent manifesting as the battle—thus energizing that intent and causing it to splash out over a larger field of space and time.

Here is a crucial understanding. It is not your actions that carry your intent to the collective unconscious, but your thoughts and beliefs, the caliber of your heart. You see, you cannot fight for peace. You cannot scream for peace. You cannot fast for peace. You cannot protest for peace. You cannot march for peace. You cannot hurl epithets at your leaders for peace. You cannot scorn the atrocities of others and bring peace. You cannot hate war and bring peace.

The contents of your heart bind you to all others of your species. At the level of the psyche, the collective unconscious, whatever you feel and believe contributes to the store of potential global experience. The more people who carry love and compassion, the more likely that events of a harmonious nature will manifest. The more people who carry hatred in their hearts—even silently—the more likely that events of enmity and war will break out.

If you stand at a nuclear test site and defiantly raise your fists against those working there, you create war. If you join in mass rallies to protest the government's conduct of foreign relations, hurling invective at your leaders, you create war. If you stage counter-demonstrations against those espousing racial hatred, you create war. If you carry private anger and hatred toward others in your heart, you create war.

Begin to appreciate that from the contents of each heart and mind are drawn the seeds of mass experience. Your heart and your mind feed the flow of your thoughts into the pool of the collective unconscious. Examine the nature of your contribution. Where you find angers, hatreds, and resentments against other persons, other groups, other nations, you find the seeds of war.

What, then, is one to do? If one cannot scream for peace, fight for it, protest for it, write angry letters for it, what can one do? How can one lone heart help bring an end to war?

You must be peace. You must clean and purify your heart. That, ultimately, is the most powerful tool you have for ending war and ushering in peace. Not by hating war, for you thereby strengthen the pool of hatred.

Not by spewing venom at warmongering leaders and generals, for again you contribute your private store of hatred to the mass pool. Only by being peace, only by loving peace, do you create peace.

A fine way to begin being peace, living peace, is at the close of each daily life creation session. After conducting whatever affirmation and visualization work is necessary for your own growth and fulfillment, take a few deep breaths and turn your gaze outward, toward the larger human community. Holding warmth and love in your heart, say aloud, "I am peace." At first, as usual, the brain will register confusion and the body will lie frozen in response, offering no resonance. Over time, the phrase should tingle a small opening in your heart or mind. Consistently affirming the phrase each day, ultimately you should find the body joyfully tingling in affirmation: Yes, I am peace.

As with all other mental work, this must be matched with everyday experience. Begin to listen to the nature of your thoughts and speech. How do you react to negativity, ignorance, or dishonesty in others? How do you respond to the mendacity and warmongering of politicians and the war machine? If you react in hatred and anger, you strengthen war. Further, any time you speak such anger and hatred aloud, a discordance should grate uncomfortably inside, signaling that the brain cannot easily process the words. For, having installed "I am peace" as the guiding vibration of life, expressions of hatred are violations and will be felt as such.

Mass experience builds from the beating of five billion private hearts. Let yours beat in purity, love, and compassion. Let your soul rest easy in the comfort of its divinity and immortality. Feel for those wallowing in quicksands of ego, separation, fear, and violence; allow their words and deeds to fall lightly from you, denying them invigoration from your anger. Steer steadily on the path of oneness. Celebrate your common bond with all others, and with the natural order. Tithe your heart's share to the universal pool of love.

Be peace.

Forty-Two

∾

The Revolution

You create your own reality.

So we began this book, and so we end it. Between first chapter and last lies an exploration of the forces and processes humming beneath everyday life, building the earthly medium in which you find private and communal experience. Everything we have outlined—physical universe construction, human consciousness seeding into the earthly medium, the nature of events, the power of mind—works together to offer you virtually unlimited power over the flow of your life's events. For that is your purpose, the reason for your choice to participate in earthly life: to find your thoughts and beliefs magically reflected back to you in symbolic, physical form.

In every realm, in every corner of creation, consciousness strives for growth and fulfillment. This is the purpose of existence, that through Its infinite realms of creation, the Source may enjoy a perpetually expanding field of activity through which to know and fulfill Itself. A life without care or challenge contradicts the purpose of earthly life, and a conscious life is hardly an eternally smooth sail over glassy waters. Rather, a conscious life is one lived in appreciation for the innate yearning toward growth propelling all consciousness; and as growth entails struggle toward fulfillment, challenges met along the way must be effectively understood and overcome. A conscious life is one embracing challenge as the nourishment of the soul, the food of spiritual growth.

While humanity has always created its own reality, this understanding was hidden from view during the Era of Unconscious Life preceding your time. It was hidden because the core vibration of the race was of a lower order than allowed such conscious understanding. Each day brings a slight acceleration of the race's core vibration, its power to reach higher into the realms of truth. Only in your time does the veil between illusion and reality begin to fall away, to reveal the gleaming machinery whirring and humming beneath the mirage of physical life. Only in your time has the race reached a new peak of spiritual understanding enabling it to perceive what lies behind the chimeric symbol of a physical universe.

This knowledge has always been available to the race, and was understood by its most enlightened members. The New Testament tells the story in which two blind men came to Jesus asking him to heal their eyesight. Jesus asked, "Do you believe I can heal you?" When the men answered yes, Jesus said, "Then according to your belief, you shall be healed." The men's eyes were opened.

According to your belief, you shall be healed. You create your own reality through your beliefs. Two thousand years may have elapsed between Jesus's phrase and ours, but the underlying truth is eternal. It is only now, when the bulk of the race approaches a new level of spiritual truth, that Jesus's words echoing from two millennia past are finally understood as literal truth.

It is a Western audience we address, for it is Western culture that suffers the greatest spiritual imbalance, and threatens to mar the natural order such that the notion of growth and fulfillment becomes a cruel joke, a farce. Over time, any field of endeavor or philosophy based on divorce from the natural order will fail. Ultimately, any violation perpetrated against others, or against the natural world, will backfire. You see this now, swimming as you are in toxic and radioactive sewage threatening your health and those of countless generations to follow. Where is the opportunity for growth, for fulfillment, to children born into such a world?

That technology should devise so many ways of poisoning and maiming the world reveals in stark relief the split between science and spirituality, when in a healthy culture they are always symbiotically balanced. Science staggers forward without a moral compass, splitting the atom and genetic codes because no ethos, no shared moral understanding, guides the culture's evaluation of what may be permitted and what may not. Western culture's spirituality is trapped in an anachronistic worldview speaking to the times of Moses and Jesus, carrying little power to address the issues of today. So Western culture staggers forward, spirituality divorced from science, careening from disaster to disaster in dark panic.

The underlying source of Western culture's malaise is divorce from the natural order, spawning divorce from one another, leaving each feeling stranded in a sea of anonymity, while the world itself spins in a random cosmos. What meaning can there be to life in such a scenario? To what purpose can one strive if every act, however noble, is mocked by the black void beyond the clouds?

We have outlined an alternative cosmology, celebrating each person's uniqueness while revealing the underlying unity binding all persons into the common human family. You stand unique and eternal, couched within a web of life binding you to all others and to the natural world. You are never alone, never forgotten, and indeed your every act is heard throughout the reaches of space, in ways you cannot now imagine.

Further, yours is the ultimate power, that of creating your life's events. Nothing is thrust upon you, nothing is fated, nothing is predetermined. All is chosen. Recognizing this, taking responsibility for what has occurred before this time, you now possess the understanding to consciously fashion the rest of your life, channeling it in new directions, releasing the limitations of the past.

Yours is the power to create a conscious life.

A revolution it will be, yes, but a revolution of heart and mind, not arms. For you recognize now that all institutions, all societal structures, are projections of private intent, pooled in the collective unconscious and reflected in mass experience. Nuclear weapons are not the problem; the problem is the fear and hatred which brought them into existence. Big government is not the problem; the problem is an atomized society racked by fears, projecting personal power onto government in the vain hope of winning relief from isolation and emptiness. The spiritual bankruptcy of religious institutions clinging to ancient dogma and spewing ignorance and venom is not the problem; the problem is projecting one's personal power and morality onto others and a willingness to toe the narrow line they insist you follow.

The revolution, then, is unique in all of human history: It has no leaders, and it fights no battles. The revolution occurs in the heart, where one fashions the energy one contributes to the pool of mass experience. Recognizing this, the ultimate revolutionary act is to restore oneself to the natural order, casting off fear and existential insecurity, embracing the natural order, cherishing all others as your brothers and sisters in the common human family.

The revolutionary recognizes that, in deepest terms, an act of violence against another is an act of violence against oneself. Not only does violence toward others infect one's karmic agenda with the need to suffer violence, it also contributes to the collective pool of negativity, that single violent act rippling across the globe to strengthen the pool of hatred and violence from which warfare springs. Knowing this, true revolutionaries renounce violence as a tool of revolution. World peace can bless the globe only when each heart beats with peace. The means does not justify the end; the means must be the end. A peaceful world springs from peaceful hearts.

The revolutionary casts off cries of outrage and helplessness at life's unexpected twists and turns. No revolutionary wails, "Why did this happen to me!" The revolutionary asks, "Why have I brought this onto myself?" The revolutionary takes responsibility for life's events, peeling away the surface facade to uncover the themes and symbols lying beneath. Understanding these, the revolutionary can release the limitations of the past and embrace a higher order of life.

The revolutionary feels safe and secure in an abundant world. Feeling the divinity pulsing through all creation, the revolutionary knows he is an invaluable part of the fabric, blessed and eternal for the mere fact of existence. No longer need he struggle to hoard surplus in expectation of later want, nor build buffers of territory against the threat of enemies. The revolutionary is secure.

Great contrasts in wealth diminish not through taxation and social engineering, but because great wealth is as burdensome a weight on the soul as fat is on the body. Seeing money as energy, and knowing energy is healthiest when unhindered and undammed, the revolutionary matches the flow of money-energy toward him with an equal flow back into the world. The revolutionary increases his abundance by increasing his generosity.

The revolutionary appreciates the extraordinary resilience of his body. He recognizes that, although certain substances may carry potential harm, they alone can cause no damage when the soul carries no need to experience disease. The revolutionary gravitates toward natural foods, those unsullied by avaricious intent, not out of fear but out of loving appreciation for the body's divine harmony, and a desire to respect and work within that harmony. The revolutionary listens to his body's messages and heeds them. The revolutionary knows radiant health as a natural fact of life, requiring no more fret and worry than trusting the body to breathe. The revolutionary knows better than to create disease through fear of disease. The revolutionary's physical health reflects a soul at peace.

Peace. The revolutionary understands that war and peace spring from the blended heart-stuff of billions. Where separation and fear prevail, there is war. Where love and understanding prevail, there is peace. The revolutionary purifies his heart, releasing the soul-cancers of fear and hatred, appreciating the underlying commonality binding him to all others. The revolutionary neither expects nor requires all others to agree with him; he carries too much respect for the uniqueness of each human soul, the primacy of private experience.

Neither does the revolutionary feel compelled to false demonstrations of love for all others, recognizing that some have strayed so far from their natural grace as to be beyond mutual devotion. Instead, the revolutionary offers respect, respect for the struggle that being human entails, respect for each to follow the path of his choice. Respecting all, loving some, the revolutionary offers his heart's pure radiance to the pool of peace.

When the revolution is finished, and each heart beats safely and securely in a natural world of abundance and freedom, buoyed by the love and respect of others; when each treads lightly upon the earth in wise stewardship; when the pool of peace descends from the clouds of hope to blanket the globe—then shall the chorus swell to the far reaches of the cosmos in thunderous exultation: The revolution is complete. The Era of Conscious Life is upon us.

Our blessings on your journey.

Other Alexander Books by Ramón Stevens

Spirit Wisdom II:
The Enlightened Warrior's Guide to
Personal and Cultural Transformation

A world in crisis is also a world ripe for transformation. In *Spirit Wisdom II*, Alexander encourages us to become Enlightened Warriors—to recognize the deeper meaning beneath today's ecological and social crises and to bring about a transformed global society founded on natural and spiritual principles. Ranging from global warming to astrology, from terrorism to music, from dreams to astrology, *Spirit Wisdom II* will transform your understanding of our troubled world and your place in it.

Spirit Wisdom:
Living Consciously in an
Age of Turmoil and Transformation

Spirit Wisdom offers a comprehensive look at our age's most compelling and controversial issues. Alexander illuminates the deeper meanings behind abortion; drugs; AIDS; sexuality; aliens; reincarnation; health, cyberspace and the Internet; spirituality; UFO's, spirit guides; and more.

Earthly Cycles:
How Past Lives, Karma, and Your Higher Self Shape Your Life

Alexander offers a richly detailed exploration of the cycles of life, death, and reincarnation, illuminating the hidden influences on your life. *Earthly Cycles* begins with a thorough description of how your higher self has crafted your life's foundation (choosing your parents; soul age and aspect; gender and nation; sexual orientation, etc.). Alexander then illuminates the mysteries of death, karma, and reincarnation, detailing how karma is accrued and released, and how karmic bonds are recast into other lifetimes. Finally, he describes how you can heal your karmic wounds and make the world a more peaceful, loving place with the support of angels and spirit guides.

Pepperwood Press

available from www.amazon.com

Made in the USA
San Bernardino, CA
21 December 2014